INSIDE
IBM

INSIDE
IBM

A Personal Story

JACQUES MAISONROUGE

Translation by Nina Rootes

McGRAW-HILL PUBLISHING COMPANY
New York St. Louis San Francisco Toronto

First published in France by Robert Laffont, S.A., Paris, 1985
First published in Great Britain by William Collins & Sons & Co., Ltd., 1988

1   2   3   4   5   6   7   8   9   FGR   FGR   8   9   2   1   0   9

ISBN 0-07-039737-6

Library of Congress Cataloging-in-Publication Data

Maisonrouge, Jacques, 1924-
    Inside IBM.
    Translation of: Manager international : 36 ans au
coeur d'une multinationale de l'informatique.
    1. International business enterprises—Management.
2. Maisonrouge, Jacques, 1924-   . 3. Executives—
France—Biography.   4. International Business Machines
Corporation—Management.   I. Title.
HD62.4.M3313 1989   658'.049'0924 [B]   89-2275
ISBN 0-07-039737-6

In writing this book I wanted to express my gratitude to all those men and women who helped me rise to positions of responsibility in a company which I both respect and admire. Not all of them are mentioned here, since this would have required many more pages. But I have thought of them all, and I wish to thank them for their support and their friendship.

In my life there has been one constant: the love of my wife. It is to you, Françoise, that I dedicate this book — you whose exceptional qualities of steadfastness and equanimity have, just a little perhaps, rubbed off on me.

CONTENTS

Introduction   9

1 1924–1948: A Happy Youth   11

2 Xenophobia   36

3 The Discovery of America   41

4 True Liberalism   55

5 I Want to be a Salesman   65

6 Sales and Marketing   84

7 My Apprenticeship in International
   Management   93

8 Internationalizing Management   118

9 My First Great Responsibilities   141

10 A Defence and Illustration of Multinationals   193

11 The Joy of Leadership   225

12 The Entry of Women into Professional
   Life   255

13 My Last Three Years at IBM   266

14 Some Contemporary Debates on Data
   Processing   283

15 The Conditions for Success   303

CONTENT

INTRODUCTION

It is 7 p.m. on 28 September 1984. I am sitting in seat No.5K aboard an Air France Boeing 747, Flight 070, New York–Paris. During the last ten years I have taken this flight more than a hundred times, and each time I have felt so nervous I have been unable to do any serious work while aboard the aircraft. Today, in addition to my usual tension, I feel enormously sad; at 5 p.m. I lived through the last minute of my employment with IBM.

It had been a normal week: two management committees, several meetings with my immediate colleagues, and a mass of correspondence. But it is very hard to take part in meetings and events in the knowledge that they will never be repeated, especially when each of these events has, in the past, brought intense satisfaction and intellectual stimulation.

Leaving an organization in which you have worked for thirty-six years, three months and two weeks is painful and difficult to accept. On 15 June 1948 I became one of IBM's student engineers and spent a year in the USA. Then I was made a sales manager, acting as an assistant to the sales manager. In 1956 I was moved into the company's European sphere of operations, and in 1962 into its world-wide activities in the capacity of Vice-President of the IBM World Trade Corporation in New York. Later I became President of IBM Europe; President, then Chairman, of the IBM World Trade Corporation; and finally Senior Vice-President of the IBM Corporation. In November 1981 I joined the management committee of IBM and it is this office I have just left today.

Ten years ago, the Board of Directors decided that executives in top management should retire at the age of sixty. The aim was to have a young management team and to permit people who were still full of energy and spirit to rise quickly to the very highest positions within IBM. However, my problem is that I do not feel

9

my useful life is over, and I shall sadly miss my colleagues.

This morning, our Chairman, John Opel, surprised me by coming to see me in my office and spending forty-five minutes with me. How many chief executives of an organization of this size would have made such a friendly gesture, especially when it was already arranged that we would be seeing each other shortly, during the farewell dinner? For me his visit was one more example of the excellent quality of human relations at IBM. But the very pleasure that I took from this added to my regrets.

Now the plane is moving, and I have the impression that hundreds of ideas are crowding into my consciousness without my being able to put them in order. Little by little, I organize my confused thoughts, too numerous to be dealt with at once. I must get a grip on myself. I have no right to make a drama out of my departure. Since I am bold enough to believe that at sixty I am still capable of more than just cultivating my garden, I must think how to organize my future life.

'Fasten your seat-belts!' I wake up. The steward informs me that we are entering a zone of turbulence. This is the moment when I always wish I could be up there in the cockpit, giving advice! Reduce speed; increase altitude by 2,000 feet. I am a true Frenchman! And, what is more, a man of action and of intervention. We are landing; for me the best moment of any flight. As we taxi towards the terminal my spirits rise. I have made my decision.

Fasten your seat-belts! I am going to describe my thirty-six-year adventure in data processing with one corporation, IBM.

1

1924–1948: A Happy Youth

Dr Moscovici, our family doctor, presented my mother with her newborn baby with the words: 'Your son has the cranium of a dictator.' He was not a phrenologist and in 1924 the word 'dictator' had a different connotation. I have always liked to think that if the doctor had known a little English, and understood the workings of big business, he would have said: 'Your son has the cranium of a *leader*.' My birth took place in my parents' bedroom.

From 1924 to 1931 I lived in a suburban house in Cachan, just south of Paris, with my parents and my mother's parents. I was about to write 'little' house, influenced by that French fondness for putting 'little' (*petit*) in front of everything they possess.

Louis Armand explained to me one day that this should not surprise us, since in the nineteenth century *petit* meant pleasing or pretty. I often met M. Louis Armand during the closing years of his life. Our first interview in 1968 was very simple: I had asked him to meet me so that I could invite him to join the international board of IBM Europe, and he accepted at once. Born in Savoie in the French Alps, this man, who had had a brilliant career and received all kinds of honours including election to the *Académie Française*, possessed human qualities at least equal to his vast knowledge. Louis Armand was, moreover, a convinced European with a broad vision of the future. He did not believe that patriotism in itself precluded internationalism; his book, *The European Challenge*, written with Michel Drancourt, remains a splendid testimony to his enthusiasm and his faith in Europe. To me, he was a kind man and a great one. Incidentally, the use of 'little' in the language of my compatriots is compensated for by the use of 'big' and not 'great' when speaking of others. A Frenchman has a big job and works in a big firm run by a big capitalist.

But in my family's case, it really was a little house: tall and narrow, three floors above a ground floor that was almost a basement, with two rooms plus a kitchen and a washroom on each floor. The staircase took up a great deal of space and the whole building was as ill-conceived as some of the 'brownstone' houses in New York. My grandparents' drawing room, which we all used, was on the second floor. All five of us gathered there every evening and the first family radio set was installed in that room, which often meant that conversation was replaced by listening to rather mediocre programmes. My grandfather, avid for news, would hold his right hand to his ear and move close to the loudspeaker, thus giving us to understand discreetly that we had to be quiet. My maternal uncle lived in a room on the ground floor, but he was not there very often. Already at the age of seventeen he was longing to spread his wings and fly.

It has become the custom in all the industrialized countries to classify people into large social groups. Even Americans speak not only of a 'middle class', but more precisely of a 'lower middle class' and an 'upper middle class'. If I had to define my family at that time, I would use the term 'lower middle class' or what the French would call the *petite bourgeoisie*.

I was born into a circle of 'achievers', people who wanted to succeed in whatever they undertook. They had ambitions, aims that had varied and evolved from generation to generation. One constant factor governed their lives: their work, mental attitudes and relationships with other people were always placed at the service of their ambitions, so they might reach fixed objectives and endeavour to instil in their children still loftier objectives.

Of my four great-grandfathers, one had been a coalminer, one a farmer in Auvergne, one a master tailor and one a '*bourgeois*' — a building contractor from La Rochelle. Only one of them, my Basque great-grandfather Cazas, the master tailor, had been up-rooted. Three of the sons from his peasant family left Saint-Jean-Pied-de-Port in the Basque country in search of adventure. Two went to the United States, the other to Paris to learn the cutter's

12

trade. My great-grandmothers, my grandmothers and my mother took care of their children and kept house; one or two of them had gone out to work for brief spells.

I never knew any of my great-grandparents. In their day human life expectancy was short. All that I know about them is what I was told with extraordinary filial piety by my grandparents, and all that remains with me are a few memories, revived from time to time by yellowing photographs in the family album.

I never knew the Christian name of the farmer from Auvergne. His family name was Séguy but he was always 'Grandfather' in the family and 'Gentil' with the neighbours. The tailor, Cazas, was arrested during the Paris Commune, although he had not been a *communard*; he was denounced by a priest which accounted for the anti-clericalism and atheism of my maternal grandfather. Fortunately my great-grandmother, who had been brought up in a boarding school for orphans and servicemen, knew the Military Governor of Paris who had him released. Settled as their generation had been, the next one was mobile.

My paternal grandfather, Théophile Maisonrouge, started his career as an assistant in a retail clothing shop. Soon after my father's birth, he left Aubusson with his young wife and went to Rouen where he was promoted manager of a shop and then transferred to Mâcon. Later he went to Paris to be employed as a travelling salesman.

My maternal grandmother, Agnès Séguy, was an Auvergne peasant; the third of a family of nine children, she came to Paris when she was very young to work as a salesgirl in a dairy store belonging to one of her sisters. Then, thanks to a family loan, she was able to buy another dairy shop; she married a model employee of the postal service who was my grandfather, François Cazas. He, too, started work very young. At fourteen he was a telegraph boy; not having had much education, he studied a great deal on his own and became a passionate opera-lover. By passing competitive examinations he ended his career as a Postmaster.

My father, born in 1900, received most of his education in Mâcon. How vividly he talked of his childhood and early youth! He was one of the first Boy Scouts in France and made firm friends among them, some of whom influenced me considerably. On their scouting expeditions they often made the Roche de Solutré their objective. This high hill, surrounded by vineyards which include the ones that produce *Pouilly Fuissé*, is a few kilometres to the west of Mâcon. Seen from the *autoroute du Sud*, it appears to be a right-angled triangle whose hypotenuse is the slope that rises towards the south and whose base is the long side of the right angle. The short side is a steep cliff and it is said that the earliest inhabitants used it as a slaughtering-place for horses. They forced them to gallop up the long slope and the poor beasts, carried headlong by their own impetus, were unable to stop in time when they reached the summit and so plunged to their deaths tens of metres below.

My father soon had to abandon his walks to Solutré. World War I had begun and at the age of sixteen, after passing his school certificate, he was sent to Lyons to work as a shop assistant. He was unhappy there, alone, fifty miles from his family, but the war ended before he was called up and he was able to go to Paris. He spent his military service as a Horse Guard with the French Forces of Occupation in Mainz, and on his return worked in a small company with 100 employees which manufactured raincoats. There he remained until his retirement. Loyalty to the company that employs you is a family trait.

My father was a travelling salesman – and an excellent one to judge by the constant improvement in the family's standard of living – up until the beginning of the last war. I remember how sad he became on Sunday evenings before departing for a tour of northern or eastern France. His visits to clients lasted a week or two and we all eagerly awaited the Fridays that brought him home.

When he returned to Paris after the 'phoney war' in 1940, the Jewish family, who owned the factory and who had excellent reasons for wanting to escape from the zone occupied by the Germans, asked my father to take charge of their business. Thus, for the next five years, he became head of a medium-sized company and ran it very well in spite of all the immense difficulties of those times. In 1945 my father handed over his post to his old employer and became the sales manager. He accepted the fact that he was no longer the big boss with good grace for he had never had the slightest doubt as to where his duty lay.

After receiving her high school certificate, my mother worked as a secretary and book-keeper up until my birth. At the same time she took piano and singing lessons and accompanied her father to the *Opéra* or the *Opéra-Comique* with a frequency that never ceased to amaze me.

This, then, was the family into which I was born. I grew up in Cachan surrounded by love and encouragement, and in the constant presence of good example.

I do not have any very distinct memories of my pre-school years. I can, however, recall my mother teaching me the 'three R's', and my father being 'astounded' at the results, although he very often gave me additional lessons.

I remember the holidays spent with my maternal grandparents at Neyrebrousse, a little village in the centre of Auvergne. I had already spent holidays by the sea, at Le Portel and Riva-Bella, but this much more intimate contact with nature, with the beauty of the Auvergne mountains, the odour of stables, the smell of country bread, the kindliness of the poor farmers of the region, remains engraved on my memory. I remember being amazed, and I should have been shocked, to discover that the men of the house sat down to lunch while the women served them, snatching a bite when they could. I was five-years-old at the time of these holidays, and my grandfather and I were the only ones who could not speak the Auvergne *patois*. This drew us together in a kind of complicity and we remained close right through to 1961.

While my mother was wheeling me around the streets of Cachan in my pram, she met another young woman who had a son six months older than me. We formed a friendship which lasted for many years and spent much of our school life together. Our parents instilled in us a sense of rivalry and right up until we were in the top class of the *Lycée Voltaire*, Michel Juillard and I were a little nervous when we took home our school reports at the end of each term.

15

My first years at school were very happy. My parents had not only given me a head-start by teaching me at home, they had also taught me to respect my teachers. Today I still feel the same high regard for teachers that I felt in my primary school days. The dedication of my own teachers was extraordinary and it is to them that I owe my very strong attachment to state education. My parents expected me to be top of the class and I did not disappoint them too often.

I have few precise memories of this period, except two or three which made their mark on me. In the house next to ours lived a very distinguished but unobtrusive couple who came from Angoulême. Mme Geneix was an English teacher and, when I was five years old, she suggested to my mother that she should give me lessons. I was therefore able to start learning English well before the normal age which proved a considerable advantage. There is another episode in my childhood that my parents remember more vividly than I do, but they have recounted it to me so often it has become my own. The distance between the school and our house seemed to me very long, and I stubbornly refused to make it longer by taking a walk with my mother (who took me to school and collected me) on the way home. I wanted instead to do my homework and learn my lessons which my mother made me repeat at once, and still have time to enjoy myself afterwards.

I also have a confused memory of an event which was to have important consequences, particularly for me. In 1929 I sensed that my grandparents and my parents were suffering from some deep sorrow as there were conversations from which I was excluded. And then one day my father told me my mother was about to enter hospital to undergo 'a little operation'. He reassured me as best he could, but I was very uneasy. They kept me informed of her progress and, ten days later, mother came home. It was not until a few years later, when they judged I was old enough, that I was told the truth. It shattered me: my mother could never have another child. This was not only very distressing for my parents but also for me. I was very fond of children and often asked: 'When shall I have a brother or sister?' From that time on

16

my parents did everything they could to ensure that I did not behave like a spoiled only child.

Michel Juillard, also an only child, was often with me; we even spent our holidays together. At least twice a month I also went to see my two cousins, Michèle and Raymonde, daughters of my father's elder sister, and they often came to our house. I believe that by inviting children of my own age to our house my parents managed to stop me suffering from the egoism of an only child, but they could not prevent the precocious maturing which is inevitable in a child who mainly lives amongst adults.

In 1931 my parents decided to leave Cachan and we went to live on rue Stanislas-Meunier in the 20th *arrondissement*, because the clothing factory which employed my father as a travelling salesman was in that district of Paris. A little later our friends the Juillards came to set up house on the same floor of our building. First Michel and I went to the elementary school on the Avenue Gambetta then to the *Lycée Voltaire* on the Avenue de la République.

On entering the *Lycée* I met with a stumbling-block; the headmaster considered me too young to be admitted. My mother tried to persuade him, but in vain; I had to repeat one class which had both good and bad consequences. I gained a little more maturity, studied under an excellent teacher, Mme Clément, but it left me with one year less to prepare for my final examinations eight years later.

Three or four pupils stand out clearly in my recollection of those years: my friends, Grunberg, Perlmutter and Pareau (who became the youngest Dean of a mathematics faculty in France). Michel Pareau was first in Greek as well as in mathematics, but happily for me we were not in the same class so I was able to walk off with a few prizes.

During these pre-war years, however, I was most strongly influenced by the atmosphere of my family and by my parents' few but faithful friends. One of these, M.E. Dargaud, an old comrade from my father's Boy Scout days, made a brilliant career in the Treasury Department and was Treasurer-Paymaster General

17

at Chambéry and later at Saint-Etienne. He persuaded me that I should try to get into the *Ecole Polytechnique*. I was good at maths so it seemed a logical conclusion. For ten years I had an ambition and a definite target to aim for.

The *Ecole Polytechnique* was founded by Napoleon and was one of the first *Grandes Ecoles* in France. It is a post-graduate Military Academy specializing in Sciences and Engineering. Graduates go on to serve in the army — more particularly in the Corps of Engineers — or in the civil service or private industry.

Every year I spent all my holidays with my maternal grandparents who had bought a house in Puchay in Normandy. I had a very enjoyable time with them, but missed my parents very much as they only came at weekends. To keep me from being lonely, they invited my childhood friend, Michel Juillard. Our games were very simple, especially since we were forbidden to go out on the main roads where, however, there was not much traffic. We cycled around the garden and played cowboys and Indians, alternating the roles. There were just the two of us, but our imaginary forces were formidable and we discussed their manoeuvres endlessly. Everyone found buying Christmas presents for us easy — simply child-size soldiers' 'uniforms'.

When I look back over this period I notice how attitudes changed from 1937–8, thanks to the paid holidays introduced by the French government in 1936. Up until then the villagers had seen few Parisians. I remember the rather tart comments made to my grandparents when Michel and I ran races against each other wearing only shorts and singlets. But from 1937 plenty of 'city folk' from Paris and Rouen came to spend their holidays in the country and . . . slowly . . . slowly . . . people's ideas began to change.

These long peaceful holidays gave me plenty of opportunity for talking to my grandparents. My grandmother was an exceptional woman — immensely kind with great sensitivity of feeling. Her letters were larded with numerous spelling mistakes, but those who received them never noticed for the spirit, the wit and delicacy with which they were written were so outstanding. I never saw her in a bad mood and I never heard her complain.

She was a woman who created happiness around her and good will amongst all her family. My first great sorrow in adult life occurred when she died in 1956 when I was 32 years old.

My grandfather, on his retirement from the postal service, was a very straightforward man who never had a disagreeable word to say against anyone. For several years, he had been the leader of his union and I still have an article from the union's newspaper praising his powers as an orator. Here is an extract taken from his farewell speech: 'I shall continue to follow the activities of this trade union and my heart will always be with you. None of you need blush for the work in which you are employed. You are not highly-educated men it is true, but you have striven hard and through your effort, your perseverance and your solidarity, you have merited your due place.'

Therefore, pulling me in one direction was my father's friend, the Treasurer-Paymaster General, who wanted to see me enter the *Ecole Polytechnique*, and pulling in the same direction but without such lofty ambition, my grandfather, who wanted me to be a civil servant since he believed service to the State the only noble course of action. Very soon I combined the two and decided I wanted to be a government engineer trained to build bridges and highways.

There were many other influences at work on me. My grandfather was a radical socialist.* His son, my uncle, had been a union leader in the firm where he was working during the 1936 strikes. My father sympathized with the Left, and the only newspapers I read were *L'Oeuvre* and sometimes *Le Populaire*. For me the model politicians were Léon Blum, Edouard Herriot and Aristide Briand; I followed my family's tradition and paid homage at the latter's tomb in Cocherel. The men of my family were all agnostics and I had still not been baptized which distressed my religious mother. I was avid for justice, but I discovered early on that contrary to claims made by the men of the Left (who were not always men of the people), there were no apparent inequalities in the educational system. Many of my schoolmates at the *Lycée*

---

* In the French political spectrum a 'radical socialist' is to the right of a socialist.

came from very modest backgrounds. Very often the best pupils were Jews, the children of immigrants from Central Europe or Germany.

My grandfather suffered from facial neuralgia which caused him a great deal of pain, and had to undergo a serious operation. This was the moment when I discovered prayer – the prayer of the supplicant. I hid myself away in a room in their house which was called the workroom because there was a bench and a number of tools in there, and I asked God to save him. How often I went to that room, and how much time I spent on my knees! I was always asking for something: for my grandparents' health to improve or for my parents to have a safe journey when they came to visit us on Friday evenings. At the beginning I forgot to thank God when things turned out well. A little later I did this regularly, then my need for an explanation of the origins of man led me on to the idea of God as the Great Architect and then to God Himself. Reading the Gospels brought me to a still-wavering faith. Whenever I return to Puchay, I go into that room which my uncle has transformed into a pleasant bedroom, and in my mind's eye I see myself again as a little boy kneeling in prayer.

In 1938 I began to worry about the state of France and the academic year of 1938–9 became a year of great anxiety. As the only other child in my immediate family was my cousin, Francis, and he was only four years old, I shared the anguish of the grown-ups around me. My father, a man who had great insight into the future, began to have serious doubts about the 'bleating pacifism' manifested by his political friends. I drew up plans for military campaigns and was alarmed to learn that the air force, although it had some good prototype planes, had mass-produced only a very few.

The horrors of Nazism, which I had been hearing about since 1933, and the French Army's lack of preparedness, reinforced my fears. On July 14th my father and I went to watch the military parade, but we were not reassured by it.

During this period, another of my father's friends, Dr Rouquès, also had a great influence on me. He was a member of the

Communist party and had fought with the International Brigades during the Spanish Civil War. He was a warm-hearted generous man, a great surgeon, and totally devoted to the cause he had espoused. We did not see him very often, but I liked him immensely and admired him for his courage.

1939. I had been promised two much-appreciated awards for winning the *prix d'excellence* at school: a three-speed racing bicycle and a month's holiday at Saint-Jean-Cap-Ferrat on the Riviera. For my parents as well as myself, this was our first discovery of the Côte d'Azur. I had loved other holiday resorts on the Channel and on the Atlantic coast, particularly Saint-Jean-de-Monts and Hendaye, but this trip to the South of France by car was enchanting. My parents had also given me my first good tennis racket, and I remember my delight when I cycled from the villa they had rented at Cap Ferrat to Beaulieu to play a match.

Those were the most glorious holidays of my childhood and they came to a sad end with the general mobilization for the war. My father had to join his regiment on the first day, so our holidays were cut short, and we set off on the road to Mâcon which was where he had to report. He was in the Commissariat. My parents decided to stay where they were and I was enrolled in the *Lycée Lamartine*. It was an interesting experience for a Parisian to be integrated within a group of Mâconnais. My outlook was prejudiced in their favour since my father had spent his youth in Mâcon, and we still had relatives in the area. But I was looked upon as a refugee, an outsider, and I was teased about my Parisian accent. The masters were hard on me and during the first weeks the phrase, 'Now let's see what the Parisians can do,' was repeated in almost all my classes. The maths master was the sternest, but as I came first in the December tests he was forced to admit that I 'had been lucky' — always that French emphasis on luck!

My father rediscovered some of his old friends, all former Boy Scouts, one of whom, M.R. Legros, gave us a particularly warm welcome. My cousin, Michèle, came to live with us and it was a new experience for me to no longer be the only 'young one'.

Our sojourn in Mâcon made me realize how unwelcoming the French are, and nowadays allows me to explain to the Americans,

Germans, English, Swedes and other foreigners with whom I rub shoulders in the course of my work, who complain of the cold attitude the French adopt towards them, that it is not a question of anti-American, anti-German, etc. feelings, but rather a general attitude the French have towards anyone who does not belong to their town or its immediate environs. The larger the city, the truer this is, and the Parisians are a prime example.

We were living through the 'phoney war'. My uncle sent us news from the front where he was stationed with an artillery regiment whose guns were still being pulled by horses. Everything we heard during this calm early phase of the war made it plain that our military and political leaders were not taking advantage of the precious lull to improve the fighting capacity of our forces. There was no sense of a national effort being made to mobilize industry to fight a war and I suffered profoundly as a result. I blamed the pre-war governments. My father was outraged by the muddle in the Commissariat and regularly threatened to write a book entitled: 'Where is the tax-payer's money going to?'

In the spring of 1940 I cycled through the region with some companions from the *Lycée*. The Roche de Solutré also became the destination of some of our long walks and I relived the Scout patrols my father had enjoyed as a youth. My mother was always worried about me, and if by any ill chance she reached home before I was back from one of my walks she would wait anxiously behind the door of the apartment. In answer to the call of patriotic duty she had started working again as a secretary/book-keeper at the military hospital, and she was lucky enough to be working for a head of department who was both courteous and competent. To this day we still enjoy friendly relations with 'Lieutenant' Gaillard.

A new element had entered my life: along with the presence of my girl cousin in my home walking groups with my friends now included girls as well. It was intriguing for me to have companions of the opposite sex because at that date neither the elementary schools nor the *lycées* were co-educational. Ever since I have been in favour of mixed schools; I believe they give young people a better chance to understand each other.

Then came May 1940 and the Germans' victorious attack. We could not believe the speed of their advance. I remember, too, the Norwegian expedition and the words of Paul Reynard: 'The iron road is and will remain cut!' It was at this point that I began to have even stronger doubts about the past administration of France. The Germans continued to advance. I had become a volunteer first aid worker and we were receiving refugees from Belgium and Northern France at Mâcon railway station. The exodus had begun. I underwent my baptism of fire on the *quai* of the Saône near the statue of Lamartine: *Adieu bois couronnés d'un reste de verdure!* ['Farewell forests crowned with tattered foliage!'] It was summer, but my thoughts dwelt on autumn, on decline and fall. The Italians had entered the war, and while aiming at the railroad station had hit the Saône river and its *quai*; as I lay under a lorry, I felt anything but proud of myself. Where were our fighter planes? What were our anti-aircraft batteries doing? My scepticism grew and I no longer believed those who said, 'We'll stop them at the Loire.'

Our turn came and we, too, joined the exodus with Lt. Gaillard, another lieutenant, my mother and myself in the same car. My father remained behind in Mâcon since the Commissariat would withdraw last of all. The final destination of our flight was Tour-de-Faure in the Lot. But what adventures we had on the way there, including two air raids! Those seven or eight days on the road made me mature quickly.

I do not know by what miracle we heard about General de Gaulle's appeal on 18 June, but I was tremendously excited and proud. At last a senior French officer had taken up the sword! I carried the message from group to group, adding my own comment: 'I hope plenty of officers will go to join him and make their way to Spain.' I received the two hardest slaps of my life from a captain in the air force, who evidently felt both more at ease and braver when facing a kid of fourteen than he did when facing a Messerschmitt. It was not the force of the slaps that made me cry for quite a while, but my disgust and disillusionment, and the feeling that the soil of my motherland was crumbling beneath my feet.

We had no news of my father, but after a trip to Cahors, where they were gathering information regarding the withdrawals of the various military units, we learned that the Commissariat from Mâcon had fallen back to Pézenas, not far from the Mediterranean coast. We had no way of knowing whether my father had arrived safely at this destination but I did my best to reassure my mother.

Then came the Armistice and our return to Mâcon. The *Lycée* reopened and I spent several days there along with the few teachers and pupils who had also returned. What a lot of fighting and squabbling there was at that time! The partisans of de Gaulle to whom I belonged formed a small group mostly composed of various 'foreigners' from the North; we were wondering how on earth we were going to get back into the Occupied Zone.

My mother was still waiting for news of my father. Late one evening we heard his familiar whistle, but only the first note for overcome with emotion he could not get out the second. What joy! I rushed down three flights of stairs jumping over at least two-thirds of them as I ran, and at last we were together again.

A few days' rest for him and then we all decided to return to Paris. My father really had to get back to his work and we were anxious for news of our relatives, especially my uncle who had been with a unit that had seen quite a lot of fighting.

Father obtained an *ausweis* [identity papers], and ever since I experienced what it was like to cross back into the Occupied Zone, my heart still misses a beat when I cross a frontier, even though I never fail to declare any taxable goods at Customs. I never have had any problems, but on that occasion the strength and organization of the Germans made a disturbing impression on all of us.

We arrived in Paris. To our great joy, all the members of our immediate family had got back. My uncle had escaped the unhappy fate of becoming a prisoner.

Paris under the Occupation has been described many times. During that period I lived under a weight of sorrow. I went back to

24

the *Lycée Voltaire*. There were some absent faces and some new ones, but I rediscovered almost all my old companions. Passive resistance began. We, who ranged in age from fifteen to seventeen, were very closely supervised by our main (French and Latin) teacher, who was moreover a good teacher but a collaborator. We all believed that the headmaster was a collaborator, too, whereas it may simply have been that he tried at times to protect us. Racism began to make itself felt and we were greatly concerned about the fate of our Jewish friends.

On 11 November 1940 there was a demonstration on the Champs-Elysées. Students from the *lycées* and the universities had spread the word and, although all assemblies were forbidden, several thousand young people gathered together to shout: '*Vive de Gaulle!*' The Germans charged and some casualties resulted, my friend Colson among them; he came back to the *Lycée* a few days later after a bullet was extracted from the calf of his leg. During the days that followed mini-demonstrations were held and Michel Juillard and I were arrested and frog-marched to the Commissariat of Police on the Place de l'Opéra. Twenty or thirty of us were dumped there with no idea as to what awaited us. Very late that evening my father, who had learned from a police commissioner who was a relative of his that some young people had been arrested in the streets, found the Commissariat where we were being held. After some argument, he managed to get us released. He did *not* reward us with hearty congratulations on the way home! We were, however, lucky to have been arrested at that time before the Germans started adopting sterner measures. They were still behaving with 'soldierly courtesy'.

Life in our classroom was somewhat isolated from the outside world. Many of my schoolfriends' fathers were POWs. We all suffered from malnutrition and the vitamin biscuits they doled out were not sufficient to appease our hunger. Above all, however, we were suffering morally at seeing our country occupied, and we felt a great deal of shame at her swift defeat. We could not go out much and the masters were delighted to have such studious pupils.

To demonstrate our spirit of resistance and our hopes, we

decided to adopt Latin mottoes. Mine was: *Age quod agis*, somewhat loosely translated as: 'Whatever you do, do it well.' It was to mark me for life, and I must confess it was not very modest!

Our whole family suffered a very painful experience. My aunt, the wife of my mother's brother, is Jewish and I shall never forget the day when she had to present herself at the town hall to collect a yellow star. My father went with her to demonstrate both his affection for her and his disgust at Nazi methods. Two of my schoolmates at the *Lycée*, Grunberg and Perlmutter, had been deported and their departure had shattered us, although we did not know in 1942 what was going on in the concentration camps. Another sorrow followed when my grandfather Maisonrouge died; it was the first crack in the ranks of our closely-knit family.

During this extremely painful period I learned what hatred is. I learned to hate racism, to hate the oppression of one nation by another, and also to hate traitors who indulged in every kind of compromise to gain immediate personal advantage. This nascent hatred within me was modified when I read Voltaire whom I admired, and who made me understand what tolerance is. I was also drawn to the church.

From the end of 1942 up until the Liberation, I studied Higher Mathematics and then Applied Mathematics at the *Lycée Saint-Louis*. Mine are not at all the happy memories that one normally has of the years of early adulthood. The war, the Occupation, all the severe material hardships, some air raids, and in the subway those appalling notices listing the names of hostages who had been shot the night before, very quickly turned us into adults. René Dufaud, one of my old friends from the *Lycée Voltaire*, and I took part in meetings of the Resistance movement and of the Gaullists. We had enrolled with the F.T.P. [*Francs-Tireurs et Partisans*].

My parents and I had moved to another apartment. My father wanted to be within walking distance of the factory he was running, so we lived on the rue Henri-Poincaré where I could see from my bedroom window the factories and the offices of the

Bull Machines Company. I do not know whether it was this view that pushed me in the direction of data processing!

From 1940 to 1945 life in Paris was quite difficult. In addition to our moral turmoil, the material situation was very bad. We had to have coupons for everything. There was a shortage of basic foods, including bread, but perhaps the worst of all was the lack of coal and gas. Cars, if they had not been requisitioned by the Germans, were left in garages, and during those wartime winters we burned paper and wood in a stove which had been installed in the entrance to the apartment; central heating was out. In the evenings my parents and I sat together in one room and I studied there. As I had the habit of reciting my maths lessons aloud while writing on a blackboard, my parents' reading was rather disturbed.

I was lucky enough, however, to be able to spend my summers during the war with my grandparents in Normandy. I had to cycle there, or take the train as far as Gisors, then a horse and cart from Gisors to Puchay. From time to time my parents came down and took some provisions back to Paris: butter, eggs and potatoes from the local farmers. They had become friends of ours because three of my schoolfriends from the *Lycée* and I had spent two months of our holiday working in their fields. They told us quite kindly that a pitchfork was heavier than a pen, but they appreciated our willingness. During those three summers I learned what the life of an agricultural labourer is really like, and I can still feel the crick in my back whenever I see a bale of hay.

In 1943 I was carrying false papers to avoid the risk of 'forced labour': the Germans had decided to send young Frenchmen, born in 1922 and 1923, to Germany. My turn was coming up so my birthdate was changed to 1926 and my name to Jean Martin. Everybody in the village knew me but I was never denounced, and this left me with a very warm affection for the inhabitants.

In the same year my parents had bought a beautiful house at Chennevières-sur-Marne. The previous owners were M. and Mme Dauphin; Colonel Dauphin was one of the leaders of the Resistance in Paris. Their two children, Jacques and Denise, became my friends. We were living in that house on 6 June 1944,

27

the day of the Allied landing. What a wonderful day that was for us; at last we could hope for an early liberation! There was an all-out strike on the railways. I had recently met Dr Deplus, one of the organizers of the local Resistance group, and had offered him my services: 'Nothing to be done at the moment but you'll be able to act as our interpreter when the Americans arrive.'

The waiting was long: I no longer went to the *Lycée*. I had made several friends and from time to time we went swimming or boating on the Marne. Life in our little commune was very tranquil. My father took the train to Paris every day from La Varenne station to the Bastille. M. Dauphin had introduced him to two of his friends who also worked in Paris: Dr Barreau, a medical specialist with the social security department, and M. Gustave Féron, manager of the Paris office of the Saint-Quentin cotton mill. All three of them travelled by train every morning and evening. Without realizing it, they were leading the same sort of life that Americans who work in New York and live in the pleasanter suburbs live nowadays. They also talked about their children and I learnt from my father that M. Féron had two daughters and a son, and Dr Barreau had a daughter.

On July 24th Jacques Dauphin rang me to suggest a picnic on an island in the Marne. He explained that there were more boys than girls in the party he had gathered and asked me to invite Danièle and Françoise Féron. He also said that their father was very strict and would not let his girls go out except to the *Lycée*, on a shopping expedition, or from time to time to attend dancing lessons. 'As you're new to the village, perhaps you'll have a better chance of success,' he explained.

I managed to overcome my shyness and called Mme Féron and asked to speak to Françoise. I explained our plans to her, and after several seconds' discussion with her mother Françoise replied that she and her sister could come on condition they got home before their father did.

We spent a lovely day on the Island of Love! At the end of the day I climbed the hill to Chennevières, walked into the house, and announced to my mother that today I had met the girl I was going to marry. My mother began by reminding me that I was not yet twenty years old, and secondly asked a question that had never entered my head: 'Have you told this girl you intend to make her your wife?' She added that in any case I had to finish my studies. I was annoyed at this 'reasonable' reaction, but understood it perfectly well, especially since I knew that the examinations had been cancelled for the time being. I had no hope of entering the *Ecole Polytechnique* before 1945.

So began our 'courtship' and a little less than four years later, on 30 March 1948, Françoise Féron married a student in his third year at the *Ecole Centrale de Paris*.

The liberation of Paris produced tremendous jubilation. But Chennevières was not liberated and the fort at Champigny was held by German troops who were covering the retreat of an armoured division heading for the northeast. For several days armoured vehicles rolled through the streets, passing regularly in front of our house. Chennevières was finally liberated, but profound disgust stained my joy. How busy some men were shaving the heads of women accused of collaboration . . . men who had never lifted a finger before! I knew that it was difficult for the Resistance to keep large numbers of fighters in the Paris area, but that was still no excuse for the stay-at-homes to try to earn themselves good-conduct medals by indulging in vengeful acts once the danger was over.

During the whole of that summer and well into the autumn I worked as an interpreter in an American supply unit stationed at Chennevières. I made friends, improved my English, and admired their organization.

In 1945 it was back to the *Lycée Saint-Louis*. René Dufaud, our friend Tabouret and I organized military training for the war was still going on and we thought that when the academic year was over – the last year of preparation for the exams – we would be able to leave. Every Saturday and Sunday we did our drill. Then came May 1945. The war really was over and the examinations were to be held at last. I failed my entrance exam to the *Ecole Polytechnique*, but I was accepted at the *Ecole Centrale*. Farewell to a career in the civil service. Farewell to my hopes of one day becoming a Chief Government Civil Engineer. It was a great shock, and during the ten years that followed I very often dreamed about that examination, and of our mathematics professor at the *Lycée Saint-Louis* who used to say to me from time to time, 'So, you're not even capable of. . . .'

Life returned almost to its normal tenor. I worked hard. I wanted to gain high marks because each graduating class had the opportunity of winning two scholarships to the United States and I was keen to get one of them. On 7 July 1946 Françoise and I became engaged. I had just finished my first year at the *Centrale*. I still had two years to go and there was no question of bringing forward the date of our wedding; our parents were determined that I must first have a 'position'.

That summer I went to Ugine Steel Mills for a period of training and learned everything I could about steel, but I missed my fiancée and nothing in the work really excited my interest. At the end of the second year, still determined to go to the United States in a year's time, and wanting to improve my English, I obtained an apprenticeship at the Loughborough Brush Electrical Company in England. My work was repetitive: I had to start up the little diesel engines at the end of the assembly line, make a number of measurements, give them to the foreman, and tell him whether or not the engines were in fit condition to be delivered to the customers. During my first week I was astonished to see that all my fellow-workers queued up in front of the punch time clock to wait for 5 p.m., the hour at which the factory closed. During the second week I was always near the head of the queue at clocking-off time. I only spent six weeks there, but it was long enough to learn what it means to do a tedious job.

In 1947–8 I spent my third year at the *Centrale*. I had matured considerably, and I had found an admirable priest with whom I had long discussions. I had myself baptized and asked my future father-in-law to be my godfather. My father's youngest sister acted as my godmother.

Our two sets of parents began to weaken on the subject of our wedding date and now they agreed to March 30th. My parents persuaded the landlord of their Paris apartment to make the lease over to us, decided that they would settle permanently in Chennevières, and we left for a short honeymoon at Villefranche-sur-Mer.

I submitted my application for a one-year scholarship to the USA, offered by the cultural relations department of the Ministry of Foreign Affairs. These scholarships are given to those who wish to continue studying after their Master's degree. As I had been passionately interested in Professor Lehmann's electronics course which was optional at that time, I chose as the subject for my obligatory thesis: 'The use of electronics in calculators'. I learned that the $2,500 scholarship would cover the expenses of a student at the Massachusetts Institute of Technology where I was hoping to go. But how could the two of us live on it? A solution had to be found, and when I was awarded the scholarship the cultural relations service authorized me to do the same work within the industry itself. I had to try to find a firm which was sufficiently interested in my field of study to take me on. I discussed it with my father-in-law who knew the Sales Manager of IBM France, M. Desouches. I was interviewed by him, by M. Blanchard, the Assistant General Manager, and then, last lap, by M.W. Borel, the Chairman. One week later I was accepted: IBM France took me on — I would start work on 15 June 1948.

Shortly before we left school the student society organized a ball. I escorted my very young wife to it and felt extremely proud. We all talked about our future employment and I came away discouraged. 'You should never have agreed to work for IBM. They squeeze people dry in that company and there's a rapid turnover of staff,' I was told. This image was false, as I can testify after spending my working life with the corporation, which, in fact, has one of the lowest turnover rates in the industrial world — a rate comparable to that of the Japanese.

There was no time for holidays between leaving school and entering IBM in the Commercial Methods and Applications

31

Department. In 1948, IBM France was a medium-sized company. At that time there were 1,048 employees, but there was already a laboratory on the rue Michel-Bizot in the 12th *arrondissement* of Paris, a factory at Vincennes, and a manufacturing workshop at Essonnes. Amongst the items manufactured and sold were electric typewriters, time clocks, and punch-card machines. The fastest of the tabulators could print 100 lines per minute. In 1948 the IBM Group, with the sixty subsidiaries it already possessed throughout the world, realized an annual turnover of $150 million. This is less, much less, than the turnover achieved today by the American subsidiaries of some French companies — such as Renault, Saint-Gobain, l'Air Liquide, Michelin and many others.

The total number of IBM's employees, world-wide, in 1948, was 25,000. When speaking of today's industrial giants, people all too often forget that they were once small firms and that it is the will to grow that has led them to be what they are today; it is this growth, moreover, which is so favourable to employees, to clients, to suppliers, and to the countries in which subsidiaries are set up.

In 1948 sending a young, newly-hired engineer to the United States posed certain problems for the management of IBM France. It required, in particular, the agreement of the International Division and even that of Mr T.J. Watson, the Chairman and founder of the company. Further, it was the first time since 1939 that a European employee was to work in an establishment belonging to the mother company. I felt rather at sea because nobody could tell me when I would be leaving.

In August Mr T.J. Watson, accompanied by his closest associates, visited Paris. This was his first trip to Europe since the war. I went to see M.G. Blanchard, Assistant General Manager of IBM France, and asked him whether the question of my scholarship to the USA had been brought up. He replied, 'No, not yet, but why don't you apply to Mr Watson personally?' I was scared stiff, but I plucked up the courage to request an interview with the Big White Chief. His secretary called me soon afterwards: 'Mr Watson will see you at 10 o'clock tomorrow morning.' I spent hours pondering on how best to present my case.

Mr Watson received me. I was in a terrible funk, but fortunately managed not to stammer too badly. He put me at my ease, congratulated me on having won a scholarship, called Mr Saber, one of his managers, and asked him to organize my stay in the USA immediately. I left his office on the Place Vendôme, impressed and shaking. What an extraordinary lesson in human relations IBM's top American executive had given me! I have never forgotten it, and throughout my entire career I have tried to make myself accessible, to see all those who wanted to see me quickly, and not to allow telephone calls to interrupt an interview.

And so everything was arranged. Françoise and I were to leave on the French liner, *De Grasse*, in early September, travelling in fourth class since there wasn't a fifth. It was a great adventure. Our parents were very sad and we went from farewell visit to farewell visit. Our parents, a few friends, and M. Blanchard accompanied us to the Gare Saint-Lazare. Anyone would have thought it was a pair of famous film stars they were sending off. We ourselves were simultaneously happy to be tasting adventure and sad to be leaving our loved ones for a year. Our parents were all the more sorry to see us go because our stay overseas would prevent them from being with us for the birth of their first grandchild who was expected in early January.

I was already convinced that the concept of European class struggle was outdated. Even before 1936 my wife's family, as well as my own, had shown to me that each generation could do better for itself than the preceding one, but that this could only be accomplished by work, motivated by ambition for oneself as well as for one's children. Having had grandparents, parents, uncles, aunts, male and female cousins, amongst whom were to be found – and can still be found – labourers, clerks, peasants, managerial staff, heads of smaller businesses, members of the liberal professions, and civil servants, and having felt a great deal of love and affection for them all, I do not see why there should be any hostility between the classes whatsoever. This is particularly true as I believe in equal opportunities and that schooling, further education, and training give everyone the chance to change his circumstances.

Another conviction I acquired very early in my life was that egalitarianism becomes an absurdity when it is pushed to extremes. It is idle to hope that every young man will be six feet tall and a fine basketball player. Or that all boys and girls will be equally successful academically or have the same ambitions and attainments in their careers. Nor can one hope that everyone will be ready to accept the sacrifices involved in taking up the responsibility of leadership. In 1948 it was my belief (and still is) that society has a duty to give all adolescents the kind of education that will permit them, if they wish, to enter a calling or profession that will bring them job-satisfaction.

My third conviction is that laxness, the abandoning of effort, the negligence of our leaders, the sterile political in-fighting, and a certain amount of treachery led to the disaster of 1940. I already felt as a young man that a change of mental attitude was needed in France, and that people should be made to understand that without definite aims and without effort nothing could be achieved.

My fourth conviction was the necessity of tolerance. My parents had allowed me total freedom of political and religious belief. Naturally, they influenced me, but they did it by example. I had learned the hard way how much suffering is caused by authoritarianism and by racism.

And lastly, I had already learned to respect others. Respect for my family, my teachers, my friends, and, still more important, the chance encounters that had brought me into contact with foreigners, had taught me to respect them, too. I had known Armenians during my childhood, and Americans and Englishmen during the war; my period of work in an English factory had revealed to me that not all inventions were French. I had come to the conclusion that it was a good thing to be a patriot, but a very bad thing to be a chauvinist.

Thirty-seven years later, it still seems to me that chauvinism is one of the greatest obstacles on the road to peace. When it is transmuted into xenophobia, as is the case in many countries, it damages the country and retards her development. I would like to offer some reflections on this subject.

2

Xenophobia

'Love enhances knowledge, and knowledge enhances love,' said the art critic, Emile Male. The trouble is that many people apply this formula only to their own countries, which they love and know profoundly, to the exclusion of all others. However, this maxim is true everywhere: as soon as one learns to know a new country, one begins to love it. Xenophobia is indeed a sign of ignorance. A great many people, who have never been out of their own countries except for the odd tourist trip, retain false ideas about other nations. And, since it is easy to blame others for the troubles that befall us, foreigners are declared to be responsible for all our ills. We have all heard this kind of talk, and it must be said that certain sections of the press delight in making similar declarations. The argument contains a common denominator: it is easy to make the foreigner your scapegoat! But this is a lazy solution and if we would only recognize that it is we, ourselves, who generate certain problems perhaps we could resolve them.

When you leave your own country you meet compatriots who have lived and worked abroad. You discover then a very different environment, composed of people who have shed many of their prejudices, and who, from a distance, can regard their home country with great objectivity. If they love it, it is with a greater love than before for it is not a blind passion, nor is it at the expense of other countries. Very often they have also learned to love and respect the country they currently live in. And they are sick of the old clichés.

This has been my own experience; from 1948 on I have spent more than fifteen years living outside France and I have worked in every country in Europe, as well as in the USA, in South America, Japan and Australia. I have also travelled in the USSR and in China.

When I graduated from the *Ecole Centrale* in 1948 I was the product of a nationalistic and chauvinistic education: at that time I believed Americans lacked culture; South Americans were idle firebrands; the Germans were hard and industrious; the Italians a little frivolous; and the English insular egoists. The French, of course, possessed all the best qualities: they were, according to me, intelligent, shrewd, hardworking, and resourceful. As for recognizing their faults, that would have been difficult – I had never allowed myself even to suspect they might have any!

Today, after working for thirty-six years in numerous countries, I have a very different vision of the world for I have met many highly-cultured Americans; ambitious and dynamic South Americans; very quick-witted Germans; very hardworking Italians; Englishmen with a truly European outlook; and, unfortunately, some Frenchmen who were dour, insular, and uncultured. I have come to the conclusion that those who attribute the same general characteristics to an entire nation show an astonishing lack of knowledge. The statistical distribution of vices and virtues has been made on a democratic basis.

While attending dinners in Paris, I have very often heard people explaining the United States to their neighbours, laying down the law, and saying the most damning things about New York. When they are well-launched into their critical diatribe, I ask them whether they have been to New York and the USA. It may seem incredible, but quite a few have replied that they have never been there, and, what is more, have no desire to go. I have had the same experiences with Americans in New York. They met one nasty cab driver in Paris – who may not even have been French – and so, all French people are bad.

We all run the risk of extrapolating on the basis of limited experience. We meet two or three Germans and then we dare to state categorically: 'The Germans are like this.' When it comes to comprehending countries as vast as the United States, Russia or China, the difficulty is even greater. A knowledge of the United

States is, however, easier to acquire since you are permitted to travel freely there, meet whomever you wish, and ask without reservation all the questions you could possibly think of. Ignorance very often accounts for xenophobia, but it can also have another origin: the difficulty or embarrassment one nation feels in showing recognition of the aid brought to them by another.

One day, after our second two-year stay in the United States, I happened to be travelling from Le Havre to Paris. It was 26 August 1964 and we were celebrating the twentieth anniversary of the liberation of the French capital. As I listened to the radio, it occurred to me that if I had not known the true facts I would never have believed that the Canadians, the British, and the Americans had played any part at all in the Liberation of France. The commentators recalled only the exploits of the French forces. They did not lie, they simply ignored all the others, but such selective information has a profound effect on public opinion.

At that time it was *chic* to be anti-American. The Americans were not only strong, economically and militarily – a condition not likely to win them much sympathy – but they were foreigners as well. In September 1966 I wrote the following on this subject:

We are approaching the situation, at once laughable and grave, where anyone who dares to say he admires or loves the United States will be considered unpatriotic. And yet the USA has not changed. Everyone I know who has lived in America has a profound admiration for that country. Unfortunately the information available, whether on TV, on the radio or in the press, is incomplete. They tell us only the bad side of things. They should give us the total picture.

Let them show us the efforts the American government is making to fight poverty; let them show us the outstanding achievements of American science; let them show us the aid the Americans are giving to the Third World; let them tell us about the new methods of education in America and let them explain to us the secrets of American productivity.

Let them explain to the French people that Americans are

not the efficient but barbarous brutes some people imagine them to be, and that the fourteen scientists who have won Nobel Prizes for their achievements, the talented painters, writers and musicians who live in the USA are all contributing to the evolution and progress of the human race.

In the United States, France enjoys considerable prestige. There was a time when we did not understand that our hostility would have grave consequences. Nationalism is good when it stimulates and gives due importance to a nation's strengths, and when it promotes healthy competition. But when, on the other hand, it becomes xenophobia and draws its strength solely from denigrating others, it will rapidly become sterile.

If this happens, France in a few years will find herself isolated from her old friends, and her new friends will be unable to trust her. Scientific and economic progress will be seriously retarded because we shall no longer benefit from vital international exchanges. Let us realize this, and move with the times.

I would not repudiate one word of what I wrote in 1966.

It is natural to be attracted to those with whom we share a common heritage, particularly in the cultural domain. It is natural, but only so long as this attraction towards our compatriots does not lead us to reject others. Young people, happily, are more open to the world than their parents were at the same age. My hopes of one day seeing the creation of a United Europe spring from the confidence I have in these adolescents, who travel, get to know other countries, speak foreign languages and have friends in many different lands.

It is my own children who have taught me to understand how this is happening: my eldest daughter married a Frenchman; the second, an American of Irish origin; the third, a British citizen whose father was Scottish and whose mother is Italian; and my son married a lovely French girl, whose father and mother are Italian. Now I wonder who will marry my youngest daughter, who speaks fluent English, good German, and can get by in Russian. I already have eight grandchildren of whom five have grandparents of at least two different nationalities. The environment they live in will certainly influence them, and I believe I am entitled to hope that they will acquire very open minds.

In spite of a certain increase in racism which I deplore, it seems to me that the primary reactions of xenophobia have tended to disappear. It is also a striking fact that it is precisely by drawing on their national culture that numerous artists and writers have, in this century, evolved a language which has been recognized throughout the world as a universal language. Lastly, one recognizes that the supreme values belong to the whole of humanity. Each one of us can draw a very simple lesson from this: the love we feel for our own country can and must form a part of our universal outlook.

3

The Discovery of America

The *De Grasse* took nine days to make the crossing from Le Havre to New York. For Françoise and myself it was a second honeymoon. There were few people of our own age on board since, at that time, young people rarely had sufficient means to travel. We read a great deal in order to begin to 'know' America. We were on deck when the ship sailed into New York harbour, and the moment when we first caught sight of the Statue of Liberty was a very emotional one. Young as I was, I took a certain pride in knowing that the metal structure which supported Bartholdi's work had been conceived by one of the most famous graduates of my school of engineering, Gustave Eiffel. Even today, I sometimes amuse myself and faze Americans by quoting this fact.

It was a Saturday. There was no one to welcome us, and we experienced a moment of panic as we did not know which hotel to go to. Impossible to get hold of anybody from IBM. I telephoned a friend of a friend who had supplied us with the affidavit necessary to obtain a visa.

'No problem, come to my apartment,' said Jacques Artel who, as a very young man, had left his native Russia to come to France, had fought in the war, and then in 1946 decided to try his luck in America. We arrived at his home on 24th Street between 2nd and 3rd Avenue. He welcomed us with amazing kindness and warmth. We were confused, but he soon put us at our ease and suggested we stay with him as long as we liked. We lived at his place for a month; on the following Monday, when I arrived at the IBM offices at 590 Madison Avenue on the corner of 57th Street, I discovered that while they had made a 'little' preparation for my working studies, they had made no arrangements whatever for our accommodation.

I was interviewed by E. Saber: 'We suggest that you spend a month in New York where you will work in the Computing Department. Then you will go to Endicott to follow a customer-engineering course for six months, and finally the rest of your stay will be spent at the factory in Poughkeepsie, where you will work on the final testing of a new electronic calculator.' I accepted, of course, but without having any clear idea of what all this meant.

Mr Saber took me up to the first floor of the building where the 'scientists' were to be found. And there for the first time I heard those 'Pleased to meet you's' and 'Wonderful to have you on board's' which accompany all introductions in the United States.

They gave me a desk in a large room where about twenty engineers and mathematicians worked. They showed me the library where, it seemed, I would find all the documents I could possibly need. After that I visited the machine-room on the ground floor. The monster Selective Sequence Electronic Calculator was housed there; its little neon tubes flashed on and off, the printers crackled, and boxes full of punch-cards littered the room. A demonstration, followed by several hours of explanation, took place. Not much theory: they were teaching me to drive a car rather than the functioning of its engine.

This was my first cultural shock! From the very first day I discovered American pragmatism. I had expected that they would explain to me the functioning of an electronic calculator, and then show me an electrical diagram of the machine. But no, instead I was told: 'It can make 3,500 additions per second; the programme is recorded; you feed in the cards on which you have punched the data connected to the problem to be solved and you press the start button.' My colleagues were the men who used the machine, not the men who built it.

After this brief introduction they gave me several problems to solve. They were new and difficult and – my second shock – I realized that not all mathematicians trained in Applied Mathematics, and not even those from the *Ecole Centrale*, were thoroughly up-to-date with the most recent discoveries. I came to the conclusion that our training was not downright bad, but that it had not been systematically up-dated!

I set myself the task of learning matrix computation with the help of the books in IBM's library. I also learnt the binary system and the theory of circuits, for I wanted to have a complete understanding of what went on inside the guts of the monster. After a month I had made good progress and knew, at least, what a double triode, a flip-flop circuit and matrix computation were.

On 12 October 1948 we left New York by train for Endicott. This little town, situated half way between New York and Niagara Falls, was host to two companies: IBM and Endicott-Johnson, a shoe manufacturer. IBM had factories, a research laboratory and a training centre there. We settled into the only hotel in the place, the Frederick. It was rather dreary! We had to find ourselves an apartment. This was not easy because we soon discovered that $250 a month was a very lean income. Through IBM I heard that one of the company's employees was willing to share his apartment with us. And so we met a very likeable man, Mr C. Edson, about fifty years old, who immediately said to us: 'Call me Charlie.' He lived alone in an apartment which had two bedrooms, a kitchen-dining room, and a living room. We moved in with him and our life *à deux* in America began. Having just left Paris, where food was still rationed, we marvelled to find all the shops absolutely stuffed with goods of every kind.

I was assigned to the 'customer-engineering' school, where engineers responsible for the maintenance of punch-card machines were trained. The course consisted of teaching us the basic theory of these machines – their mechanics and the electrical relays – and the practical work of repairing them when they broke down. It was the first time I had done any intensive manual work. I was a little disappointed for, while everything I had learned in New York was going to be very useful to me when I came to write my thesis on electronics, this course in electrical and mechanical maintenance was taking me right away from it. I was tempted to ask for a transfer but did not dare; the only solution was to do what I had to do as well as I possibly could. I learned all the maintenance manuals by heart and recited them at home in the evenings, aloud, so as to improve my English; I began to handle screwdrivers, pliers and a voltmeter with ease. I thought of the motto – *Age quod agis* – I had adopted in my penultimate year at the *lycée*, and I was one of the top students at the end of the Endicott course. It was my own way of thanking those who had made this training period possible for me, and still more of demonstrating to the Americans that a Frenchman could be competitive.

During this time Françoise found that the change from the Sorbonne, where she had been studying for her degree in English, to Endicott, where she spent her time between our gloomy apartment and the not very well-stocked municipal library, also represented culture shock. But her optimistic nature, and the anticipation of the birth of our first child, enabled her to be very happy. She spent hours writing home to the family and keeping up her diary. We had no car, so our weekends were very simple: perhaps a little stroll through the village and always a great deal of reading.

The inhabitants, even those who were working for IBM, were not particularly welcoming which is rare in the USA. During the first three months we were never invited anywhere, except to official dinners at IBM, which were given when VIPs visited. These dinners always ended with two or three speeches of variable interest. I remember one, however, given by the president of a university who embroidered his theme with a quotation from Pasteur: 'Luck favours prepared minds.' I was pleased that he had chosen to quote a Frenchman, and still more delighted with the quotation itself which I have never forgotten.

Françoise knitted and sewed for the coming baby. We bought everything that would be needed. Our visit to the Lourdes Hospital in Binghamton, a nearby town which boasted the best obstetricians, produced another shock. The fee for a few visits and for the delivery itself was $500. That was exactly the amount we had been able to bring out of France, since at that time there were exchange controls.

On the evening of 31 December Françoise had to go into hospital; the baby was about to be born. It had been snowing for several days and our landlord, who had offered to drive us to hospital on The Day, was away. I went to the local taxi stand and waited there a long time, but in vain. I decided to go to the company manager who at once offered to drive us there himself. We set out along a road covered with snow and every five minutes he turned round to ask: 'Are you all right, Madame?' He was terrified the baby would be born in his car.

We entered the hospital. After Françoise was examined she was told the baby would be born in the morning. I asked if I could stay, but the rules were strict. I returned to Endicott on foot, more than eight miles through the snow. No sooner did I get there, at about six in the morning, than the telephone rang. It was the hospital calling: 'You can come back now; the baby is about to be born.' Fortunately, our landlord had returned, I woke him up, and he took me to Binghamton. I arrived just as they were taking my wife into the labour room. I waited, tramping up and down, then a nurse appeared and told me we had a beautiful little daughter and that my wife was doing fine. An hour later they were both brought back to the ward. We were so happy! Christine was a really pretty baby; my wife was radiant and smiling. I returned to Endicott and made my first telephone call to Chennevières (where both sets of our parents lived) since our arrival in the USA. Such joy and excitement at the other end of the line; my parents-in-law said they would pass on the message.

I carried on attending my courses, and in the evenings took the bus to visit my wife and daughter. For nearly a week I did not eat; I just drank milk and nibbled a few biscuits for I had not a single dollar left. My monthly scholarship payment was overdue.

I was so happy when my wife came home with Christine. Then we enjoyed a big surprise: an American tradition in small towns at any rate demands that the birth of the first baby to arrive each year should be celebrated. We read in the local newspaper: 'Christine Danièle Maisonrouge – the Winner'. This was a great stroke of luck for us because all the shopkeepers offered our baby a present. At a time when our resources were desperately low, their gifts were extremely useful and enabled us to save money, and rent a car for a month later on.

A new life began for us: our life as parents. Obviously we had had no experience and we had no one to advise us either. In America, medicine was already highly specialized. The obstetrician had given us the name of a paediatrician. Two weeks after her birth, we discovered that Christine was not putting on weight in accordance with the graph we had been given. My wife rang the paediatrician who asked if it was serious. We did not know of course and asked him to come . . . 'Oh, no, bring the child to me!' We pointed out to him that it was far too cold to do so and he came, found the child to be perfectly healthy, made a few recommendations and reproached us for having disturbed him for nothing.

An event now occurred at Endicott that was to change our lives. Jimmy Johnston, the Vice-President responsible for all IBM's factories world-wide, returned from a long trip to Europe. His wife was French. One Saturday shortly after his return we were invited to lunch at his home. In this little provincial town, everybody knows what everybody else is doing, and from that day on we were invited by a great many families.

The Junior Chamber of Commerce also heard about this foreign couple in their midst. I was asked to give a lecture; I talked about France under the Occupation, the destruction caused before and during the Liberation, and the efforts that were then being made to reconstruct my country. Very few Americans knew what had happened. The Endicott newspaper printed a long article about my lecture. This was my first public appearance.

A new course to do with the first commercial electronic calculator, the 604, was announced by IBM. Now here was a course that really interested me, and I was the only 'new boy' among the experienced maintenance engineers who came to study the new machine as part of their continuous training programme. My best friend was Hans Fietze, a colleague of German extraction. At the end of the course we were at the top of the class; he was first and I found myself in a place I was to remain in for a long time during my career – second.

IBM's Education Center at Endicott was already important. The steps leading up to the main entrance bear inscriptions which surprised me: 'READ ... LISTEN ... DISCUSS ... OBSERVE ... THINK.' As well as the traditional courses for salesmen, engineers and maintenance engineers, there was also a full programme of general education. I was invited several times to take part in the French courses given to all members of the staff who wished to attend. I studied this system of 'continuous training', and discovered that even as early as 1949 it was one of the great strengths of this corporation! There were also management courses which all employees worthy of promotion were obliged to attend. So here was a company of average size whose president, even before the war, had already perceived the importance of continuous training. The number of 'students' was considerable. Ever since 1949 there have been optional courses in electronics.

By now my wife and I had learnt a great deal about the real, underlying America. The more time passed, the more we came to understand and to love it. In those six months at Endicott we learned that one should never make hasty judgements, but wait and try to understand. We met people from every stratum of society. One of our best friends, whose wife was French, was a lathe-operator at IBM. My fellow students in class were generally people whose level of education was equivalent to a French school leaving certificate or an American high school matriculation. The instructors were 'old men' of thirty-five or forty who had fought in the war, but they never talked about it. The Americans' reticence regarding their service records never ceased to amaze me. We also knew the Director of Training and the Vice-President of Manufacturing. If I add to all these IBM employees, the people we also met through the Junior Chamber of Commerce and the university professors who completed the 'faculty' at IBM, I think I can honestly say that in those six months we got to know a representative cross-section of American society.

We were invited to dinners which were invariably preceded by a prayer, sometimes given by a pastor, a rabbi or a Catholic priest, and we realized how extremely tolerant this nation was in religious matters.

When Dick Watson, son of the Chairman and President of the International Division, was passing through Endicott, he invited us to dine at the company club. Like his father he understood the meaning of good human relations.

Certain company traditions, however, surprised me. No alcohol, not even wine, was ever served on the company's premises, nor during official dinners held elsewhere. Every Friday morning from 8 to 8.30 a.m., all the 'students' in Endicott gathered together to sing. That was how I learned traditional American songs, and also two hymns to the glory of Mr T.J. Watson. I must admit this seemed rather bizarre to me, but I realized that this kind of exercise contributed to the forging of a company *esprit de corps*.

Today employees of the Matsushita Company in Japan still gather together to sing songs glorifying their industry and its boss, Mr Matsushita. When you see the results, you are not inclined to laugh. Some years ago I discovered that many of the Japanese management methods that astound Westerners were, in fact, borrowed from the Americans, adapted to Japanese culture and rigorously imposed.

My six-month stay in Endicott taught me a good deal about the administration of a large business. I was too inexperienced to understand everything and in too lowly a position to interpret correctly the things I had been able to observe. Nevertheless I had been instantly impressed by the importance given to the training of personnel. I did not know exactly how much IBM spent on staff training at the end of the 1940s but it was already a considerable sum. Never, during the courses I followed at the *Ecole Centrale*, nor within French industry, in spite of all the contacts I had made, had I heard anyone speak of the necessity for training people in order to promote them. This emphasis on training was one of the aspects of IBM's policies that was well-ahead of its time, even in the United States. It was Mr T.J. Watson who had conceived this policy. In 1930, in the early days of the Depression, and when

IBM was still a small company, the Chairman had decided that there would be no dismissals for economic reasons.

He decided that the factories would continue to function and that the machines produced would be stock-piled, since very few clients were taking delivery. When President Roosevelt launched his New Deal to bring the country out of the crisis, numerous social services were established in particular Social Security, and this meant a sudden demand for punch-card machines. IBM, who had stock, was able to supply them at once, while its competitors, who had ceased production, had to ask for very long delivery schedules.

It was during this stay that I also learned the main principles of the company such as its respect for the individual. Even on a course as technical as the one for maintenance engineers, we had seminars on human relations and on management-labour relations. The policy regarding salaries and internal promotion was also explained to us. Even in those days the rule was to promote company employees rather than to engage trained personnel from elsewhere. No outsiders were ever 'parachuted in'. This policy, still flourishing today, had already created excellent morale.

Another IBM principle was and still is to try to promote satisfaction among employees, customers and shareholders alike. I must admit that at the time I did not understand too clearly why it was important for an organization to state principles that were already known and approved by everyone. I was also taught the process by which everyone could progress right through the company: assessment by the management, in-job training, and promotion.

Another thing I observed at Endicott was the mobility of Americans. The instructors in the different schools came from their specialist fields and were assigned to the Training Center for two or three years, then they were sent to another area, generally to a post which carried promotion with it.

In March, I attended the final course of my training period: the product to be studied was a new accounting machine, the 403, a machine which could print 150 lines per minute. What speed!

A Frenchman from IBM France came to Endicott soon after my

arrival there. He had been sent to the sales school where almost all those who had attained, or were to attain, important positions in the corporation had been trained, or were to be trained. Three times, at intervals of a few days, he asked me what I was doing at Endicott. His contempt for the 'manual worker', which I had become, was apparent. Françoise and I invited him to lunch, thinking he would enjoy being with other French people again. Although we never drank wine, because it was too expensive, we had bought a good bottle for the occasion. When I came to serve it, he refused and gave me a lecture: 'Don't you know it's against company policy to serve alcohol at meals amongst colleagues!!!' I had not realized he was incapable of interpreting a policy, and when he became a subordinate of mine several years later I refrained from reminding him of this incident.

My assignment at Endicott came to an end and we departed for Poughkeepsie. This time everything had been prepared for our arrival. We were warmly welcomed by the senior staff of the factory where I was to work. Two families were particularly helpful: the Deuells and the Ritzes. Paul Deuell was head of the Personnel Department; Francis Ritz was a production engineer who was about to leave for Europe to launch the manufacture of typewriters there. These two couples treated us like members of their own families by introducing us to their friends and showing us around the area.

My work at Poughkeepsie was interesting: three weeks on the key-punch assembly line (this product has virtually disappeared during the 1980s). I was lucky not to find myself in the same kind of routine boring job I endured during my spell in England. Far from it, in fact. Two or three years earlier Mr T.J. Watson had initiated the idea of job enrichment. He was one of the first to understand how onerous production-line work can be, and how tedious repetitive work can become. He eliminated the job of the assembly-line inspector and made each assembly-line worker responsible for checking his own work. And more importantly, instead of having the assembly belt move along in front of the workers with each man carrying out just one or two very simple operations, the machine remained stationary and each worker assembled a whole unit from A to Z, checked it and sent it on for final inspection. I cannot say that I would have been willing to do this job for years and years, but I was not bored while I had to.

At last, as my final job during my probationary period, I undertook the final testing of the Electronic Calculator 604. This machine allowed an operator to perform several dozen functions per second; the data was fed in and read by punch-cards that passed through at the rate of 100 cards per minute. The 604 contained an important technological innovation: the electronic circuits were mounted on a support that could be disconnected like a lamp. This allowed a defective circuit to be replaced very simply, thus eliminating the long and costly business of dismantling and re-assembling the components. Apart from the very big machines, such as those at Harvard, the ESSC at IBM or the ENIAC, there was nothing on the market that gave a comparable performance. I knew the circuits very well and believed that I was making myself useful.

My wife was much happier here than at Endicott. The spring and then the summer were much more pleasant than that snowy winter of 1949. She was able to take our little girl out into the beautiful gardens of Vassar College, one of the most famous women's colleges in the USA. It was there that Christine learned to smile and to say 'mama' and 'papa'! During May, we managed to rent an old Plymouth and take trips to Washington and Boston. In Washington, we were greeted by the most delightful man, Red Lamotte, Vice-President of IBM, who treated us as if I were a 'top executive'.

In Boston, I paid a visit to the MARK I, conceived by Professor Aiken and constructed with the collaboration of IBM in 1944. It was a very powerful electromagnetic calculator. I had requested a meeting with the Dean of the Engineering Faculty at Harvard; he gave me a friendly reception and a good lesson in humility. After questioning me for several minutes about IBM, he asked:

'What education have you had?'

'I graduated as an engineer from the *Ecole Centrale des Arts et Manufactures.*'

'Good! What else have you done?'

'I passed my *baccalauréat* in Mathematics.'

'Ah! That's excellent!'

From this conversation, I realized that the great French schools of engineering, or at least the *Centrale*, were not well-known in the United States. Many times during the years that followed I had to explain the French educational system to people who only knew about the Sorbonne.

We often went to the company club for walks. The club had a golf course, bowling alleys and tennis courts. Every employee, no matter what his rank, was entitled to join and to play with the various teams for an annual subscription of one dollar – yes, really, just one dollar!

Every day, I had lunch at the factory and I saw that here, as at Endicott, there was just one cafeteria. The assembly-line worker and the managing director of the plant were served the same menu and ate in the same room; this was very different from what I had seen in France and England. I felt very comfortable.

An event now occurred which was to have an important bearing on my career. Each year, at the end of June, Mr Watson visited the plant on a Friday and stayed over on the Saturday so as to attend a grand dinner in the evening, during the course of which he presented the trophies that had been won by the company's best sportsmen. During the latter part of that afternoon, the employees strolled over the lawns of the country club with their families and watched some of the finals in the tennis and golf tournaments. My wife and I were pushing the pram through the crowds of spectators when we ran into Mr and Mrs T.J. Watson. Mr Watson asked me a great many questions concerning my work and Mrs Watson cooed over our little girl, who was just six months old.

At the end of the afternoon while we were waiting for the dinner, it occurred to me that Mr Watson might ask several of the guests to speak. As there were two French couples present I guessed that he would call upon at least one of the men to make a speech. I told myself this onerous task would probably fall to Monsieur X, but recalling the quotation from Pasteur, 'Luck favours prepared minds', I began to consider what I should say if it turned out that I was the 'chosen one'. I decided to speak about the Marshall Plan which I considered to be the catalyst in the reconstruction of Europe.

And so we went in to dinner. The saying of grace, the meal itself, a speech by Mr T.J. Watson, the presentation of the most important sports cups – phew, finally all that was over! But then Mr Watson stood up again and announced that there were two French couples in the room and asked Madame X to say a few words. She spoke well, with great charm and in perfect English. Monsieur X was called upon in his turn; he said, in essence, that he had visited the factory and found it to be run with remarkable efficiency – again in flawless English. I thought that was the end of it. But, no! Mr Watson went on to ask my wife to come forward. Françoise has always been rather shy. She went up to Mr Watson, opened her mouth, but not a word came out and she fainted straight into the arms of the Chairman. It all happened very quickly, but Mr Watson was equally quick to offer the following tactful and felicitous words: 'Don't worry, Madame, I've never asked my wife to speak in public since the day she fainted in my arms.' Encouraging applause for my wife broke out as she came back trembling to our table. But Mr Watson did not leave it at that; he called me up and I gave a four-minute talk on the Marshall Plan. At last Mr Watson announced that the reception was over and invited us to have our photographs taken with Mrs Watson. He then congratulated me: 'I am happy to see that a young man like you has other interests beyond his own trade.'

The time for our departure from Poughkeepsie was drawing near. This time, at the farewell ceremonies, Paul Deuell presented us with a magnificent photograph album with the words 'Our first trip to the United States' embossed on the cover. As we gratefully accepted the album, we allowed ourselves to hope that our first visit would be followed by many others.

In July we returned to New York for a few days. The hotel had no air conditioning and we suffered from the heat and humidity until it was time to leave, once more aboard the *De Grasse*, for France. But we did have the opportunity to see some of our friends again, including the directors of the International Division of IBM. I also went to say *au revoir* to Mr Watson and his son, Dick, who had always been so nice to us.

We were, however, happy to be going home where we would be reunited with our families and be able to show off our little treasure, Christine. As a result the voyage seemed painfully slow to us. Late in the morning of the penultimate day of the crossing, we entered Southampton harbour. In the distance we could see the tender returning from shore with a number of people on board. We thought these people a little crazy to want to take the *De Grasse* from Southampton to Le Havre; we turned away without bothering to look at the new passengers since they were responsible for delaying the ship. We strolled about the deck and just as we were going down a companionway I suddenly caught sight of my father-in-law, then my parents, mother-in-law, sister-in-law and brother-in-law. What a reunion! Without writing to tell us, they had decided to spend a few days in England so as to be able to rejoin us at Southampton.

It was their first trip to England and, during a prolonged dinner, they told us in minute detail about their great cross-Channel adventure. Our own trans-Atlantic one seemed to pale by comparison. But then my father-in-law was always a marvellous raconteur and my own father also knew how to tell a good story.

4

True Liberalism

On my return I was assigned to the laboratory of IBM France to 'develop the electronics department', as my job description put it! A little later the Sales Manager, Jacques Herbart, asked me to give a lecture to the sales staff to tell them what I had seen and done in America. I spoke to them primarily about IBM, and the new products I had studied which were not yet available in Europe. Naturally my descriptions of the 604 electronic calculator filled them with wonder. I also described the plants I had visited, the two laboratories at Endicott and Poughkeepsie, and then gave them my general reactions to the USA. What had struck me most forcibly about the Americans was their sense of optimism and spirit of enterprise. Once the war was over they got back to work with terrific zest. The GI Bill had been passed: it allowed war veterans to study free of charge and hundreds of thousands of young people, upon their demobilization, instantly enrolled in colleges and universities.

Their spirit of enterprise could be seen in the desire for promotion manifest amongst the men and women who worked for large organizations, and in the existence of a large number of small and medium-sized businesses. When I first went to America this had surprised me, for I had imagined that over there there was nothing but General Motors, General Electric, Ford and a few other megafirms. The 'Jaycees', members of the Junior Chamber of Commerce, had taught me to understand the country's industrial structure otherwise.

I had read de Tocqueville and I referred in my lecture to one of his sayings: 'To the Americans, nothing seems impossible.' Although they did not talk about their war, they were happy to have emerged victorious. Their generosity was evident every day, and the Marshall Plan was a fine example of it. The cynics will say that it was in America's own interest to help in the reconstruction of Europe. Of course this is true, but perhaps other countries in similar circumstances might not have interpreted their interests in the same way.

I gave an illustration of American optimism by telling a joke I had heard a little while earlier in New York: 'A man leans out of a window on the thirtieth storey of the Empire State Building and falls out. Some people sitting by an open window on the tenth floor, immediately in the line of his fall, hear him utter these words as he free-falls past them: "Well, so far, so good!"' My colleagues smiled politely.

Then I told them that what had left the deepest impression on me was the Americans' respect for success. In France if a man is successful, we say he has been lucky, or someone has pulled strings for him, or he's married a rich wife; in America they say: 'He really deserved it.' This remark, made in 1949, was not very profound perhaps, but it seems to me to be just as true today. Such a difference in outlook has important consequences: the moment one acknowledges that success is related to personal merit and hard work, one realizes that the rewards of success are fair and well-earned. In specific terms one is no longer amazed to see that successful people earn a lot of money. Americans respect the well-paid, since this is proof that they possess certain admirable qualities.

Now in France (as in Italy and in England), people are more willing to forgive those who simply have money than those who earn it. A man whose family is well-to-do or even rich, and who can therefore live well on a small salary, would be quite acceptable to the Left, whereas a man who had acquired the same standard of living by his own efforts starting from the bottom would be considered a member of the 'trusts' or as a *nouveau riche*.

In a poll run by a French public opinion survey company, the following question was asked: 'Do you consider it should be normal practice for businesses to place a ceiling on high salaries, just as there is a guaranteed minimum wage?' Eighty per cent of those questioned answered, 'Yes'. On the other hand, only 50 per cent were in favour of a more rigorous, sliding-scale of inheritance tax in proportion to the amount of money inherited. These figures demonstrate our atavistic attitudes as an ancient nation of farmers.

Respect for success, even measured in terms of material goods, seems to me to have encouraged a desire for constant progress in the Americans. They are certain that by working hard, by learning, they can rise up through the hierarchy. Seeing so many people taking training courses had convinced me of the strength of their personal motivation.

I had also seen that human relations within IBM were much simpler and more egalitarian than in the French (and one English) organizations where I had served my time as a student-engineer. The work force's conviction that they can rise up through all the echelons of the hierarchy, no matter what their social origins, renders them totally impervious to any idea of class struggle. This is doubly so given the existence of a system which allows them to buy shares, and which thus gives them some access – however small it may be – to ownership of the means of production. In 1949 the number of shareholding employees in IBM was already considerable, and today more than 70 per cent of the 220,000 employees of IBM in the USA are shareholders. This is also true of the majority of large US corporations.

In my opinion, the redistribution of capital is the factor that has done most to modify modern capitalism. American capitalists did not wait for the French system of *participation*, nor for the Germans' *Vermögensbildung* or profit-sharing, to allow the mass of their workers to benefit from the profits of industry. But they did it American-style, that is to say, by maintaining a sense of individual effort. Every employee can buy shares at below the market price but is required to make the effort to save up for them, and to take a risk since the price of shares can always fall. Personal effort and willingness to take a risk are the two fundamental principles of true liberalism.

The results of such redistribution of capital have been extraordi-

57

nary. In the United States, as in all countries that have a market economy, the number of shareholders in any one business is generally greater than the number of its employees. There are 41 million Americans who own stock, and very often the New York cab drivers I chatted with told me they had shares in IBM and wanted to know why the price was not higher.

Here are some figures for 1984 which illustrate this point.

	Number of Employees World-wide	Number of Shareholders
General Motors	748,00	957,000
Exxon	150,00	838,750
Mobil	178,900	270,400
Ford	383,700	285,200
IBM	394,930	792,500
Texaco	68,088	331,300

In the case of IBM 30 per cent of its 93,000 employees in Europe are shareholders; in 1984 employees bought 1,052,409 shares. Such redistribution of capital is not widely recognized. Even the rulers of the Eastern bloc countries are ignorant of it, or choose to ignore it.

In 1971 I had the opportunity to organize IBM's reception for one of the first Soviet delegations to visit the United States. The highest-ranking participant was Professor Zhimerin, a member of the Academy of Sciences in Moscow and the Under-Secretary for Science and Technology. In the course of a general introduction to the corporation I explained our redistribution of capital, without mentioning who were the principal shareholders. Professor Zhimerin asked me: 'But, M. Maisonrouge, since Mr Watson is the Chairman, he probably holds more than 50 per cent of the shares?' I replied that the Watson family – two brothers and two sisters – held about 500,000 shares, in fact less than 1 per cent of the total capital. Soon after this I paid a visit to the Professor and several other members of the delegation in Moscow, and I realized I had not convinced them. These are, however, accurate figures published in the United States because the number of shares held by the company's directors is always given in its Annual Reports. In 1974 I had the same experience with another Soviet delegation, led by Mr Ponomarev, an important member of the Politburo.

Moreover an enquiry carried out in the United States during the 1970s proved to me that even young Americans who have access to all the information they could require and live in a liberal environment – one in which the State interferes far less than in most European countries – still do not have a clear understanding of the redistribution of wealth being brought about by large business organizations. One of the questions put to the sample of college and university students taking part in this survey asked: 'Do you believe that businesses pay out more money to their employees in the form of salaries than they do to their share-holders in the form of dividends, or is the opposite true?' Seventy-six per cent of the students replied that more money went to shareholders than to employees. In fact at the time of this enquiry a medium-sized company, whose shares were quoted on the Stock Exchange, distributed 96 per cent of its money in the form of salaries and other benefits paid to employees while only 4 per cent went to the shareholders.

One striking feature of the new capitalism is, therefore, that a great many people, including the company's employees, share in the profits of production. But the great evolution in modern capitalism also results from changes in the management structure.

Historically the initial entrepreneur, the creator of a new business, has not always been able to supply all the new capital required by his enterprise, and hence his share of the capital investment has diminished progressively. In part this explains the difficulties that have been experienced, and are still being experienced, by many medium-sized and small companies whose shareholders are also its owners and directors. In wanting to retain possession of the whole or the major part of the capital investment, they run the risk of putting the brakes on their company's development, especially in times when there is a credit squeeze. Moreover, when the majority of important posts are occupied by members of the family and, in extreme cases, there is a danger that they might one day sell out to an international corporation, this can prove a strong disincentive to some of the higher levels of management. It would be interesting to examine the management structure, and the redistribution of capital in those medium-sized businesses which have been taken over by major groups during the last twenty years.

In any case this evolution has affected all the big organizations: the founding family has gradually been replaced by employee-managers. The 'manager-employee' has replaced the 'manager-owner'. IBM is an interesting example. The founder had two sons who made brilliant careers within the company: Tom, the elder son, became its Chairman; Dick, the other son, became its Vice-Chairman and Chairman of the IBM World Trade Corporation. These two brothers and their two sisters had eighteen children between them. And yet, today, not one of the eighteen grandchildren of the founder is to be found in an important managerial position, nor on the Board of Directors. This transformation – which applies to most modern industrialized countries – has had important economic and social consequences.

First, the 'manager-employee' is more mobile. It is much easier for him to leave the company, and it is easier for the Board of Directors to dismiss him. He can never feel totally secure in his presidential chair, and knows that each year he will be judged on the results he obtains alone. At any rate this is the way things must be done if the Board of Directors is to pull its weight. One cannot be a true liberal and refuse to accept the consequences of bad management.

During the course of a meeting at the French Consulate in New York, I heard M. Michel Rocard, a leader of the [French] Socialist Party, explain the nationalization of some large companies to a group of American industrialists: 'We decided to nationalize because the owners of these businesses were not running them efficiently.' This was of course an explanation presented for foreigners, and I told the Minister how strongly I disagreed with him, but I am bound to admit that if those responsible for the running of private enterprises will not accept sanctions in the case of failure, the liberal system loses all its value. It is a good thing that shareholders can voice their opinions at the Annual General Meeting and through the intermediary of the Board of Directors. But it is obvious that if the owner is the principal shareholder, he will not willingly submit to sanctions and that is a serious matter for the company's employees.

Secondly, the attitudes of the 'manager-employee' are different. There are of course some excellent owner-managers who understand the human problems of the organization, particularly if they founded it themselves. But directors who began their careers as workers, even if they had a degree in their pockets, are much more likely to have experienced and confronted all the problems that face the work force and the executives. Because they have lived through them, generally they understand them.

When I was a salesman with IBM France, I was elected Delegate of Personnel. This gave me the opportunity to study my colleagues' problems and to negotiate with the management. What I still retain from this experience is the ability to put myself into the position of others who cannot possibly have the same outlook as the general management, since in most cases they have played almost no part in defining the company's objectives and are not sufficiently familiar with its problems.

The new executives are not 'capitalists' in the classic sense for, although they receive handsome salaries, they are not in a position to accumulate much capital. One must not forget, in fact, that the higher echelons of the executive staff pay their taxes in full without cheating, and when looking at their salaries one must compare their net incomes after the deduction of taxes, and this greatly reduces the differential margin.

It is my profound belief that a man or a woman who rises up

through the hierarchy of a corporation must justify his or her position every single day. They must also be in a state of perpetual anxiety, the healthy anxiety that makes one reject complacency. Long ago I observed that one of IBM's strengths has been that its leaders were never entirely satisfied with the company's performance. I wish that mental attitudes in Europe would change correspondingly, and that young people, when they graduate from prestigious schools, would stop thinking their careers are guaranteed. In order to bring about such change in their thinking, they must become aware that progress in their chosen career is no longer assured simply because at the age of twenty-five they carry a degree or a diploma in their pockets. They must learn to think of their degrees as a *proof of potential*, an advantage at the outset, and nothing more.

Fortunately, businesses are changing. Once they set up evaluation systems for their executives, past achievements are less important and more weight is given to present performance. A new category of executives is coming to power: those who are good at their jobs no matter what early training they may have received. It is, in fact, in the United States, the country which is the very symbol of capitalism, and in Sweden, the country which symbolizes liberal socialism, that one still finds the largest numbers of people who have not had the privilege of an élitist education holding managerial positions in the large corporations. These are also the countries in which one finds the highest percentage of young people in higher education.

I have visited the USSR and I have visited China, and it is my observation that those who carry the responsibilities of leadership there are not so very different from those who lead the Western democracies. In these two countries there is a meritocracy; work is considered an essential virtue. Those who contribute more than others to economic development are rewarded in various ways: in the USSR they spend their vacations in a *dacha*, in Peking they live in a modern apartment. And differences in salaries, although less extreme than in the West, nevertheless exist.

At a certain moment egalitarian regimes always discover

that men need to be motivated. There are numerous factors that provide this motivation (political, ideological, moral, psychological . . .), but economic motivation is and always will be important. The real problem is, therefore, a fairer distribution of the wealth created by the enterprise and a fairer share-out of the power to make decisions. When criticizing the capitalists of the nineteenth century, Marx often saw things correctly. But capitalism today is so different, the changes in structure so fundamental, that the vast majority of Marxist objections are out-of-date.

Lastly, like all those who at a certain moment of their lives have experienced oppression, I have a passion for freedom. And, in my view, freedom of enterprise is profoundly related to other forms of freedom. That is to say, there is no incompatibility between the new capitalism and democracy.

In writing these last paragraphs, I have skipped happily on from 1949 to 1984 and now must retrace my steps. In September 1949 my wife and I dined at my parents' home in the company of Dr Rouquès. I explained my new views to him, including my enthusiasm for America, and described what I had seen over there especially in the domain of labour relations. He replied that all this was only made possible by the Americans' exploitation of a sub-proletariat of Blacks. I could not manage to convince him. Nor he me. He decided that I was a lost soul, a total prisoner of what he called the capitalist tyranny, but we remained excellent friends. Today I regret that I did not have the opportunity before his death to explain to him all that the leaders of American industry and business had succeeded in doing to change the conditions of the Blacks and other minorities over the last twenty years.

On my return from my first stay in the USA, I had become a fervent partisan of a free-enterprise society. And year after year everything in my experience, including the comparisons I have been able to make by visiting in the course of my work countries such as the USSR, China, East Germany, Bulgaria, the one-party countries in Africa, and Latin American countries ruled by military regimes, has reinforced my convictions. The efficient running of business and industry, and of a nation to the benefit and increased happiness of the employees of the first, and the citizens of the last, demands freedom. And freedom, properly understood and upheld by a spirit of good citizenship, never engenders anarchy.

5

I Want to be a Salesman

On my return from the United States my first job with IBM France was as an engineer in a little lab with a staff of 150 people. The programmes were limited and the technology was based on electrical and mechanical engineering. It was here that a punch-card accounting machine, the 421, was developed; this was to become for a period of several years the most important machine in the catalogue of IBM products sold in France.

My first project was to reproduce with the aid of such electronic tubes as were available in France, the electronic calculator 604 that I had studied in the USA. In 1949 it was difficult to find on the market tubes which were sufficiently reliable for data processing machines, which required much more precise specifications than those needed for the manufacture of radio sets. The director of the laboratory was a man of great imagination, a remarkable inventor, but essentially he was a mechanical engineer. He did not have much faith in electronics and refused to allocate the necessary resources to this newly-created laboratory. A single technician – a most delightful one, however – worked with me and we did manage to construct a copy. Two or three engineers who were a little older than myself took an interest in the project and one of them, Eugène Estrems, a Spanish engineer of great talent, gave me moral support throughout this venture.

I was back doing manual work and handling a soldering-iron much more frequently than the pencil, Indian ink, and T-square which together with a drawing-board represented for me the symbols of the engineer's profession. The fact that my boss was not interested in my work also dampened my own enthusiasm for it.

After several months and many long discussions with my wife, I decided to go to the Assistant General Manager, Monsieur G. Blanchard, and ask for a transfer. This was rather a rash step but it paid off. I suggested to him that we should set up a scientific computing service in France and he was very quick to accept the idea. During my first training period in the United States, I had noticed that scientists in all disciplines were finding it necessary to pass on from the slide-rule to instruments that could perform much more complex functions and carry them out much faster.

They set me up in an office on the Place Vendôme with instructions to sell the idea to French scientists and engineers. This was my first experience of salesmanship and it was absolutely enthralling! I was helped by Jean Guilhaumou, one of the colleagues I had met during my first months with IBM France in 1948. He had worked with Professor Rose, head of the crystallography laboratory at the Sorbonne, and had perfected a method for calculating the Fourier series with the aid of punch-cards. I carried on this work and met the first scientist in France to have used electro-mechanical calculating machines. I got on extremely well with Professor Rose and he gave me some useful introductions to colleagues of his who worked in other disciplines. However, trying to convince these gentlemen that a sound knowledge of mathematics and physics, in addition to using tables of logarithms and slide-rules, were not themselves sufficient to ensure rapid progress, and, above all, persuading them to initiate new projects, was a pioneering task.

I recall a visit to Monsieur Kowarski who was then one of the heads of the Atomic Energy Commission. His response was very plain: 'Monsieur, we shall never need these machines; all we need is to have good physicists.' I was not discouraged by his lack of enthusiasm, however, and many years later felt extremely gratified when I visited him at CERN (European Council for Nuclear Research) in Geneva which had become the most important centre for scientific computers in Europe.

I managed to find a few clients here and there, and their computations were carried out on the machines in the company's service bureau. This was a department which executed data processing work for clients whose businesses were too small to justify the cost of installing their own machines, or for people who had to handle peak load work that their own equipment was not sophisticated enough to deal with. This service had a very heavy workload, but the head of the department was kind enough to lend me some machines on Saturdays and Sundays. It was here that I learnt that ambitious men cannot be content to work a forty-hour week.

Monsieur G. Blanchard took an interest in the development of this service of which I was for some time both the head (which looked good on my visiting-cards) and the sole employee. Mlle Coutanceau came to join me and took over work on the machine with devotion and competence and, what is more, with constant enthusiasm and good humour. I was able to spend more time selling the service and studying new ways to apply it. Operations Research became fashionable and I came to realize that the potential for computation was not limited to university laboratories nor to important research centres – industry also had need of complex calculations.

A lucky contact was made with the National Centre for Aeronautical Research, and the service took off rather timidly with gathering and evaluating the results of the wind-tunnel at Chalais-Meudon. I needed more help and management agreed to increase the size of the staff by 50 per cent, in other words to recruit one more engineer. After two or three engineers had turned me down, saying they were not interested in any hole-in-the-corner computer work (I suppose they knew that the machines were only available on Saturdays and Sundays), René Rind, who had graduated from the *Ecole Centrale* the year after I did, accepted enthusiastically. Now there were three of us united by our conviction that we were undertaking something new and difficult. René Rind immediately revealed his talent for mathematics which was streets ahead of mine.

The electro-mechanical calculators in the service bureau were no longer capable of carrying out the computations we needed; we were impatiently awaiting the arrival in France of the first 604 electronic calculator to be imported from the United States. It was delivered and all the salesmen realized that it could be of immense service to them in handling their own important customers. The Sales Manager, Jacques Herbart, asked us to take it on a demonstration tour of the principal towns in France; so René and I, accompanied by the maintenance engineer, Monsieur Ludman, set off to demonstrate scientific computation and this marvellous machine all over France.

This was the first time I had seen evidence of the general public's fear of technology. For its day the 604 was a rapid machine, but much less powerful than a programmable hand calculator is today. And yet during the question time after each lecture, whether we were in Paris, Lille, Metz, Thionville, Lyons or Marseilles, the same question came up time and time again: 'What you have told us is very interesting, but with machines of such speed and capacity there will soon be no more need of engineers!'

In 1950, no matter how carefully we explained that these machines were nothing more than tools, fear remained. In 1984 now that computers are thousands of times faster and great numbers of them are in use, almost all Western countries have one problem in common: a shortage of engineers graduating from university each year. For example, the students who graduated from the *Ecole Centrale* in 1984 each received, on average, eight offers of employment on leaving school.

After our demonstrations of the 604 our prospective sales potential looked excellent; we were at last able to offer our clients a powerful means of computing. But in 1950 restrictions were placed on imports into France and because of them I came to understand exchange controls and the necessity of exporting. An IMPEX agreement had been signed by IBM which allowed us to import goods to half the value of those we exported. After the great difficulties we had encountered in convincing scientists to use our machines, we now had to 'sell' them the reasons for long delivery delays.

I was passionate about selling and soon discovered that all the most important jobs within the company, except for those in the factories and the laboratory, were held by managers who had started their careers as salesmen. In the United States people were proud to be known as 'salesmen'; but in France the title *vendeur* had to be improved upon. At that time a sales job, whatever you sold, was not considered very glamorous. Young graduates wanted to be engineers, scientists, production engineers, doctors, pharmacists, lawyers, but not peddlers. Although the majority of the staff in the sales service were not engineers, they were duly christened *ingénieurs commerciaux* or sales engineers.

Once again I had a meeting with M. Blanchard, then M. Herbart, who allowed me to join the sales force. I was assigned to the government branch office, whose employees are responsible for sales to the various departments of the French government. Newcomers were not given an easy option and the old guard defended its territory jealously. The remuneration consisted of a fixed salary plus commission on machines or services sold, and those who had succeeded in persuading a large government department to 'mechanize' itself could not bear to see their potential client assigned to a colleague. Christian Boussus, the director of our branch, was charming and courteous and a one-time ace tennis player, but he was also a little weak when facing the tough old guard; but perhaps it was a deliberate policy of his to give young salesmen a difficult job at the outset in order to test them.

'Your clients and your territory will be the Paris Public Transport Services; the Ministry of Posts, Telephones and Telegraph; the Ministry of Public Works and the Office of Tourism,' he told me. Naïve as I was, I asked no questions. The salesman who had been my predecessor in this sector was in great haste to hand over to me, since the transport service was his only client with any computer equipment; and the other two 'prospects' in my new territory had bought nothing, neither machines nor service contracts. I was not discouraged, however, and looked on the bright side of things: I thought that in any case the postal service must have formidable potential, and I told myself that the grandson of a 'postman' must surely be able to succeed selling it computers.

Each salesman had a precise target: a quota which corresponded to a certain volume of business. Each machine and each service arrangement corresponded to a certain number of points. Each point was roughly equivalent to one dollar of monthly rental.

A key-punch represented ten to twenty points, an accounting machine as many as five hundred. This system, which with some variations is still in force, was already an application of management by objectives. Moreover it created healthy competition because any salesman who reached the fixed targets for the year was considered worthy of entry to the '100% Club'. This Club still exists and its motivating value is recognized within the company.

'You will have a quota of 1,200 points,' Christian Boussus said to me. This did not seem too difficult to me until the day I discovered that my predecessor had put in an order for some accounting machines for the transport service which his client really did not need. I began to clean up the account, and cancelled an order worth 1,200 points which appeared to be unjustified. A fine start: wiping out the amount I was supposed to sell in one year! As a matter of fact I finished my first year as a salesman without 'fulfilling my quota'.

During the whole of that year, 1951, I assisted my colleagues who wanted to present the electronic computer to their clients, by giving demonstrations and visiting American installations in France. On 12 January 1951 I accompanied Inspector General Forestier and M. Ballereau, who were responsible for data processing in the Army, on a visit to the administrative headquarters of the American Air Force at Châteauroux. The Americans had the most modern equipment at their European bases and how they made use of it was streets ahead of us.

That was a great day for me. Very early in the morning of 12 January our second child, Florence, was born. 'Another pretty little girl,' Dr Ravina told me. 'She has the largest eyes of any baby I've ever brought into the world.' But I did not have much time to see my wife and baby before the train for Châteauroux left at 7.30 a.m. Her birth was nonetheless a stroke of luck: the important men I was accompanying came to the conclusion that the father of two children must be more mature and competent than they would otherwise have guessed from my physical appearance as a young man of twenty-seven. It was a successful day; the French client was astounded by such American innovations. I also was a little envious of the salesman who was running this account; he would certainly achieve his quota. But he had introduced me to these gentlemen as 'our demonstrator' and I had not been too pleased about that.

It was during this year that the IBM World Trade Corporation, the company which supervised the overall activities of IBM outside the United States, set up a European management group. The General Manager was Jack Brent, a former Chairman of IBM Canada. He was a very impressive man, dynamic and bursting with energy. From the beginning, he created a small multinational management team and situated his offices in IBM France's building on the Place Vendôme. There were some fifteen people in his team, including Francis Ritz, my friend from Poughkeepsie, who was given the task of setting up the manufacture of electric typewriters in Europe. He was the first man to think up the idea of an integrated European industry long before the creation of the Common Market. IBM did not yet have the capacity to produce all the parts for these machines, which were often very complex, in their own factories. Francis Ritz sent out invitations for tenders to several European countries. Suppliers in England, France, Switzerland, Belgium and Italy all won various contracts, but each supplier manufactured only one specific part for the whole of the market. By this means the company organized in 1951 the production of a machine so that all the parts could be mass-produced, thereby reducing its cost. These parts were then sent to the assembly plant. The sales of IBM typewriters began to increase very rapidly.

During the war IBM's subsidiaries, sequestered by the Germans in the countries they occupied, were independent from the mother company. As soon as Jack Brent got to work, assisted by an English financial manager, Percy Taylor, he decided as far as it was possible to standardize the methods of accountancy and the reports sent to Paris from the subsidiaries, and to co-ordinate the commercial and industrial activities of the company. This Canadian, used to wide-open spaces, refused to admit that frontiers or differences of language could prove an obstacle to the organization of a vast market.

I was one of the few salesmen who spoke English, Jack Brent did not speak French – a happy coincidence! – and the management of IBM France asked me to participate from time to time in meetings between him and his staff. Towards the end of the year, he asked me:

'Have you reached your quota?'

'No, and I've no hope of doing so.'

'You know you will have to reach it next year or else you'll have to leave the sales department.'

I was in a bit of a panic – the boss for the whole of Europe was going to keep an eye on me. I explained to him what my territory consisted of and he replied: 'Poor salesmen always find that their territory has no potential, the competition is too tough and economic circumstances are unfavourable. As for the good ones, they sell whatever the circumstances.' I have never forgotten the lesson he gave me, although Jack Brent was not nearly as tough as he liked to appear. A few days after this conversation Christian Boussus sent for me and said, 'Don't worry about your results for this year. We are well aware that it's quite impossible for you to achieve your targets. From 1 January 1952 your territory will also include the Ministry of Defence.' Jack Brent must have mentioned my case to the Chairman of IBM France, Christian de Waldner.

The years 1952–3 were great years. The French Army needed a lot of equipment. I was very familiar with such equipment and knew how it had been made use of by the American Army; so, basically, it was only a matter of persuading our customers who were already using large quantities of the equipment to introduce American methods of administration.

On 19 February 1952 I once again escorted several officers from army ordnance, and also some from the air force to Châteauroux. Last year's demonstrator was this year's salesman. Early that same morning I'd also been to the American Hospital in Paris. At about 5 a.m. Dr Ravina had told me of the birth of our third child, Sylvie. He had come out of the labour room and said, 'You have another beautiful little girl,' before walking away immediately without giving me a chance to say a word. No doubt he was worried about the possible reaction of a father who'd just been told he had a third girl. The verdict of the officers I was accompanying was very different. 'Every time you come to visit the American base at Châteauroux, you have a little girl,' they teased.

I thought I was seriously handicapped in my relationships with the generals, colonels and other officers whom I was seeing almost daily, because like all men of my age group I had been given a dispensation from obligatory military service, and so was a 'second class' soldier. I did not yet know that salesmanship has no need of gold braid but only of competence, keenness and a certain amount of aggressiveness. So I asked for an authorization to serve short periods with the army, so as to become an officer in the reserve. In 1952 and also in 1953, instead of taking a holiday, I spent the time at the Ordnance School in Fontainebleau. In 1952 I benefited from a rather special regime. We were renting a house near Fontainebleau and after a week of nights spent in the dormitory of the barracks the Colonel authorized me to go 'home' every evening. The Colonel had taken a liking to me.

In 1953 during my second period of military service, the major sent for me. 'Maisonrouge, almost all the officers are on holiday. You're in the habit of studying. Here, take the syllabus and the instruction manuals, you can go and work in the lecture hall.' In minute detail, I spent three weeks learning about the management of supplies in the Army Ordnance Corps. My examination results were 19.5 out of 20; the commanding officer was delighted and I became a second lieutenant.

After my 'holidays' I felt better equipped to tackle the officers with whom I was working, and I was able to sell the IBM equipment required for the management of supplies by the French Army and Air Force.

On 23 December Jacques Herbart sent for me and congratulated me, 'You've done good work. I've decided to offer you a substantial promotion. I am proposing you as director of our office in Saigon. Give me your answer after Christmas.' Never had my wife and I spent such a miserable Christmas Eve. In accordance with family tradition we spent it at my parents-in-law's house, with my parents, my wife's brother and sister, and our three children. We did not want to cast gloom over the family with the prospect

73

of our departure, but with three young children, we finally decided we could not go to live in Vietnam which was then at war. I therefore took the risk of refusing promotion and opted to remain a salesman.

On 23 December 1953 Jacques Herbart called me in again. It was becoming a habit! 'Monsieur Viguié, the manager of our Algiers branch office, is coming here to HQ to be my right-hand man. I'm asking you to take on the job in Algiers.' This time, the request was more urgent. And once again it produced a rather topsy-turvy Christmas. But, on returning to the office, I said yes. Two or three days later Jacques Herbart called me in once more:

'The situation in Algeria is very difficult just now, I believe it would be best if M. Viguié, who knows the country well and is well-known there, stayed where he is. I suggest that you take on the position I had had in mind for him.'

'Certainly, sir, when do I start?'

'On the 2nd of January.'

I had not felt that it was necessary to discuss this with Françoise. The offer was an exceptional one: an important promotion in Paris could only be accepted with enthusiasm.

Nevertheless I felt some regret at leaving the sales department where I had found complete satisfaction in my work. On the other hand, IBM had received a request for tenders – the most important in its history in France – from the army's data processing service and I could see that commissions would be disappearing. My promotion meant, in effect, a transition to a fixed salary. Jacques Herbart gave me permission to take a continuing interest, together with my successor, in the business of the territory I was leaving. However, I also left with a sense of failure. The only machines I had succeeded in selling the postal service were six bank proof machines set up in the department issuing postal cheques.

I had, however, made great efforts to obtain more information and had carried out numerous studies aimed at achieving the mechanization of Post-Giro and telephone billing. The enormous volume of transactions entailed in such an enterprise proved a stumbling block as our machines were not technologically sophisticated enough to handle it. Also, we continually came up against the conservatism of the administration. The Swiss postal service had already demonstrated what advantages were to be gained from the use of punch-card machines for the invoicing of telephone calls, and Hans Luethy, the Swiss salesman who landed this splendid contract, had become the leading IBM salesman in the world for 1949. But the French Under-Secretary for Telecommunications whom I often visited would nonetheless say to me, 'You see, I'm like the swimmer who stands on the end of the diving-board and dare not take the plunge because he's afraid the water will be too cold.' This setback did nothing to alter my conviction that the postal service would eventually become a very large-scale user of data processing.

I had suffered another failure by losing business to the Bull Machines Company. They were strong competitors and I came up against them in dealing with all my clients. They had produced the Gamma 3, a machine that performed better than our 604, and this gave them a big edge especially with the banks.

Despite such setbacks, Jacques Herbart entrusted me with the following responsibilities in my new position: recruiting the sales staff, sales training, the sale of scientific and commercial computers, and customer services. It was a hefty portfolio. Large computers had just been announced in the United States and it was decided to put them on sale on the European market. The machines concerned were the 701, a scientific computer, and the 702, a commercial computer. They seemed very complicated to me; they had memories on magnetic tapes that could read 15,000 characters per second, and they had specially stored programmes. They also gave rise to two new professions: programming and systems analysis. When launching them I made a mistake; it seemed to me they were so complex that only the young, and preferably people with an engineering background, would be able to understand them. So I formed two small teams, headed by Georges Parisot, a graduate of the *Ecole Polytechnique* and already a salesman, for the commercial computers, and by René Rind, director of our scientific computing centre, for the scientific ones.

Each of them had a staff of four or five engineers. This specialized sales force became, in fact, a support group for the other salesmen who knew far better than we did what their clients required. There was some conflict, and I realized later that it was necessary to train all the salesmen to sell these computers, rather than have specialists. In spite of our fumbled start the launch went well, and the first user of the 705 (successor to the 702) in France was the Drouot Group, managed by the remarkable M. Tattevin who knew at least as much about data processing as we did.

Developments in technology led us towards a considerably different kind of recruitment. Most of the salesmen taken on before 1954 were real, hard-headed salesmen, enterprising go-getters with a passion for their work. As the equipment was fairly simple, what we looked for in these men were the essential qualities of salesmanship, as well as some useful contacts. Among my colleagues there were members of the great French families, four marquesses, some counts, and also several ex-Rugby International players and other well-known sportsmen. After the computers arrived, we engaged engineers from the major postgraduate engineering schools, graduates from business schools, and men and a few women with Masters' degrees from universities, and even a few Ph.D's.

I interviewed a great many prospective employees, and if ever a candidate asked me about retirement, or about the length of holidays, he was almost certain to be eliminated. The applicants my colleagues and I judged to be promising were then seen by Jacques Herbart; there were no psychotechnical tests given, no graphological analyses made, but simply an analysis of their CVs undertaken and their powers of communication assessed.

There was only one woman in the sales department. I had noticed that she got excellent results and I asked why we did not hire more women. No one could give me a valid reason, only the traditional clichés: women were more often off sick; the clients (all men) had less confidence in them; they could not make a career with IBM because the men in the company would not consent to report to them. I found myself up against one of the most ridiculous of prejudices, but I was happy, however, to recommend employing a young woman graduate from the women's *Ecole Polytechnique* who, furthermore, had a Master's degree in aeronautics from the University of Seattle.

During these two and a half years I learnt what management really was: recruiting, training, motivating, promoting, rewarding. Some people today seem to think the need for reward is a little antiquated, and yet men and women in 1954 desired, as they still desire more than thirty years later, to see their efforts and their devotion recognized.

IBM, in France and in Europe, generally delivered to their clients equipment that had been developed in the United States and which did not suit the needs of the local market completely. Jack Brent, the Chairman of IBM Europe, was aware of this and decided to create a committee to study the market and the planning of new products. His idea was simple: the sales department had to define the customers' needs and explain them to the engineers in the laboratories in terms of the general specifications for the machines required, then quantify what the customers wanted so that the factories could make production plans which would correspond to the demand.

I was put in charge of organizing the Market Research and Product Planning Committee. This was my first experience of working with managers from other European countries. Every three months we held meetings that lasted two or three days. We prepared analyses of the quantities to be sold for each of the new products announced in the United States. We studied what requirements would be needed by European clients and discussed with the laboratories what modifications should be carried out to the machines. Several new models resulted from our labours, one of which was a machine that combined a tabulator and the electronic calculator 604. This was extremely successful with the banks. For the first time I went to Germany, Sweden, Spain and Holland, and I made return visits to England and Switzerland. Our estimates of the market were not very accurate, but they were improving with time.

In 1955 a new technology was born: magnetic disc memories were developed which had a huge capacity and the RAMAC computer was soon put on the market. Remembering my vain attempts to automate the handling of postal cheques when I was a salesman, I saw in the magnetic disc memories a solution to the problem. The directors of the Dutch Post-Giro were interested in the question and a study group was formed made up of members of their organization plus Philips and IBM. The journey between Paris to Amsterdam became a familiar one for me. It was the start of my travels and of our daughters' collection of dolls.

The work of the Market Research and Product Planning Committee grew to the point where the European management decided to transform the study group into a department, and in June 1956 Jack Brent appointed me Manager of Market Research and Product Planning for Europe.

I left my friends at IBM France to join IBM Europe. A short trip since my office was still in IBM France's HQ on the Place Vendôme. We started to organize ourselves: René Rind became Manager of Product Studies and Ted Gehring, a manager from IBM Germany, became Manager of Market Studies. Identical departments were created in the major European subsidiaries and in the management of the IBM World Trade Corporation in New York.

One of my essential tasks was to establish good relations with the laboratories. The directors were in the habit of starting with the technology and moving on to the product. We wanted to start with customer needs, utilize technology, and define the product. The American department responsible for the same projects had a little time advantage over us, and each important laboratory had on its staff some employees who had come from the sales department. The problem was they knew only the American market, and it took considerable persuasion to get them to take European requirements into account. It was not easy for them to adjust their thinking to an electrical current supply of 50 cycles, instead of 60, as in the USA.

Between 1956 and 1958, however, a profound transformation in methods of research and development took place at IBM. One of the needs of some of our clients was for sufficient technological power to carry out complicated procedures that required a large memory capacity in the computer, and printers which would be less costly to run than those of the 705 Systems. This was particularly true for the banks, which already represented an important proportion of our clientele. My functional manager in the United States and I discovered that the Endicott laboratories in the USA, the Boeblingen lab in Germany, and the Paris lab were all working on a hardware solution to the same problem. A meeting of the chief engineers working on these projects took place at Boeblingen and we came to the simple conclusion that it was absurd for three groups to be running three projects to solve one problem. It was then decided to define what we wanted in a single machine capable of serving both the American and European markets. Each of the chief engineers vigorously defended his own project. A very important French innovation – the variable length of word – invented by Maurice Papo and Eugène Estrems was, however, retained. Up until then computers had words of fixed length, for example, ten letters. This 'used up' more of the memory. By introducing words of variable length substantial economies were made in the amount of memory used.

After a stay of more than two months in the United States – in Poughkeepsie which I was delighted to visit again – we were able to define what sort of machine we needed. Working on the programme from the European side were two engineers from the German laboratory, Dr Ganzhorn and Dr Einsele, two from the French laboratory, Maurice Papo and Eugène Estrems, and two marketing people with an engineering background, Claude Erulin and myself. We spent all this time writing programmes, work which I found somewhat less than enthralling. What is more, we almost missed the family Christmas of 1955, for there was a snowstorm in New York and a strike by air traffic controllers in Paris. We flew from New York to Brussels, and then on 24 December took the morning train from Brussels to Paris. We just made it!

After my stay a decision was taken to produce the same machine for the States, Europe, and the rest of the world. And so was born the 1401, which served as the IBM work-horse for a number of years. This project, and the decision to have a product that with just a few minor modifications could be sold in Japan, Brazil, the USA, Canada, and Europe had a decisive effect on the organization of the company. I believe it was the first time a company that had laboratories and factories in several countries, and sales departments in more than eighty, had planned a single product which would be adapted to the local market but would utilize the same technology and the same architecture. We had endeavoured to use the greatest possible number of electronic components, sub-assemblies, magnetic tape memories, disc memories and mechanical parts in common.

The aim was to make optimum use of the funds for research and development, to simplify the training of sales staff, and to satisfy our clients. Large companies often had computers in their subsidiaries in several countries. The machines that had been in use up to this time varied considerably from one country to another, which compelled those who used them to have programming services more or less everywhere. Even when one country perfected an efficient method, it was difficult to apply this method elsewhere.

This decision to 'universalize' research and development was taken by Tom Watson Jr, at that time Chairman of the IBM Corporation and by his brother, Dick Watson, Chairman of the IBM World Trade Corporation. Shortly thereafter Jack Brent returned to the States as President of IBM World Trade and was replaced by two General Managers, one for Northern Europe and one for Southern Europe. They shared the same staff and this was the only period in my career when I had two bosses simultaneously. From an organizational point of view it was not a very tidy solution, but we all got on sufficiently well together to make it work.

During my last two months in this job my colleagues and I had an idea for a new product. In our market studies we had noticed that the new machines were designed primarily for our big customers and a few medium-sized ones. We realized that we were tending to ignore the great potential represented by small and medium-sized businesses. We launched the idea of the 3000 series, a small computer whose cost price we hoped to bring down by using a new punch-card that was much smaller than the preceding one. Innumerable meetings were held, but our

American friends were not convinced of this market requirement.

In the middle of 1957 IBM called in a famous consulting firm, McKinzey, to study its operations in Europe. This study followed very closely the reorganization of IBM in the States, where they had just created product divisions, marketing divisions, and a central management board to co-ordinate the whole. This new form of organization was to be the first step towards decentralization, since the company had now passed the figure of $ one billion turnover.

The conclusions of the McKinzey study were presented at a meeting in Zürich, attended by the managers of the World Trade Corporation and all the directors of the European subsidiaries. Europe was divided into six geographical units: Germany, England, France, Italy, and two regions which regrouped all the other countries. Dick Watson called me in and asked me to take over the direction of one of these two regions.

This was the era of rapid promotion and I agreed enthusiastically to change from a functional to an operational role. He gave me responsibility for the IBM organizations in the following countries: Holland, Belgium, Luxemburg, Spain, Portugal, Switzerland, Greece, Turkey, Iran, and Israel. There did not seem much similarity in their markets which bothered me; moreover, I was a little worried because I was only thirty-three yet I would have to supervise experienced general managers; fortunately, I had made the acquaintance of many of them in my other jobs at IBM and they recognized I possessed some technical competence.

During my apprenticeship in selling, marketing and creating good relations with my colleagues from other countries, I was helped enormously by my wife. From the start Françoise showed her exceptional ability to adapt, to remain calm and good-humoured under all circumstances. She participated fully in my professional life, very often helping me when I worked over Saturday and Sunday, agreeing to sacrifice holidays, letting me go off on long journeys without jeremiads, and greeting me on my return with a joy that made me very happy. She took on full responsibility for family relationships, with my own parents who from the beginning of our marriage had called her 'their daughter', just as much as with her own. She brought up the children with an abundance of love that did not prevent her from using a firm hand when this was needed. A family tradition was swiftly established: we spent one weekend with my parents, the next with my parents-in-law. We knew nothing of 'generation gaps'.

In those days holidays were not long. I do not remember ever taking more than two weeks in summer and sometimes one in winter. Several times our parents had our daughters to stay with them so that we could be free for romantic intervals. We loved the Côte d'Azur and some generous cousins lent us their villa at Cannes for three years running. Then as the family increased we found an old mansion, Les Cassiflores, where all five of us went to stay several times.

Most of the people we entertained were colleagues from work. Many of our present friends were originally colleagues. Françoise accompanied me on some of my business trips and so discovered Holland, Sweden, England, Spain, Italy, and Switzerland. For us, this represented the period of our European education.

At this time, I left my position as European Director of Market Research and Product Planning, but I had begun to acquire the habit of looking back over the past and asking myself: what had I gained; in what way had I contributed to the development of the company; what mistakes had I made; what more could I have done? Each time I left a particular position, I had the same reactions: some satisfaction given the work I'd accomplished; the very great pleasure of having helped my colleagues and prepared them to step into my shoes as soon as I left; but also a sense of regret that I had not been more successful.

In 1956 my maternal grandmother died. During the weeks preceding her death Françoise and I went to Puchay, the little village in Normandy where she had lived for a long time, and I do not think I ever covered the ninety-five kilometres that separated us so fast. Before our last trip the doctor had telephoned to ask us to bring some medicines that were available only in Paris. I tried several pharmacists without success, and each time I came out I said to myself that the fate of my beloved grandmother was in my hands. At last I found them and we arrived at Puchay in less than an hour. She was very weak, but I continued to hope. Two days later she died with a smile on her lips, looking at all those around her, saying nothing, but with an *au revoir* in her eyes that were brimming with an immense goodness. I swore that I would take her as my inspiration, try to emulate her example, but that was – and still remains – an aim impossible of attainment. It is too high a target.

6

Sales and Marketing

Many words have been written about marketing. Courses in this subject abound in universities throughout the world and I am not going to present any recipes. My experience on the job has taught me some things which do not always correspond with what is written in the manuals.

For a long time the public has tried to analyse the reasons for IBM's success. The management, on the other hand, is more interested in understanding why the company hasn't been still more successful. Mr T. J. Watson, the founder, used to say: 'Never be satisfied.' But various reasons for IBM's success have been forthcoming, and personally I agree with Peter's and Waterman's analysis in *In Search of Excellence*. First, principles, then precise objectives known to the entire personnel and, lastly, a sub-culture of its own, has made the company a success throughout the years. One cannot, however, dispute the valid opinion of those who attribute IBM's recovery in the 1950s to superior marketing when Tom Watson Jr, surprised by Univac's sweeping successes, decided to take the plunge into computers.

It is recognized that IBM has a good management system, and among the six members of the Management Board today, four began their careers as salesmen. The Chairman, the President, the presidents of all the most important subsidiaries except one, IBM Japan, have all been salesmen at some point in their careers. I do not believe that this is a result of co-option or of corporatism. Modern management demands a certain form of consensus. Not necessarily Japanese-style consensus, but decision-taking by senior levels of management who can communicate well with one another, who have a perfect understanding of the objectives,

84

agree with them absolutely, and can explain them to their subordinates. This method applies particularly to large business organizations which without this approach would be paralysed, but it applies equally well to medium-sized firms that without it would find themselves in serious difficulties if the boss, with his centralizing authority, retired or left the company.

The first necessity, then, is for the executive staff to agree on their objectives and be able to communicate well amongst themselves; this in no way detracts from the authority of the chairman or the president, who carries final responsibility before the Board of Directors.

Today's employees – and by 'employees' I mean factory workers, laboratory technicians, shorthand-typists, programmers, etc., all the non-executive staff – who like the management itself no longer accept the old style of management (still too widespread in Europe and even in the United States), which consists of giving orders without ever explaining them. Management today must be founded on the competence of the leader; he must explain the objectives and share them with his associates. He must motivate them and have the courage to blame as well as the grace to compliment. Above all, he must listen, give others the chance to express themselves, and accept ideas 'from below' except where he can prove they are non-viable. In particular he must persuade and not command.

Adherents of the old system generally believe that the new one wastes time. This is not true. The time spent in preparing a decision is largely compensated for by the shorter time required to execute it thanks to the good will and understanding of the people doing so, and also their desire to play a successful part in the outcome. There are certainly other advantages. The social climate is better, as is the quality of the work accomplished. Job-satisfaction, one of the most important factors motivating people, is assured.

Everybody must be able to express his ideas; this system of management leads quite naturally to 'quality circles', to a programme of active suggestions and creativity. Employees at all levels are given responsibility, but they are also given greater security, since having participated in the decision-making or at the very least, having had future changes explained to them, nothing comes as a shock, provoking anxiety, but as an expected evolution.

Let us return to selling. The salesman must master a number of techniques: he must know the products and the services he is offering very well indeed, together with their uses; he must understand something about their manufacture and the administrative structure governing their ordering; he must know whether delays in delivery are likely; and he must have good contacts. As well as this, he must possess very sound human attributes: he must listen to others, win people's respect, persuade, be pugnacious, make himself indispensable, reply quickly and precisely to questions put to him, and never hesitate to show himself as amiable with the receptionist as he is with the head buyer. His love of his job, and the pride he takes in representing his company, must be apparent to all and sundry. By the time he reaches the final stage of the signing of the contract, which in a field such as data processing often takes the form of a discussion with the president of the client company, accompanied by his senior staff, the salesman's reputation as a man or woman of ability must be established and his capacity for rendering useful services obvious.

Sometimes he may have spent months persuading people that what he has to offer will benefit the company concerned, now he must convince the man who has to sign the bottom line of the contract. Here we have a man or a woman – and women are just as capable as men at being salespeople – who without any hierarchical authority over the people he or she is dealing with has convinced them to make a major investment, and has done this through personal ability, by winning the client's approval and through an evident desire to provide the best possible service while inspiring the client's confidence.

When you have spent several years engaged in this profession, it is not difficult to manage your associates in your own company, especially since you have hierarchical authority over them. Several other qualities are necessary, therefore, including your own willingness to work as part of a team. Unfortunately in many companies the role of the salesman is not given the importance it deserves.

I will not describe in detail what marketing is, but only some of the activities essential to good salesmanship. In other words what must be done to achieve a strategy for developing the business that will allow for growth, which is the only means of attaining competitiveness through socially-acceptable increases in productivity.

How many companies set up adequate market research? The boss sends one of his henchmen on a week's visit to a foreign country with instructions to find wholesale buyers, retailers, and sometimes even the eventual customer. If it is a government minister who organizes the trip, the boss himself will go, but he will spend so much time at official receptions that he will usually come back without having made any useful contacts with the 'locals'. However, this will not prevent him on his return from knowing all about the country he has visited.

A serious study of the market requires considerable investment; men and women who speak the local language and are trained in investigation techniques; serious people who are always at the right place at the right time. They must know who will ultimately be using the commodity; what the competition is; how the system of distribution operates; the importance of advertising; and, with all this information in hand, be able to analyse market needs: the type of product required and in what quantity.

Obviously the aim of market research projects may be to determine whether an existing product can be sold on a foreign market, but the most valuable type of research attempts to see whether some similar or modified product would give better results. This confirmed, the development engineers and the manufacturing engineers try to invent and produce the most suitable products. Such an approach is diametrically opposed to methods adopted in many industries, especially in the Latin countries. For a long time, inventors simply said to management: 'Here is a new product, now let the salesmen go out and sell it.' Today, the sales department must be able to say to the general management: 'This is what the clients really need; ask the engineers to create the product and the factories to produce it at a competitive price.'

I have shown that market research is the first step towards good marketing. Now I would like to consider two others – the product and its after-sales service.

When times were hard in France during the war, one could sell even poor products. At one time women wore wooden-soled shoes, we ate swedes, warmed ourselves as best we could with rolled up newspapers or compressed coal-dust bricks, and suffered many more hardships than I could possibly mention. Today the market is world-wide. The finest products from all the industrialized countries are available in all other industrialized countries, except in those with a planned economy who defend their frontiers because they would not be able to compete in a free economy. If domestic products are not of sufficiently high quality and reliability, or if the price is too high, foreign products will penetrate the home market at an accelerated rate. There is one solution to this problem, which is as facile as it is absurd: close national frontiers. Facile because imports can easily be stopped for a few months (at the risk, however, of seeing the country of supply take its revenge by also banning imports); absurd because France, like other European countries such as Britain, cannot survive except as a member of the Common Market, and because there are certain products which must be imported, like petroleum, for example. The real solution lies with industry and consists in supplying goods and services at competitive prices.

The ideal is to be able to offer unique products and services which, for several years at least, will not meet with any competition. This calls for a knowledge of market needs plus thorough market research and adequate development. The inventor, stimulated by the market, can be the originator of technological breakthroughs that will ensure commercial victory on condition that innovation follows invention. In the case of IBM various products such as the 360 computer, disc memories, and many others have given the company an important advantage over its competitors for a given time. It was the same for Apple in the early days of micro-processing. Manufacturers of pharmaceutical products have long understood the fact that the discovery of a new molecule can enable them to make a great leap forward. Research and development must be considered as forming part of a global marketing strategy.

Nonetheless one often has to launch products after other companies have already put them on the market. For instance, IBM commercialized large computers after Remington-Rand had launched the UNIVAC. In any company the development engineer still has his part to play. He must find products that are sufficiently different to avoid problems over patent rights, but similar from the market [i.e. the consumer's] point of view. He must also come up with products that are easy to manufacture. By doing so the industrial engineer can then play his true role: in other words to allow the manufacture of high quality goods at the lowest possible cost.

Quality has been too much neglected by big business. It has taken the extraordinary results achieved by Japanese business to wake up Western countries. When I returned to Armonk, HQ of the IBM Corporation in the United States, in December 1981, I was astonished to see that my four colleagues on the management committee were driving German or Japanese cars. When I asked them why, they all gave the same answer – quality. American industry has now got the message and in 1983–4 Chrysler made a spectacular recovery. Three factors were involved:

1. The general management and the union (United Auto Workers) signed an agreement on 'quality programmes' in 1980. In three years the cost of repairs to one of their new cars after 20,000 miles was reduced by 50 per cent.

2. Production was modernized and robots were introduced. In 1984 this company was profitable on an output of 1,100,000 vehicles, whereas in 1981 it had had to produce 2,200,000 to get out of the red.

3. Advertising was expanded considerably, but centred on the quality of the cars rather than their appearance. And then there was a fourth factor – a great boss in the shape of Mr Lee Iacocca.

I will also cite an example from IBM. IBM France's company

newspaper carried this headline in December 1984: 'Quality is the key to mastery of the future.' The editorial, written by the President, Jacques Lemonnier, began thus: 'In the highly competitive environment of our industry, resolute research into quality in all areas is the key to our success.' In this number, there was also a very interesting article by Gilbert Stora, the Quality Director. First, he recalled two of the company's great principles: to strive for excellence and to be of service to the client. He went on to describe IBM's basic principles, including a definition of quality: 'Conformity of our products and services to the needs of our clients at home and abroad.' This, he stated, applies to all aspects of the industry, as does our policy of prevention and the tracing of any faults back to source to eliminate them. The company's standard of quality aims for zero faults and perpetual improvement in all company procedures.

He then set out the principles governing the management of quality:

1. Everything emanates from the commitment of the management.

2. All personnel in all functions and at all levels must adhere to the quality programme.

3. A national approach to the improvement of product quality must be maintained. This must be based on correct standards; on research and analysis of the causes of non-conformity in specific products; on the subsequent elimination of such causes.

But the company must make available the means to ensure the success of such a programme. This must include the constant training of staff; the evaluation of client-satisfaction; a coherent strategy of 'quality' goals needed to implement the company's objectives; group work; an analysis of the staff's perception of what is being undertaken and why; good communication within the company and its recognition of individual merit.

Doesn't this correspond to what I have already said and am going to say about marketing? It is simply an extension of all other activities taking place within the company. But nothing can be achieved if the men and women who work for the company don't consider their role to be crucial to the enterprise. IBM France employs just over 22,000 people; forty-one executives have as their sole goal to maintain quality. Let me give one example of the practical results obtained by these procedures: in 1984, 150,000 export invoices were sent out containing 150 errors. In 1982, for the same volume there had been 300 errors.

Good products are essential, but one must sell them. I have already spoken about the role of salesmen, but a company must also ensure its customers' fidelity by giving them satisfactory services. After-sales service is one of the most important aspects of marketing. Here again the Japanese have set us an example: it is good to sell, but it is better to sell a second time to the same client. The client who is dissatisfied with the after-sales service will buy from a different supplier next time. Good after-sales service requires reliable repairmen, well-trained maintenance engineers who arrive promptly with the necessary spare parts when the client sends out a distress call. The total time lost through the breakdown of equipment is what matters most to a client. The average time that elapses between breakdowns is also important, but depends more on the quality of the equipment supplied in the first place than on the quality of the after-sales service.

Every country needs to export in order to import raw materials, manufactured goods and services which it does not have on its native soil. Even the United States and Soviet Russia, countries with abundant natural resources, must do so. In the States the customer is very demanding; he wants to be able to buy the best product, or the one that gives the best value in terms of cost and quality. Over the next ten years those organizations which succeed in exporting and in making overseas investments will be the winning companies. They will be the ones who, to quote the fashionable expression, will 'reconquer the home market'. A company's success in selling its products abroad is proof, generally speaking, that they are good. Thus businesses that succeed in foreign markets demonstrate that they are offering good products and that their sales departments are competent. Having triumphed beyond their own borders, their victories at home are easily won. Reconquest of the home market is achieved through the conquest of export markets.

7

My Apprenticeship in International Management

In January 1958 I was appointed Regional Director for ten countries, eight of which were in Europe. My new job entailed reviewing plans, giving advice, and obtaining the support of the key European staff for these countries. From the outset I decided to approach my work not by looking at these companies from the outside, but by trying to make myself part of their own management teams. Above all I would have to help them discover their weaknesses and how to correct them, and obtain for them the support of experts in manufacturing, marketing, service and maintenance, as well as finance, from IBM's HQ in Paris or in the various companies belonging to the group.

During the preceding years I had established excellent relations with the Managing Director for Holland, Mr J. Schotte, a man close to retirement age who knew the company very well, and who, the first time I visited Holland in my new capacity, said to me, 'Look out, young man, do not forget that you are standing before the Vice-President of IBM Europe.' I was a little surprised, but he explained to me that Mr Watson had nominated him Vice-President for IBM Europe just before the war but no one had told him he no longer held the post when a president was appointed.

I quickly undertook a series of visits to all the countries in my group, and made my first discovery of Greece, Turkey, Iran, and Israel. I shall never forget my first visit to Israel at the beginning of 1958; when I offered a tip to the porter at the Hotel Dan in Tel Aviv who had conducted me to my room, he said, 'No thank you,

93

sir, the French are doing so much for Israel, I couldn't accept a tip. It is I who am indebted to you.' During this first stay I met a great many individuals and made many friends who are still friends today. I discovered an extraordinary pioneer spirit in the country and my visit to a kibbutz was very instructive. The company General Manager was Mr Alex Rathouse, a Jewish South African, who had come to fight for Israel in 1948, and who at heart was not very keen on his position as General Manager. On each of my visits he said to me, 'I would like you to find a replacement for me.' He was a man of extraordinary intellectual honesty and he felt that the sacrifices demanded of a general manager were more than he was prepared to accept.

I spent a whole week in Greece, arriving on a Monday morning and leaving on a Friday evening. I went to the office every day and on this first trip I did not even visit the Acropolis, which might of course be interpreted as a lack of intellectual curiosity or even of culture, but with so many problems to resolve I could never take an hour off to become a tourist.

In 1958 Turkey appeared to be several decades behind not just Europe, but even Israel. I have never forgotten an incident that occurred during my first meeting with an important customer at his Ankara office. He was a courteous businessman and offered us some coffee. A few minutes later his assistant returned and announced to him, 'We are extremely sorry, sir, but there is no coffee today.' The client knew this perfectly well since at that time coffee was unobtainable in Turkey, but tradition demanded that coffee should be served to all guests at a meeting and he wanted to observe all the rites of hospitality. I met all the company employees as I did on each of my visits there, and learned of the immense difficulties experienced by a country 'on the road to development'.

My first visit to Iran was also interesting because I learned from that trip what corruption means. At that time we did not do any business at all with the Iranian government for in accordance with the principles clearly established by IBM, there was no question of offering anyone whatever a percentage on deals concluded, nor would we hire someone close to the seat of power to be our local representative, nor reduce our prices for Iran since ours were international prices and hence non-negotiable. Our local manager – a Frenchman moreover (and at that time it was already a rarity for the manager of a subsidiary to be other than a national of the country) – told me that it would be very difficult to do business if we were not prepared to 'do what everybody else does'. I had to have long discussions with him, explain company policy all over again, and tell him that when it came to making an evaluation of his results we would not hold it against him if business deals were lost for these reasons. For a number of years we did not sell a single machine to government-controlled installations because one of our competitors employed a cousin of the Shah as its representative. But our company ethics remained unscathed.

In Iran, as in Turkey and Greece, and most certainly in Israel, I noted the high quality of the company's personnel. I had been struck, particularly in Israel, to learn that several of the maintenance engineers held doctorates in the sciences, in mathematics, and in physics. Israeli industry had not yet been developed, and young people who had studied long and hard to obtain valuable degrees could not find employment commensurate with their qualifications, but they did not hesitate to accept a position for which they were over-qualified. The result was that the quality of the middle rank of staff was superior to that found in European countries, and I soon observed that with regard to the number of suggestions made per man per year, for example, Israel was always well ahead of all European countries.

Such a system of employee suggestions, which was already established and flourishing at IBM, corresponded roughly to what were later to be called 'quality circles' since many of the suggestions were developed by a group of men and women rather than by just one individual. They worked together on a problem then proposed an improvement in methods or an improvement to a certain machine. Owing to this system, a group of people with few resources at their disposal had managed to adapt a standard typewriter to print Hebrew. Since Hebrew is written from right to left, considerable modifications had had to be carried out.

While I am saying a few words about each of these countries, I would like to add that my visits to Belgium and Luxemburg, always very pleasant, were much easier than the others for me since I was dealing with people who shared the same basic culture as my own. There were no problems in communication, relations between French and Belgian bankers and industrialists were already very close, and the data processing requirements were the same.

I had been to Spain in 1956 and 1957 to study the problems of the Spanish banks, but I had not had the opportunity to take full account of the difficulties the country was going through as a whole. Imports were controlled; it was not easy for IBM Spain to obtain delivery of new machines from their countries of manufacture; and when visiting certain clients such as the Spanish Railways, or a small client in Barcelona whose name now escapes me, I saw installations where a very modern machine like the computer 650 rubbed shoulders with very ancient printers, such as model 285 tabulators brought out in 1934. Finding parts for these old machines was very hard since our factories had long since ceased to make them, but our Spanish maintenance engineers performed miracles, making for themselves the parts the factories could no longer supply. Every one of us who went to Spain at that time would receive a message from the Spanish general manager asking if we could bring such-and-such a spare part. I must confess that a number of us did a little smuggling in those days, carrying in our pockets one or two important parts that were needed by our Spanish friends.

My first trip to Portugal was a little difficult because business was going badly, and our local manager was distinctly lacking in authority over his associates. It was all rather anarchic. Consequently I was induced to spend more time there than I had intended, and to combine our family holiday with work. In July 1958 my wife, our three daughters, and myself left to spend a month in Portugal; we planned to return through Spain. We had reserved rooms in a family pension, La Quinta das Torres, an old private house transformed into an inn-cum-hotel. It was a very pleasant place with an immense basin of water which served us as a swimming pool.

On the second or third day after our arrival, I went to the office and began making a thorough investigation into the affairs of IBM Portugal. The situation was not too brilliant: practical marketing techniques were non-existent and budget control was absolutely deplorable. Instead of taking a holiday, I went into the office every day to work. It was a long trip because the Quinta das Torres was situated south of the Tagus and I had to take the ferry to get to Lisbon. Two weeks later we decided to leave this 'bucolic' place and move to Estoril, which was much closer to Lisbon and which was a site our daughters actually preferred. Nearly three and a half weeks went by, and the only holidays I took were the weekends. It taught me what it is like to run a small business.

These were the last days of the Portuguese dictatorship although well before the end of the colonial empire, but all levels of society seemed to be lacking in motivation. The loss of empire, which was already present in their minds, seemed to have turned them into a disillusioned people without hope for the future. One of them, who was an outside Director of the company, impressed me very much when he strongly criticized those IBM managers who came to visit the subsidiary for a day and promptly left. He was astonished to see that I had spent such a long time with IBM Portugal which after all accounted for only a very small percentage of the total European turnover, and said that such a long stay would not have been justified if it had not coincided with my holidays. He came from a family of 'brilliant intellectuals', and his brother, Fernando Alves Martins, is today the President of the Portuguese subsidiary.

I was to return several times to Portugal, and in the course of one of these visits we planned what is known within IBM as a 'family dinner'. On such occasions, held roughly every two years, the entire personnel of a regional office, a factory or a country, husbands and wives included, assembles for a dinner attended by one of the managers from HQ who comes in order to meet the staff and explain the company's aims and results to them in a fairly brief speech, for it is a dinner-dance.

This dinner had been fixed for a date which I have since forgotten; about ten days before I learned that one of IBM's American vice-presidents would be coming to Portugal. (No doubt he was uneasy because I had not yet managed to redress the financial situation. The man in question was Mr Eddie Goldfuss at that time Financial Vice-President of the World Trade Corporation.) The dates of his stay did not correspond exactly with the date set for the dinner so I telephoned the general manager in Portugal to ask if it would be possible to change the date by a few days. He called me back the same day to say that it was perfectly possible, both from the point of view of the hotel where the reception was to be held, and for his immediate associates whom he had consulted.

As it happened, while we were organizing this dinner, the President of the IBM Corporation was spending his holidays in Portugal. His name was Mr A. L. Williams, a man for whom I have the greatest admiration and who was truly a pillar of IBM for many years. So Al and his wife were in Portugal, and learning this I asked the general manager to invite them to the dinner, too. Everything went off very well, except that Mr Williams found out I had changed the date a little while before the pre-arranged time; he called me in and hauled me over the coals. As he said, 'Once you have advised the employees of the date, especially when members of staff have had to make preparations well in advance so as to attend this sort of occasion, particularly young parents with children who have to arrange for babysitters, you don't just go and change the date. You have shown yourself completely lacking in a sense of human relations.'

I admired Mr Williams very much and I still admire him, and I must say that the lesson sank in. Never since then have I changed the date of a meeting that has been planned some time in advance, unless there were absolutely pressing reasons.

Throughout my period as Regional Director I often visited our Swiss offices in Geneva, Zürich, Berne and elsewhere, and I became extremely friendly with the Chairman, Walter Herzog, who was French-speaking, a francophile, and a great business-man. I met the Sales Manager, Hans Leuthy, again and he became my best friend outside the Hexagon. I also met Kap Cassani, a young salesman with remarkable qualities – enterprising, com-petent and made of very stern stuff. Several years later he was to join me at IBM's European HQ, and later to succeed me.

In 1958 the Universal Exhibition was held in Brussels, which I visited several times with clients as we had a very important stand there. The director of the stand was Gene Saber, who had welcomed me to New York in 1948.

When we left for Portugal and Spain in July 1958, my wife was expecting a baby. On November 30th we set out once more for the American Hospital in Neuilly so that Dr Ravina could attend the birth. As usual I waited in the same room until the doctor came to announce the arrival of our fourth child, and this time he seemed to me much more cheerful than at the birth of our third daughter six and a half years earlier. He spoke to me for a long time and even asked me – something he had never done with the previous children – what we were going to call our son. François had arrived and my wife was radiant with joy.

At the beginning of 1959 a meeting of the 100% Club, the annual reunion bringing together all the salesmen who had fulfilled their quotas in 1958, was held in Madrid. It was still possible at that time to bring together in one European city all the salesmen from European countries who had done so.

Everything went off smoothly, except that the Club reunion was followed by a management meeting at which I had a violent argument with the Chairman of IBM World Trade, Mr A.K. (Dick) Watson. Dick was a very 'present' boss. He visited the subsidiaries regularly, knew all the managers very well, and did not hesitate – in any way – to share his impressions with me and pronounce judgement on all the managers in the countries for which I was responsible. He had discovered that in one country relations between the general manager and some of our big customers were not all they should have been and that this man, although perfectly competent in other respects, had not the necessary 'class', as he called it, to remain general manager. I, on the contrary, felt this manager's general competence outweighed any shortcomings in business relations he may have had on a worldly, social level with the big bosses in the country. However, Mr Watson suggested, quite forcefully, that I should replace him with another man who did not have anything like the same abilities, but who knew all the right people. After a rather lengthy argument, I told Mr Watson that I absolutely refused to replace this man and if he insisted on it, I would hand in my resignation. He said to me: 'You're wrong. Sleep on it, and we'll discuss it again tomorrow morning.'

I need hardly say that I spent a troubled night, reviewing all the arguments I could possibly bring to bear, and next morning at breakfast — 'working breakfasts' were already an established practice — I met Mr Watson and told him, 'I haven't changed my mind, either he stays or I go.' Mr Watson answered: 'I am willing to accept your judgement even though I believe it is wrong. If you can work with him and if business goes well, fine! But if not, I shall consider that you have made a serious error of judgement and you will have to take the consequences.'

That was the first time I had had a serious conflict with my management, and there have been very few since, but I was absolutely determined to take a firm stand in a case where my boss wanted me to do something that was totally against my principles, and I am happy to say that in this case the future proved me to have been right. One of Dick Watson's great virtues was that one could have a very tough argument with him, but once a decision was taken there were no unpleasant repercussions for the person who had stood up to him. However, from this time on, I acquired a reputation for being too sensitive. And I really was, but I can now confess it served me well. At one meeting in which I reacted violently, for example, one of the American executives even called me Charles!

*

The following June Dick Watson told me that I had spent long enough as a Regional Director and had been appointed Assistant General Manager of IBM Europe by the President, Louis Castaldi.

So there I was at the age of thirty-five responsible for the greater part of the staff functions of IBM Europe, especially marketing, manufacturing, service, and finance. Those responsible for operations, such as the general managers of the four biggest countries, and the two new regional directors, were reporting directly to Louis Castaldi. This new move placed me in an ideal position to tighten links with the World Trade Corporation in the United States, and from now on I began to maintain very close relations with IBM's top-ranking American managers.

One of the functions I was responsible for was directing market research and product planning, so I again found myself studying these problems which I had left off at the end of 1957. The manager was my friend, René Rind, and I was delighted to be working with him again. Together we took up once more our battle to have IBM products manufactured in Europe adapted to European markets, and for the laboratories to play a better role in doing so.

In 1958 the decision had been made to give IBM's European laboratories a world-wide mission; they were to participate with the American labs in the development of products intended for the whole world and not solely for their own country or just for Europe. The laboratories in France, Germany and England were already important; new labs were now set up in Sweden, Austria and Holland, and each laboratory had three essential aims.

The first was to develop a product, be it a machine or a programme-product, i.e. software, for the whole of the world market. Setting up this sytem was a long and difficult business because the engineers and the men in charge of marketing had to be familiar with the market in each country and find the common characteristics linking them. Obviously a decision had to be taken at the very highest level as to whether or not the company should put the product on the market, and, since the

101

American market was large and there were far more engineers working on development in the USA than in the rest of the world, it was a hard battle for the European laboratories to win the place which, in my opinion, they deserved.

In this case, as in many others, the ability and will of certain men played a considerable part; the directors of the European laboratories knew how to make themselves appreciated, not only by the European management but also by their American colleagues so that they were able to have a say in things. Several times they carried the day when it came to a choice as to where a product, which was to be marketed in the US and in the rest of the world, should be developed. The men who made the greatest contribution to the reorganization of IBM's laboratories were the Chairman of World Trade, Dick Watson, his President, Jack Brent and, later, Gilbert Jones, who became President of World Trade in 1961. These men understood the needs of foreign nations; they fought with very great persistence against the American labs' project managers and knew how to present our dossiers and our problems to the management board. This form of organization bore fruit, and quite a few of the products which today are sold by subsidiaries throughout the world were developed by our European laboratories.

The second goal of the European and Japanese labs was determined at this time; it was to develop products required by a local market which were not in demand by world markets as a whole. For example, only the Japanese needed Katakana or Kanji characters and so the task of developing the terminals and personal computers utilizing these characters was entrusted to the Japanese laboratory. Another example: only the European countries have a Giro postal system so it was the European labs which were given the responsibility for developing the special products for such European operations.

Thirdly, each laboratory now set up a department of advanced technology. The world-wide organization of research with very precise goals set for each laboratory might have led to a diminution in creativity. However, in every lab a small group was maintained which I have no hesitation in calling a centre of creativity; the engineers and scientists forming a part of each one were free to work on fundamental research.

The organization of European-wide production had already begun. The original project had been the manufacture of type-writers, the parts for which were produced in several countries — wherever the lowest costs could be obtained — then assembled in a few countries. In 1958 it was decided to organize production slightly differently — each of the factories was henceforth to manufacture one or several products for the whole of the European market, but no product would be manufactured in more than one European plant.

I believe this was a 'first' — the first time such a plan had been organized by an international corporation, and I was closely involved in the task of sharing out production and giving precise production plans to the nine European factories. I worked very hard throughout this period with the Director of Manufacturing for Europe, who was first Paul Maniéri, then Bob Dunlop. At this time, I began to realize that only co-ordination of production on a scale vaster than that possible in a single country could make Europe competitive with the United States.

In 1958 another extremely important decision was also taken: all the workers in IBM factories would henceforth be paid monthly, that is, they would have a fixed monthly salary and would not be paid 'piece rates' or by the hour. This, together with job enrichment schemes which had already been introduced in 1949, brought us definitively out of the Taylor system of production.

I believe this was the first instance of a change-over to monthly salaries for the work force in any industry in Europe, and I must admit that, at many of the meetings I attended after this decision, the leaders of European industry whom I met reproached me bitterly for having taken this decisive step in the amelioration of social relations. I had evidently upset these gentlemen, and it seemed they believed that paying the workers monthly would reduce productivity, a notion which was to prove blatantly false.

I have already mentioned that, while I was concerned with

market research and product planning, we had worked very hard on the study of a 'little' system with 'little' punch-cards since we believed that client needs in Europe were very different from the States, and that we had to be able to answer the problems of small businesses as well as those of big ones.

The German laboratory had done a lot of work on this in collaboration with all the Europeans who were involved in studies aimed at producing new products, and when I took over these functions we were getting close to a prototype, which meant that I very often travelled to the Boeblingen laboratory in Germany. As a result I decided to learn German by the Assimil Method. I am afraid I do not remember very much, although I did manage to gain a working knowledge within a few months, at the very least enough to understand what people said to me, but my capacity for expressing myself always remained very limited.

In 1960 Mr Castaldi and Mr Watson decided I needed a little further training in management, and I was sent on a course called 'The Executive Programme' which Columbia University held during July and August at Arden House, a magnificent mansion in the Harriman forest in the State of New York. I spent six extremely interesting weeks there, worked very hard, but still managed to improve my performance at tennis.

This sojourn at Columbia University was an enthralling period because the run-up to the American elections was in full swing. As a result I was able to see the famous debate between Nixon and Kennedy on television, and, after seeing it, I was convinced that Kennedy would win the election, while the majority of my 'schoolmates' who were staunch Republicans naturally thought Nixon would carry it off.

Better 'trained', I believe I was able to bring about a tremendous improvement in communications between the different functional services of the various countries, those of the European management and those at our HQ in the USA. In fact, my position allowed me to be the channel through which all communications between Europe and the United States had to pass, and when I look back over this time I am happy with a number of decisions

104

I caused to be made, particularly the one to increase the number of Europeans working at head office. Their home companies – IBM Germany, IBM UK, IBM Italy – would get them to spend two or three years in a reasonable job at HQ. This gave them the opportunity to gain an understanding of the company's overall functioning and, above all, taught them to work with their foreign colleagues.

This was the era in which Mr A.K. Watson had set us as a target a 30 per cent growth rate per year in both turnover and profits, which, in spite of the rapid development of data processing that was to take place in the 1960s, was none too easy to achieve. But having such an ambitious objective stimulated everybody and I can still remember the phrase Dick Watson often used: 'Better to shoot high and fail than to shoot low and succeed.' We all knew perfectly well, however, that failure would not be lightly tolerated.

During 1961 along with many other people, I was to live through an experience that was both traumatic and extremely enriching. The few prototypes of the 3000 System at present working in the German laboratory were at the testing stage, and we had observed that their technical performances were not all we had hoped for and worse still that the prices at which we expected to be able to rent or sell them would not be high enough to make the programme profitable. The head of the European laboratories and many marketing people were adamant that the product should be announced at the Hanover Fair, which was to take place in May. The Hanover exhibition is the venue at which all the manufacturers of data processing and office machinery present their new products.

We held numerous meetings at the Boeblingen laboratory, and some American experts came over to Paris to study the machine which led to a very worrying situation – the Americans did not seem too keen to put this machine on the US market. This would obviously reduce considerably the number we could hope to sell.

One last big meeting was held, which was attended by all those who had some say in the matter: Mr Watson, Mr Brent, President of World Trade, the Director of European laboratories, Mr Schwab, the Director of the German laboratory, Mr Rind, the Director of market studies, and myself. Only two of us, Mr Rind and myself, took a stand against announcing the new product which we did not think ready for the market, but the engineers carried the day and Mr A.K. Watson and Mr J. Brent took the decision to present it at the Hanover Fair.

Commercially it was extraordinarily successful and during the next few months we received a huge number of orders. Nevertheless, once the machines were in production, they did give some trouble – the cost price could not be brought down to the necessary level – and, although my wife and I, together with some of my wife's family, had rented a villa in Cannes for our holidays, I had to spend the whole of August in Germany with Jack Brent, working with the engineers, financiers, and market research experts to reach some definitive decisions on the product.

At the end of August I managed to snatch four days' holiday in Cannes. No sooner had I arrived than my father telephoned: Mémée Guitte, as we all called her, had died in her son's arms, the victim of an infarct. My children, like my wife and I, were grief-stricken. Of all their grandparents, she was the one they had known best for she used to come several times a year to spend a few days with us.

At the end of the year my Cazas grandfather, who at 87 had been failing little by little, died in his sleep. He was buried in the little cemetery at Puchay and rejoined his wife, whose death had affected him so deeply that he seemed to have lost all taste for life.

In the last quarter of 1961, the Chairman of the corporation, Mr Tom Watson, sent one of his immediate associates, the Treasurer, Mr R. Bullen, to investigate the 3000 machine and how the decisions about it had been made. In spite of the many orders in hand, the programme was halted. It was then necessary to launch a programme to replace these machines with slightly modified versions of our classic models so that the small clients who had ordered the 3000 system would still be able to rent or buy them.

All work connected with the launching of the 3000 machine was brought to a close.

During the latter part of that year I spent hours and hours agonizing over this decision, for at that date I still did not understand how important it was for a company to stop a project in time if there was not a strong probability that it would prove profitable, and that the product's performance would be satisfactory to our customers. This was how I learned the importance of a courageous decision on the part of a management who, although they had already invested in research and development, knew when it was time to cancel a new product.

It often happens that a development programme falls behind the dates originally set, that the product does not quite reach the performance levels envisaged for it, or that the new cost price is higher than the earlier estimate. It is at this point that the engineers who have come up with good ideas and new inventions and have worked very hard will say to you: 'Give us another six months and some more money and you will have the product the market needs.' Sometimes they succeed, but more often than not, six months later they make the same request: 'More time, more money.' If the general management lacks the courage to call a halt in time, a product will be put on the market that causes people to say, 'It's a magnificent technological achievement, but a commercial and economic disaster.'

The result of Mr Bullen's study provoked much upheaval in the management of the IBM World Trade Corporation and of IBM Europe: Gilbert Jones became President of the IBM World Trade Corporation; the Director of Laboratories was replaced and a new President of IBM Europe appointed, Mr E.S. Groo, who arrived in Paris at the end of 1961.

By virtue of the position I had taken regarding the disputed product, I retained my post and I now had to adapt myself to a new boss who was an altogether remarkable man, an American who was highly cultured but did not know Europe very well and had certainly never worked there before. I was to spend several months with him and I got on very well with this dynamic but somewhat blunt man, spending a good deal of time helping him to understand a number of things. He, too, taught me a lot: especially that one must never accept the slightest compromise in ethical principles.

At the end of 1961, I had to replace the director of marketing for Europe, the finance manager and the personnel manager. This meant a great deal of change at one stroke, and we set off again at the beginning of 1962 with a new team.

During this period, Gilbert E. Jones, the new President of the IBM World Trade Corporation, often came to Europe and I found him to be 'the perfect executive'. He was a man of great distinction whom I would call a 'world class manager'; having lived in France in his youth he spoke French well and displayed a sensitivity towards foreigners that few Americans who have reached important positions without ever having lived outside the USA could equal. It was the beginning of a long friendship that still endures to this day. His 'presence', his influence, and his intelligence made a deep impression on me at the time.

I remember equally well another event that was to be a first for me, and which I found very interesting. The President of ITT, Mr Harold Geneen, was just then looking for a vice-president to be responsible for ITT Europe. I did not know this of course, but I received a telephone message from him, asking me to meet him for lunch on Whit Monday 1962. I found it very odd that anyone should make an appointment on a public holiday, but in those days holidays were not such an important part of a manager's life as they are nowadays. I went to the lunch thinking that Mr Geneen wanted to talk to me about relations between IBM and ITT, since IBM was one of their most important suppliers. Two of his vice-presidents accompanied him to this luncheon at the George V Hotel. He said to me, 'The fact is, I need a new vice-president for Europe, and I would like it to be you.' He explained to me what the job entailed, but I told him at once that I had no intention of leaving IBM, having decided very early on that I would never leave the company, even for the most dazzling offers from elsewhere, unless I had serious problems in my relations with my management, or if my principles dictated that I should resign.

I never found out what salary Mr Geneen intended to offer me since we did not reach that point in the discussion. However, that was not of the least importance to me since I had made up my mind to stay with IBM in whom I had absolute trust, and would not have dreamt of leaving the company for mercenary reasons. Perhaps it is a weakness on my part, but I must admit that I have never understood how people who are satisfied with their situations can agree to leave their company for the sake of a 20, 30 or 50 per cent rise in salary. I felt that I had a mission to fulfil, and that as long as my management allowed me the freedom to accomplish it there was no reason to go elsewhere. A little later on Mr Geneen engaged M. Bergerac, who, as many people know, later became the President of Revlon in the United States and obtained the fattest contract ever given to a 'professional manager' up until the time when Mr Ian MacGregor became Chairman of British Steel.

In IBM, it is a traditional practice to elect members of the management at HQ to local boards of directors, so that they can work closely with the subsidiaries. This is a way of bringing IBM executives into contact with other executives, with professors and people who have been in the civil service, from whom they can get direct advice. In the period from 1958 to 1962, I became a Director of IBM Spain, IBM Belgium, IBM Congo, IBM World Trade Europe Corporation, IBM Portugal, IBM Netherlands, IBM Israel and IBM Switzerland.

For IBM 1962 was rather a difficult year, and as August approached we realized that we were very far from reaching our objectives. In September Dick Watson called me to New York to propose that I should become Vice-President of the IBM World Trade Corporation in the United States with responsibility for marketing, maintenance services, and manufacturing. I would be directly answerable to him, rather a strange arrangement since Mr Jones was already President of the IBM World Trade Corporation. I accepted of course, but my departure for the USA was delayed by the poor results obtained by IBM Europe, which led to an operation known as 'operation close'. This simply meant the entire resources of the company were directed towards the signing of contracts, in other words, winning orders. We set to work immediately and each one of us in the European management was put in charge of stimulating sales in one particular country. I am happy to say that 1962 ended well, and that within three months we had brought about a recovery.

My wife and I were gradually getting used to the idea of returning to the States, but we were very sad to be leaving our parents. On 1 January 1963 I left for New York to take part in a 'Task Force' (see below). In February I came back to accompany my wife and four children on board the *France* on their way to America. On our arrival in New York we went to a hotel until we could move into the apartment I had chosen all on my own, and our girls immediately started attending the French *Lycée* in New York. The transition was very easy for them, since give or take a few pages, the syllabus was the same, the books were the same, and they fitted into their respective classes without any problems.

The apartment I had chosen was at 16 Sutton Place, New York, but I had vetted so many before my wife came to join me that I had made a mistake in the number of rooms it contained. I was 'house-hunting drunk', as the Americans say, and on the plan I drew up to send my wife I had put in an extra room. We took the apartment anyway for it would not have been easy to find another, and for the next eighteen months of our stay we had to live in a rather cramped fashion.

At the end of December 1962 Dick Watson was in Paris. He called me up to explain that there had been a change of plan. I was a little uneasy for I had already had to defer taking up my new post from October to January. He announced: 'I've got good news for you. Tom (Watson) has decided to undertake a study to reorganize IBM which will be entrusted to a "Task Force". I'm asking you to be part of the team, and to pay particular attention to the consequences that a reorganization of the company in America could have for the subsidiaries. The study group will have to submit its findings in three or four months' time and you will take up your post as of now.'

Perhaps it would be as well if I explained here what a Task

Force – in IBM jargon – is. In all dynamic enterprises that husband their human and financial resources carefully, it happens that new problems arise which for one reason or another cannot be entrusted to any existing department. The reasons may be that the new objective is so vast and so generalized that no department can take it on in addition to its normal workload without seriously affecting the latter; or that it may call for a kind of expertise that is not to be found in any of the already established departments. Over several months the study will represent so many man-hours of work which will disappear when the study is completed. Results are good if such a study leads to new solutions. But it can only do so if the group is very creative, that is to say, if it is not a slave to existing systems of work or thought, nor to the hierarchy.

In the study in which I was concerned the Chairman determined our brief. He was afraid the company's rapid growth would lead to bureaucratization; he wanted to ensure efficient relations between existing departments, a better response to the needs of the clientele, and the strengthening of creative innovative structures – in short, to reorganize for optimum utilization of resources. He had discussions with the director of organization within the company and they both came to the conclusion that the department of organization did not have the necessary resources to carry out this study quickly enough.

A group of a dozen people was created, therefore, composed of managers who had already proved their worth, including some of the vice-presidents. It would be pointless to describe the group in detail, but there were representatives from sales, marketing, the labs, the factories, the finance and personnel departments, and the 'international' division. The work was co-ordinated by the director of organization, whose role was to assist us from the point of view of methodology, to distribute the work amongst us, organize interviews with the corporation's chief executives, and to meet frequently with the chairman to keep him informed of the work in progress and obtain his reactions.

In this group we were all equals, but as always happens in a non-structured group one or two personalities, little by little, gained ascendancy over the others. Without its ever becoming official, a self-governing system always produces its own leaders; this has led me to believe that self-government, as it has been proposed by one French Socialist, is impossible in the day-to-day running of a business. One of the outstanding personalities in this group was Frank Cary who some years later became the Chairman of IBM.

Dick Watson had told me he thought it would take about three to four months. We began in January and presented the results of our deliberations — a plan for reorganization — at the end of September. It was a very enriching experience for me. I was the only one who was really familiar with IBM's activities outside the United States, and so I had to spend a considerable amount of time explaining to my colleagues why certain solutions, which they thought were obvious for the States, would not work well in France, Germany or Japan. My attitude provoked some irritation for I had introduced a 'complication' that delayed the handing-in of the final report. Each member of the Task Force was impatient to resume his normal duties, and it took all the authority of the director of organization and of Frank Cary to prevent our throwing in the towel.

During these nine months I learned, or relearned, the pragmatic American approach to problems. But I learned more than that when I learned the importance of having a large number of people participate in the preparation of decisions. There were already a dozen of us who were familiar with the recommendations; in addition to this we had had to discuss them with many of the managers so as to make use of any original ideas they might have had to contribute and get their reactions to our new concepts. At least one hundred highly-placed managers, in many different positions of responsibility, knew all or part of our plan.

At the end of 1963 and the beginning of 1964, when the plan was put into operation, everything went off smoothly because the people affected by it who might have reacted unfavourably were already expecting major changes and even knew about the most important decisions. When changes are explained in advance, when the men and women concerned are warned of what is going to happen to them, fear disappears.

As a way of thanking us for the work done, we were invited to present the report to the management committee at Jenny Lake in Wyoming. And thus I saw for the first time the beauty of the Rocky Mountains, and demonstrated to my American friends during the course of several long rides on horseback that I could be as good a cowboy as they were. I was re-enacting in reality my favourite childhood game, but we never met any Indians along the trails.

In a buoyant mood I returned to New York. At last I would be able to begin my real work. One advantage of my new job was that the office was near my home, whereas during those long nine months the Task Force had been meeting at White Plains or in the Yorktown laboratory, both of which were more than three-quarters of an hour's drive from New York. These car trips had, however, given me time to reflect alone on the problems of yesterday, today, and tomorrow.

My stay in New York — I was the first foreigner to take up an important position at IBM's HQ in the United States — was an extremely happy one. I learned to work with Americans as virtually all the senior posts were filled by Americans, and I must say they taught me a stern sense of duty, strict time-keeping and punctuality, and availability. I settled in to my position as an international manager. A great many Europeans came to visit IBM in the United States. I received them all, and most of them were certainly impressed by American methods of management, and in particular by the American system of long-term planning.

On 22 November 1963 we were shocked and grief-stricken by the assassination of President Kennedy. That date marked the beginning of what I called the American period of 'mea culpa'. Under the presidency of J.F. Kennedy hope had been renewed; a great wave of enthusiasm had carried the American people towards new frontiers; culture, including scientific culture, enjoyed a full flowering, thanks to his personal intervention. The rights of man were one of his chief preoccupations and segregation

113

diminished day by day. All such high hopes of the great majority were shot down with him. I have never seen so many Americans crying. The French were also shocked and I received several telegrams from France in which condolences were sent to me on the death of *my* president. I was French after all, but then J.F. Kennedy was almost 'one of us' for he was a citizen of the world and . . . his wife was of French origin.

I made my first trips to South America and Canada during this period. In early January 1964 the four children, my wife and I spent a week's holiday in Quebec. It was so cold that skiing was impossible; we learned a few Canadian expressions and spent more time 'gossiping in the hotel lounge' than we did going for walks.

I heard that one of my colleagues from IBM France who was also on holiday in Montreal had had a car accident with his wife and child, and that they were all in hospital. I telephoned the manager of the local office to find out where they had been taken. Having spoken to this office manager, I felt obliged to request a meeting with him. But first I visited the hospital and found that the casualties were recovering well. I then went to the office and told his secretary I had an appointment with her boss at 4 p.m. 'Very well, sir, please take a seat for a moment.' I read the IBM Canada magazines; at 4.20 I asked the lady to remind the manager that I was still waiting. At last he received me at 4.35 p.m., saying, 'Pleased to meet you, Mr Maisonrouge, no doubt you're a salesman with IBM France.'

'No,' I told him, 'can you lay hands on an IBM Organization Manual?' He picked one up and looked for my name in the section devoted to France. I let him get on with it, then, to help him (!) said: 'Now look at the first page.' On this page there was a list of the 'officers', starting with Mr A.K. Watson, G.E. Jones, then me. He was rather surprised, turned pale, and offered me a coffee to 'recover' himself.

This incident made me realize yet again that in large organizations, the leaders of the mother company are not always known to the executives of the subsidiaries, and that communication must be improved. This experience was another clear proof of how important it is for executives to pay regular visits to their company's factories, laboratories, and offices.

During this period, the great event at IBM was the announcement of System 360. It was an extraordinary risk; our competitors were snapping at our heels, but nonetheless IBM launched this enormous project as a gamble which, had it failed, would undoubtedly have had grave consequences for the company. It was a plan for developing a family of computers which would be compatible amongst themselves, and have the same software based on the same technology of semi-conductors.

It was my responsibility through the intermediary of the vice-presidents of manufacturing and marketing, to co-ordinate the announcement outside the United States, and this led to my second or third great battle with my management. Gil Jones, the President, did not believe the Europeans were ready to announce this new product, he did not think the marketing plans had been sufficiently well drawn-up, and I must admit that he was not altogether mistaken, but at that time I believed if we really wanted to be a multi-national company, products had to be announced simultaneously, or at the very least *almost* simultaneously, in Europe and in the States. I knew the risks I was running for the scars left by our experience with the System 3000 had scarcely healed.

In the end I won the argument: System 360 was announced on the same day in Europe and in the USA. All decisions concerning its manufacture in Europe had been taken, the teams of engineers responsible for the launching had spent the necessary time in the laboratories, and I was very proud of the work of our German lab who had been responsible for the development of the less expensive end of the 360 family system.

Shortly after this announcement Dick Watson called to tell me that the board of directors wanted me to return to Paris as President of IBM Europe, to replace Mr Groo who had to return to the United States. It was the first time in the history of IBM that a European, born in a European country and retaining his nationality, was to take over the management of IBM Europe. The preceding presidents had been a Canadian, an Italian with an American passport, then an American. I was happy and proud to accept.

My stay in the US had turned out to be quite short, and because of the Task Force assignment I had not made many trips. It was probably the eighteen months in which I was able to spend the most time with my wife and children. The 'Big Apple', as New York is called, no longer held many secrets for us. We had made many American friends who lived in the vast and fabulous suburbs of the city, and some French friends who lived in New York. The great majority of executives who had children lived outside the city: not one of my immediate associates lived less than eighteen miles from our offices. We had experienced American hospitality in Poughkeepsie in 1949. Living in an apartment in New York, we found that the inhabitants of this great city behaved like Parisians – we did not even get to know the neighbours who lived on the same floor.

Before leaving the USA my wife and I decided to tour the United States, and I took three and a half weeks' holiday which at that time was exceptionally long. In early July 1964 we set off with our four children to discover America by car. We covered an amazing distance – from New York to Chicago and from Chicago to Wyoming with a stop-off at Jenny Lake, a visit to Yellowstone National Park, and to Cody with its memories of Buffalo Bill. From Wyoming we went on to San Francisco to see the magnificent beaches of the Pacific, then down to Los Angeles to return via Las Vegas where two important events occurred: neither my wife nor I bet a single cent in the casinos and my son had a 'crew-cut'. We made a film of the entire trip and called it 'America through the windshield' for we travelled so many miles that Françoise had to shoot from inside the car. Our stay in Las Vegas facilitated the editing, it divided the film into two periods: before and after the 'shearing' of François's hair.

We returned via the Grand Canyon, the Mesa National Park near Denver, the Plains, and finally New York. We had travelled some 7,500 miles in three weeks. To hold America in your arms is an extraordinary experience and I came to understand during the course of this journey why Americans from Montana, or Wyoming, even from California and Colorado, have little practical reason to take an interest in what goes on outside their own country. If they live in Montana or Wyoming, they are scarcely interested even in what happens on the East Coast.

8

Internationalizing Management

The Common Market has created a huge economic space and, on condition that they have the necessary willpower, businesses can profit from the vast markets now open to their products. How often one hears industrialists and politicians attribute this or that American or Japanese success to the size of their two markets! And yet Europe has more inhabitants than the United States and a gross national product almost as big as the American one. While I acknowledge the fact that the American market is more homogeneous, it must also be understood that there is not one American market but at least eight. I also recognize that a language common to 238 million inhabitants, the absence of frontiers, a similar system of education from one State to the next, and the federal spirit all facilitate penetration of the market and the transfer of employees from New York to San Francisco or from Chicago to Dallas.

The Treaty of Rome has given Europeans possibilities which they have not exploited to the full, because the people in power, in big business as much as in government, are still prisoners of their historical past. Around 85 per cent of Americans are of European origin, and it seems to me the United States is an excellent example of what Europe could become if Europeans would only liberate themselves from the constraints of history. The ancestors of present-day Americans, as well as today's immigrants, left their countries of origin because they were unhappy there: they were poor and without hope, subjected to political oppression, victims of racism, or more recently harassed by bureaucratic systems that prevented them from attaining the goals they set themselves. Added to which there were and still are entrepreneurs in search of new challenges. Their mobility has remained one of their strengths; a quarter of all Americans change their address every year. Their intellectual mobility in addition to the mobility of employment within the country has also helped Americans to restructure their industries earlier than the Europeans.

Interestingly when the Common Market was created, the Americans believed in it. They thought that a new market was opening up and American industry decided to increase its investments in Europe. It seemed to them possible to set up a factory in Germany, France or Holland, and they anticipated no problems in selling the products to the initial six countries comprising the Community. Certainly they had one advantage over European businesses: the existence of their world management structure allowed them to take decisions on a 'European scale', whereas European employers remained nationalistic. Getting Siemens, Philips and CII-Honeywell Bull to co-operate on common projects was harder than getting IBM's subsidiaries in Germany, Holland and France to work together.

I have already spoken of what IBM had been doing since 1958 in the realms of research and development, and manufacturing. I want to come back to this, and, by generalizing, suggest some solutions to the problems of restructuring which confront every European country today.

RESEARCH AND DEVELOPMENT

National expenditure

Since 1965 Europeans have been talking a great deal about their technological backwardness in relation to the United States. This is the famous 'technological gap'. A serious examination of the situation throughout the sixties makes clear that such backwardness was not due to a shortage of scientists or engineers, or to a deficient system of education, or to any lack of creativity whatsoever in Europe. It was and still is a question of how research and development is organized. As early as 1967 I wrote an article for a French newspaper, *Les Echos*, titled: 'The real gap is in management'.

I cannot give a full account here of the strengths and weaknesses in research and development in Europe for that would need an entire volume to itself. I would just like to stress certain points and underline my conviction, founded on experience, that European scientists and engineers are in no way inferior to their American or Japanese counterparts. They are not inferior in talent – more than 25 per cent of the scientists living in the United States who have won Nobel prizes were born in Europe or studied there – or in number, in fact, there are more qualified engineers graduating each year in Europe than there are in the USA, and the 'stock' of scientists is larger.

The total resources devoted in Europe or America to research and development are not very different. In 1981 the amount expended on it in the five most important countries in the free world was in terms of percentage of gross national product as follows: USA, 2.43%; Japan, 2.38%; France, 2.01%; West Germany, 2.49%; England, 2.47%. Since 1981 these figures have risen greatly: in 1983 America held the lead with 2.62%; West Germany reached 2.57%; and France hit 2.13%.

It is difficult to measure the concrete results of research in various countries, but the royalties paid to other countries by the users of patents give a rough idea. In 1981 American businesses paid $883 million in patent rights to foreign countries as follows: 365 million (41% of the total) to England; 111 million (12% of the total) to Japan; 76 million (8% of the total) to West Germany; 68 million (7% of the total) to France.

These figures call for comment. In my opinion, something that should create Euro-optimism is the fact that West Germany, England and France receive 4.58 times more money in patent right sales from the USA than Japan does. This proves the old continent has not lost her creativity. Rather sadder is the fact that Europeans pay more for patent rights to the Americans than the Americans pay to Europeans. However, England, a country which many Europeans consider to be living on its past, is extremely well-placed in the technological race. The last point to be made is that 'returns' on research and development vary a great deal from country to country and if one recognizes – as indeed one must – that, in future, international competitiveness will depend largely on scientific and technological performance, then neither France, nor Germany, nor England nor any other European country can be truly competitive on its own in all fields against the United States and Japan. Even if returns on research were the same, there is still the question of scale.

On the other hand it is evident to any man of good faith that Europe, as a single united force, could easily do as well as Japan or the United States. What is required is better organization within each country and then better organization on the European scale.

National organization – European organization

Here again, I could develop my argument at great length but I will simply give a few examples. The Houdry process of catalytic refining is used throughout the world. The inventors were two French engineers, Houdry and Lassiat, who, finding themselves unable to persuade any of the French petroleum companies to adopt their invention, went to the United States before the last war. Professor Guillemin, the Nobel prize-winner for medicine and father of neuroendocrinology, had to work in the USA to obtain the necessary resources to bring his research to a successful conclusion. In the November 1984 issue of the magazine, *Sciences et Techniques*, there is an article about a high resolution ophthalmoscope that utilizes laser beams. The prototype was made by the Institute of Theoretical and Applied Optics in collaboration with Professors G. Coscas and G. Quentel of the National Institute for Medical Research. The end of the article is edifying – I quote: 'The apparatus patented by the *Centre nationale de la recherche scientifique* [National Centre for Scientific Research] *could* be commercialized. The search for a company to manufacture it is now in progress.'

If instead of the NCSR a private company had conducted and financed such research, is it not reasonable to hope that the marketing of the product would have been an important consideration right from the start of the project, and that some market research, plus a study on how to set up the manufacturing process, would have been carried out?

Large *national* establishments dedicated to research and development are not necessarily the most efficient. They employ highly skilled men and women, but some of the scientists on their staff have one of two problems: either they produce excellent work, but concentrate on pure science in the belief that applied science is less noble and co-operation with industry a compromise that conflicts with their conception of academic liberty, or they are scientists who have never discovered anything of importance and continue to work in government-funded research because their jobs are protected by civil service regulations. Such establishments are also victims of the system by which public funds are distributed. For example, a research unit is set up and kept going in Brest even though it has very few students; meanwhile another research unit in Lyons has plenty of students but not enough professors.

If we move from the French to the European level, we see in each country examples of several laboratories all working on the same problem. Multiply this by six or ten and you will realize that few of them could have the capacity to rival the large Japanese or American laboratories working in the same disciplines.

Research in almost all fields – except perhaps pure mathematics and theoretical physics – demands considerable means and materials, but also men and women trained in different disciplines. For example, new semi-conductors are developed by teams that include chemists, solid state physicists, electronics experts, data processing specialists and generalists. In order to work quickly they must also have at their disposal powerful computers capable of utilizing Computer Aided Design. This may seem an obvious example, but almost all activities in new research call upon modern data processing technologies.

To summarize, research and development demand today

multi-discipline work teams; the will among scientists to move on from pure research to applied research and then to the 'product'; considerable industrial capacity so as to be able to make use of the most modern equipment without supplementary costs; regular financing not subject to budget cuts. It is perfectly obvious that to meet these demands research must be carried out on a European scale. Moreover this is already well-recognized: ESPRIT, the project set up by the EEC Commission, and EUREKA, the project proposed by the President of France, are examples of this. Furthermore, the most recent European successes, whether technological or scientific, are due to the pooling of the material and intellectual resources of several European countries. They were also successful because the Europeans who worked on them accepted the fact that there would be an international management team, and that they would have a boss. I would cite, for instance, CERN (European Council for Nuclear Research) at Geneva, which is among the foremost centres in the world and can compete with the finest achievements of the Russians and Americans; the airbus, Ariane, and in rather less spectacular fields the development of new antibiotics – the cephalosporines – carried out jointly by Hoechst in Germany and Roussel-Uclaf in France; Ford Europe's launch of its new Fiesta; research on new chemical gases conducted in common by the laboratories of Air Liquide in Chicago and in France.

I do not want to add too many examples, nor do I want to give the impression that great successes are obtained solely through international collaboration. There are numerous cases where an English, French, Swiss, German, Dutch or Italian laboratory has produced important inventions. I simply want to suggest that, in order to compete effectively against the Japanese and the Americans, it is indispensable in a great many cases to provide ourselves with the same advantages. In other words we must have a large market – Europe; scientists and engineers with a wide variety of training; cultural approaches which are not all identical (which means including people from several different nations); considerable financial means which an individual country cannot always provide; financing on a European scale;

men and women motivated by the needs of the market; and all this leads preferably to systems of co-operation between private industries.

Co-operation between the universities and industry

If we look at research and development from the economic viewpoint we get a different perspective. The essential aim then becomes to obtain results from research which will give each country a position in the front rank in as many fields as possible. I shall speak here of France, but the same comments apply to most European countries. We must have research centres of such high quality that foreigners will be induced to come and work there, thus helping us to maintain and enhance our culture which will improve France's image in the rest of the world. We must give doctors the necessary research facilities, so that they will pursue their labours in France, working with the major centres researching into new molecules and with those involved in biotechnology. We must also convince scientists and engineers that, while in no way diminishing the importance of pure research, they must not neglect or despise those activities which will provide the financing for it. To recall one example already mentioned: the manufacture and world-wide sales of a laser ophthalmoscope, that could effectively compete with ones made by the Japanese and Americans, would bring in new funds for the professors who conceived it. The proportion of French scientists who work in State establishments is too high. They know little about the importance of markets. For them, there are no sanctions – or, on the other hand, are there any great rewards – in terms of the results they achieve.

I have no illusions; it will take a long time to change the system, but there exists a method which has proved its worth in other countries and we must have no compunction about adopting it as well. It is co-operation between the universities and industry.

The United States provides a striking example. Researchers in industry and researchers in the universities have always worked together. In this case, as in many others, we find that an idea originating in Europe became successful in the USA and then was forgotten in Europe; we find the same situation in Japan and the United States. The Japanese 'quality circles', which have now been introduced in America, were created in Japan by Japanese productivity teams which had observed the 'suggestion' box system at work in the United States.

I would like to examine here how one of the most famous American universities, the Massachusetts Institute of Technology (MIT), approaches the problem. The Athena project, launched by MIT in May 1983, aimed to discover how the integration of computers into educational programmes could improve the process of acquiring knowledge for students at college level. The support from industry amounted to $50 million which came from two companies, IBM and DEC (Digital Equipment Corporation). Each company had to furnish thousands of personal computers and dozens of large computers, which would be interconnected in a single system. The companies hoped the project would bring them new knowledge concerning integrated systems, while MIT leaped at the chance to develop a revolutionary system of education.

MIT has five schools and twenty-two departments. The five schools include a business school and a school for the humanities and social sciences. The other three are scientific. There are 9,500 students, 980 teachers and 700 research workers; as is well-known, it is a private institution. It has developed three methods of co-operation with industry. The first is the *programme of industrial liaison*. This programme was started in 1948. Nowadays it includes nearly 300 companies whose combined financial contribution reached 6.4 million dollars in 1983. Representatives from the associated companies receive the following services:

1. Opportunities for discussion with research workers. In 1983 there were 4,000 meetings.

2. Access to a service supplying outstanding publications. Again in 1983, 50,000 documents were distributed.

3. The opportunity to attend symposia. 4,500 representatives from industry took part in these in 1983.

This programme is co-ordinated by eighteen 'liaison officers' who come from diverse backgrounds.

The second programme is the *sale of licences for the exploitation of patents*. Research at MIT leads to patents being taken out, for example for the production of Vitamin A, synthetic penicillin, and computer memories with magnetic cores. MIT attempts to establish which industries might be interested in exploiting the patents. In exchange, MIT asks for payment of patent rights.

The third programme is that of *research financed by industry*. In 1983 MIT received $20 million for this type of co-operation. It is, however, limited by problems of patent rights.

In spite of the long experience of co-operation between industry and the universities, certain problems remain which cannot be ignored. The main one is the fear some university men have of losing their academic independence and their objectivity; and the fear some industrialists have of not being the sole beneficiaries of the results of the research. In 1982 MIT's President, Dr Paul Gray, organized a meeting with the residents of Harvard, Caltech, Stanford and the University of California to study these questions. A kind of code of conduct was published, containing the following principal points:

1. In aiding university research, industry is looking for a competitive advantage;

2. The development of relations between industry and the university must not alter academic goals;

3. Secrecy regarding results must be avoided and full publication of agreed findings is desirable;

4. All results of research, including those indebted to contracts with industry, must be communicated to the public, although delays in publication may sometimes be necessary to protect patent rights.

The experience of MIT, like the large American companies it co-operates with, demonstrates that such co-operation benefits both parties. Perhaps the most important benefit is that this alliance has given each a·better understanding of the other, creating a greater mutual respect.

I would cite many other examples, but my aim is simply to show how deeply industry and the universities (which, in Europe, remain somewhat separate) interpenetrate in the United States. As well as contracts and financial aid universities receive from industry, a great many exchanges of scientists also take place: research workers in industry may want to spend one to three years in the universities and then return to their original company; researchers on sabbatical leave from the university may spend a year in the laboratories of a major business enterprise, or they may teach regularly in programmes of continuous training in industry.

There is very little government interference, except in the case of the very large organizations which have specific aims, such as NASA and the National Institute of Health, which is the largest centre for medical research in the world. With reference to the NIH, it seems to me interesting to note that more than 50 per cent of the doctors or biologists who work there stay no longer than three to five years, and then go on to pursue their careers and teach in the smaller research centres, either public or private ones.

Since the Nixon administration federal funds devoted to research have suffered constant cut-backs, and this has served to reinforce co-operation between the universities and industry since the universities have been compelled to turn more and more to the private sector for the financing of new projects or those already in hand. Their search for funds has made the major university laboratories and even the teaching units extremely competitive amongst themselves. In 1983, for example, IBM mounted a competition amongst the American science and engineering faculties. It had been decided that the twenty universities presenting the best projects on computer assisted production would receive a 4341 computer free of charge. One hundred and seventy-two engineering schools took part in the competition.

There are, on the other hand, those who see the intervention of business, whether private or public, as a grave threat to academic liberty. I would now like to reassure them. Here is how the budgets for higher education in the United States have been financed:

	Academic year 72–3 (in billions of dollars):	Academic year 82–3 (in billions of dollars):	Expenditure in 1973 multiplied in 1983 by:
Total budget	31.3	82.5	2.64 times
Voluntary aid	2.24	5.15	2.3 times
Aid from industry	0.318	1.1	3.5 times

It is therefore a fact that aid from industry has grown more rapidly than the total budget, but in 1983 it represented only 1.33 per cent of that budget. This is very far from being a 'controlling majority'.

I have given the American example at some length. I am not suggesting that we should copy it slavishly, and in any case that would be impossible. We must adapt, but there is nothing to prevent our taking inspiration from what has been done well in another country or on another continent. Certain European scientists are too ready to believe that only pure science will permit them to defend their academic freedom completely. But – I repeat what I have already said because it must be repeated unceasingly – the means to set up modern research are so costly that a single university, indeed all the universities in France or Germany or England together with the national laboratories in those countries, would not be able to mobilize the necessary resources. These laboratories must work across frontiers. Moreover science is universal, and if we want to return to the humanism of our ancestors and rediscover the honest man we must not hesitate to become Europeans. Leonardo da Vinci was not content to work solely in his native country!

In 1984 the Centre for Political Studies in Brussels published a study called 'Why certain countries are more innovative than others'. This document was prepared by Mr H. Ergas, principal administrator of the planning unit of the Organization for Economic Co-operation and Development.

In West Germany in addition to 120 universities engaged in research and development, there exist three private, non-profit-making organizations. One of them, the Fraunhofer Gesellschaft, has twenty-two research centres which provide technical support for small and medium-sized businesses. The universities have recently set up offices to establish liaison between industry and the universities on the model of the MIT.

The smaller countries, Switzerland, Holland and Sweden, furnish many examples of co-operation. In Switzerland private industry finances 15 per cent of university research. In Sweden the Council for Technical Development has given priority to the laboratories of research 'co-operatives', who now receive 22 per cent of the finance for research and development in the country.

France (in spite of some recent progress) and England are lagging behind other countries in this field.

INTERNATIONAL PRODUCTION

It is not my intention to write a manual on organization but simply to make a few suggestions which are the fruits of my own experience and firm convictions. I am starting from a hypothesis which some people will dispute, and go on disputing for several years to come: *we are producing goods and services for a world market.* Almost all the industries in each country have to be competitive with the industries in all other industrialized countries and even with the newly-industrialized countries (South Korea, Taiwan, Hong Kong, Singapore, Brazil, etc.).

I am very well aware that protectionist tendencies exist in every country, tendencies which become even more evident as the unemployment level rises and the balance of payments becomes worse. But in spite of the obstacles, one finds Coca-Cola in Nigeria as well as in Indonesia; Renault in New York as well as in Paris;

IBM, Apple and Burroughs computers in almost every country in the world; and Shell gas stations nearly everywhere . . .

An English product, manufactured in England, is therefore bound to be in competition – in Paris, for instance – with comparable products manufactured in France or imported from the United States, Germany, Italy, Japan, Brazil or elsewhere. Three essential things determine success:

1. A better, more attractive product, offering high quality and greater reliability at a competitive price, or a unique product;

2. A marketing department that does its job, knows the market and provides a good after-sales service;

3. Lastly, a product which costs less to manufacture than the others.

I will only elaborate on this last point, since I wish to focus upon *the internationalization of production*. Every business organization must set itself an objective: *to obtain the lowest possible manufacturing cost without in any way sacrificing quality*. In the majority of industries, where production methods are adequate, the manufacturing cost comes down when the quantity produced increases. We generally have the following curve which is intuitively evident and verified by the facts.

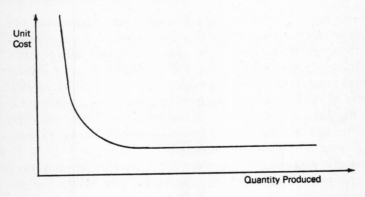

This curve simply expresses the fact that for each product manufactured there exists a minimum quantity of production required to attain a low cost. From the commercial point of view, it means that there must be a sufficiently large market potential to create profits. It must certainly be added that modernization of the methods of production has a considerable influence on the quantity that must be produced in order for goods to be competitive. A recent and significant example is that of Chrysler in the United States. In 1980 this company had to produce 2,200,000 cars per annum to avoid losses (see Ch.6). After changes in manufacturing methods, the introduction of robots, and the rise in productivity over the last three years, the company now starts making profits on an annual output of 1,100,000 cars.

For almost all products, the USA and Japan represent a larger market than that of any individual European country, even West Germany. European firms which in general have not invested sufficiently abroad, nor exported enough, sell more on their home market than outside it, and so suffer a serious handicap *vis-à-vis* Japanese and American businesses which benefit from a larger internal market.

There are three solutions to this problem:

1. *Increase the size of the market.* This is achieved by large exports and by investing abroad. Typical examples of this approach are supplied by Nestlé, Philips, Unilever and Shell, companies which all realize a greater turnover abroad than at home.

2. *Have a unique product,* which, for a few years – and only for a few years – is the only one able to satisfy the needs of consumers. This is where the rewards of high quality research and development lie. And this is what innovative businesses succeed in doing when they are not content with a new product but make every effort to improve it or to launch others like it.

3. *Call on the government for aid* in the form of various kinds of assistance, in particular, protectionism which in the long term never succeeds. This also means depending on favourable rates of exchange and they cannot last either.

For the European countries only the first two solutions are, in fact, valid since we are committed to the Common Market in an irreversible manner. Unless we are to envisage a return to the past, which is neither probable nor desirable, and which would bring about the inevitable decline of each country in the Community, we must work on the European scale. In the domain of production this is possible, as several companies have already demonstrated.

I witnessed the rationalization of IBM's production in Europe, and I played a part in setting it up. In 1958 IBM had eight factories in Europe. The four most important ones were making the whole product line, the others a part of this line. There were also products that were manufactured in five or six different factories. Each one produced, therefore, the quantity required for the local market plus some units for export to countries where there was no factory. All the services required for manufacturing, engineering, control of production and stock control, the departments responsible for orders and schedules, and those for technical publications, were duplicated. Each one of our products was badly placed on the unit price/quantity curve and our productivity levels (in volume) were very much lower than those of the American factories.

On the other hand, the machines were becoming more and more complex and the percentage of 'indirect' employees was constantly rising in proportion to the total number of production staff, which is the case however in all the advanced technology industries. Therefore, the question raised by several of our leaders was: How to organize European production in such a way that unit cost would be comparable to American unit costs, in spite of customs duties and transportation expenses?

In principle the answer was simple: divide the range of products into eight, give to each factory (and to one only) responsibility for producing several products, or parts of products, for the whole of the European market. A committee for the rationalization of production, comprising the director of manufacturing for each country and the European director of manufacturing, was given the task of sharing out production. Discussions were difficult, for each country wanted to retain production of the most profitable items, but resolving this difficulty was successful because there was a European directorate to take the decision. A federal authority was indispensable.

In 1984 IBM had fifteen factories in Europe (two in England, one in Sweden, one in Holland, four in Germany, four in France, two in Italy and one in Spain). Each had a precise role. For example, the factory at Montpellier manufactured all the computers at the top of the range and these were delivered to every country in Europe, the Middle East and Africa. This did not mean that this factory produced every single component used in the computers. Certain semi-conductors came from the factories at Corbeil-Essonnes in France, from Sindelfingen in Germany, or were bought from external suppliers. The memory-discs connected to these computers came from the factory in Mainz, West Germany, and the printers from the factory at Jarfalla in Sweden. The PC was manufactured in Greenock, Scotland.

As the quantities of these computers delivered within the geographical area comprising Europe, the Middle East and Africa are almost equal to those delivered within the United States by the American 'sister' factory at Poughkeepsie – or at the very least we have reached the horizontal part of the unit cost/quantity curve – our productivity is the same as in the United States. I am speaking here of productivity in volume or to put it in other words, the time required for assembly and testing and, what is very important, quality measured by the percentage of machines with *zero default* at the time of delivery to clients. The costs, measured in dollars, are lower than American costs.

The great lesson I have learned during more than twenty-five years' experience in European production is that with good management, modern methods of production and automation on a large scale, Europe can be competitive against the United States and Japan. I say advisedly Europe, and not Germany, England, Italy or France.

I have explained this method of production to scores of Europeans and endeavoured to convince them. This was fairly easy in the case of multinational corporations which have factories in several countries and manufacture products that are easily transported. It is paradoxical to note, moreover, that it is the multinationals of American origin who have drawn most profit from the advantages of the Treaty of Rome. National companies in the various countries in Europe have made less progress in this direction. They lacked, and are very often still lacking, the political will to create a supranational management. This is the reason why we have seen a number of mergers and take-overs within frontiers but very few between companies from several countries.

The electrical-electronic industry is a good example. In England, Germany, France and Italy, large companies have been formed which were amalgamations of smaller companies within their own countries. They have certainly attained the critical size industrially, but few through merging have enlarged the size of their market: they still prefer to sell within the national market. Now I am convinced that in order to ensure growth the size of the market must be increased *before* the size of the company.

I am well aware that sales are also increased via exports or through investments abroad, but I am convinced that three companies which were, let us say, Anglo-Franco-German, would be more successful against world competition than an English company, a French company, and a German company.

Application of European rationalization to the problems of defence

When my friend, Robert Galley, was the French Minister of Defence in 1973, I sent him a long report suggesting that France should take the initiative in creating a European arms industry which would of course be composed only of countries belonging to NATO. This idea was not taken up, and we see today that the equipment used by the armed forces in the different countries is not compatible. Even the ammunition varies.

I understand the political and even the strategic obstacles to a rationalization of the defence industry. Certain strategists would say that it would be unwise to have one single tank of a certain category, forty tonnes for example, utilized by all the land forces and manufactured in Hanover (West Germany); in the event of a conventional war the factory could quickly fall into the hands of the Russians. But let me pose this question: If the Russians occupied Hanover how much longer would the French Army need deliveries of new tanks?

There is another answer to this objection, which is to manufacture each type of equipment in at least two countries in the world with, preferably, one of the two being further from the theatre of operations.

I put the following basic proposition forward to Robert Galley:

1. First, to standardize weapons, equipment and systems in all the NATO countries.

2. To organize production in such a way that only one or two factories manufacture the equipment.

The economies achieved by each country would be considerable since the quantities of any model produced would be very much greater, and this would permit an appreciable reduction in the costs of research and development per unit.

It is quite obvious that this type of organization poses political problems and social difficulties; but difficulties need not be insoluble. In my opinion the ideal would be to have a European army, but, since that is impossible, the best solution would be to have armies supplied with good equipment that costs less than it does today.

President Reagan has offered Europeans the chance to participate in the research and development of the sophisticated material necessary for what is misnamed the 'Star Wars' programme. (It is a waste of time to try to explain that this programme is defensive in nature, aimed at destroying rockets carrying atomic bombs at very high altitudes.) Europeans are reluctant to become involved; the French government maintains that Europeans would be reduced to the role of sub-contractors. Even if this is true, I do not believe that this role would be in any way degrading for sub-contracting gives one the opportunity for important technological exchanges. But if we want to take the initiative and be the innovators, the creators, let us band together and propose some positive initiatives which the Americans will be willing to accept. Let us have some sub-contractors in America, and then we shall hold some trump cards during negotiations.

I have diverged somewhat from the problems and solutions with which I am intimately familiar, and now I will return to them.

THE INTERNATIONALIZATION OF MANAGEMENT

Some time ago, a great French industrialist, the head of a nationalized industry, and a man I respect and admire, said to me: 'We must meet, so that you can explain to me how we can internationalize our management.' I leaped at the chance because I have observed that very few large, multinational, French businesses have foreign executives on their staff, and what is worse their top management has few French executives with international experience. Until this eminent boss asked me about the problems of internationalizing his executive staff, I had not given all that much thought to the question. For me it's an obvious matter, but the question having been put to me I was bound to reply.

In order to lead one must motivate all those with whom one works including one's own 'boss'. Nothing is more tiresome than executives who come to see their boss with long miserable faces to say, 'We have a problem.' That is one of the few times when they do say 'we'. How to motivate people? *First by example and then by personal competence:* you will never obtain anything whatever of lasting value from your subordinates unless you, yourself, give constant evidence of your own desire to outdo yourself:

1. *By taking coherent decisions* – capricious or erratic bosses are never much good.

2. *By establishing precise objectives known to everybody* – objectives which you will later compare with the results so that you can discuss each person's quantitative performance with him.

3. *By paying attention to what others want to say* — you must be a good listener.

4. *By understanding*, as far as you can, the things which will give satisfaction to employees at all levels.

This last point could be elaborated at some length. I mention it last of all because it is perhaps in this respect that the internationalization of management is most necessary. I have had the opportunity to examine many studies on motivation of personnel in different countries. A significant sample of employees were asked to classify, in descending order, the importance they attached to various things influencing their motivation. I will not quote them all, but they included, for instance: salary, working conditions, relations with their colleagues and their immediate superiors, the management's image, promotion prospects, the products manufactured, the sense of responsibility towards the company, and 'their' company's reputation.

Now the same questions when asked in a number of countries produced classifications which varied from one country to another. All this is nothing more than an analytical method of arriving at a conclusion that will appear obvious to many people, namely one cannot manage Americans, Frenchmen, Germans, Italians and Brazilians in the same manner. Inherited cultural differences, reinforced by local educational systems, prevent people from different countries from understanding one another and one sees this in evidence at every international meeting.

The company must therefore make efforts to superimpose on to this acquired culture a new one — one that will permit people who have common objectives, common working methods, and who will apply identical policies, to understand one another. This cannot be learnt from books; one must go out into the field.

Therefore, it seems necessary to me that the management of large firms should include, at every level, executives from its principal subsidiaries. Such internationalization of the management will prevent a great many errors. It will also do away with that type of foreign trip in which a group from HQ sows panic for a few days in one of its own subsidiaries, whose own executives are delighted to see the back of their visitors and sometimes forget everything that they have agreed to do by the very next day!

How to carry out such internationalization? The first condition demands a process of decentralization through which executives in the subsidiaries are given real responsibilities. I have observed that the majority of the heads of subsidiaries of French companies in the USA are French. At the outset, when a company is launching a foreign investment, it may be necessary to send out a national from the parent establishment, accompanied by a few technicians. However, after the company has been operating for five to ten years – especially if it is in an industrialized country – it must evolve a policy of giving local executives the opportunity to reach the top positions, in their own countries to begin with. But this is not enough, they must also have the opportunity, if they so desire, to attain high positions in the parent company. All this seems to me self-evident, but I would like to give an example.

Let us imagine a company that has a very good standing in the market of its original country, 'A', and that it is the sort of business in which young people want to work. It will not have the slightest problem in recruiting men and women of excellent abilities who will expect to be able to make progress without handicap from the beginning.

Now let us consider a major subsidiary of this company in a country we shall call 'B', where for a long time the successive chairmen, the financial managers and the technical directors have all been nationals of country 'A'. How can one possibly expect that young people who are the élite of country 'B' will feel the slightest desire to work in this subsidiary, especially if the rival firms of country 'B' are more important than the subsidiary and have a management made up of nationals from 'B'?

There are therefore two principal reasons for internationalizing management: to increase efficiency by having executives who are highly conversant with the problems of the subsidiaries, and to get a better type of local executive in the subsidiaries. There is also a third, less easily accepted reason: it may be the case, and this will astonish the xenophobes, that an executive in one of the

138

group's subsidiaries is the best possible man to do that particular job!

To make a success of such internationalization, it is necessary to lay down careful guidelines for career progress. These plans must include the following:

1. Identify the young executives of recognized potential in both the subsidiaries and the parent company.

2. Send them, while still quite young, to work in a foreign country for two or three years. Those from the subsidiaries must be systematically offered posts in the parent company so as to 'learn' the local culture and also to show executives in the company's 'home' country that foreigners can be valuable members of staff.

3. Decide that the subsidiaries (no longer than a few years after a subsidiary has been set up) will be run by citizens of the country in which the investment has been made. Establish the following rule: no executive will be promoted managing director of the subsidiary established in his own country unless, at some stage in his career, he has spent several years at the company's international headquarters. This will improve and even radically influence communications between HQ and the subsidiary.

4. If the turnover achieved abroad represents a significant part of the company's total turnover, more than 30 per cent for example, insist on having a steadily-increasing percentage of foreigners amongst the top level executives at the parent company. These executives must have been managing directors or working managers of important subsidiaries and already have spent a certain amount of time at HQ.

These four principles cannot be as simple as they seem since very few companies have put them into practice. We all know of companies in every country in the world which have wrecked their overseas enterprises through not knowing how to adapt to the specific conditions in the host country without sacrificing their own general policies. Some time ago, when American investments in Europe were growing very rapidly, it was American firms who were criticized. A book on this subject called *Le viol de l'Europe*

[The rape of Europe] came out. Since 1981 foreign investments in the United States have been larger than American investments abroad, and in New York, Houston, Chicago and Atlanta, one is beginning to hear the same complaints once heard twenty years ago in Paris, London, Brussels or Milan.

In a large corporation with subsidiaries in numerous countries, it seems vital to me that those who are representing it abroad should be fully convinced that total adherence to its established policies and practices is a pre-condition for success. The group's directors must understand that cohesion, an *esprit de corps*, require at the same time good communications and the participation of the 'proconsuls' in decision-making. To acquire this, the executives at Head Office, as well as those in the subsidiaries, must have international experience.

9

My First Great Responsibilities

In August 1964 the Maisonrouge family came back to Paris after seventeen months in the United States, a stay that had given us the chance to get to know the country and its people well. I rejoined the headquarters of IBM Europe, in the *cité du Retiro*.

I must say a word here about how IBM was organized from 1964 to 1974. I will not speak about the very frequent reorganizations of the company that took place in the US or other major countries, but will give instead a brief description of the general concept of organization in use at that time.

In the United States the corporation was presided over by the Chairman of the Board, Tom Watson Jr, and a group of executives who met regularly every week to study the principal problems brought to top management and make the major decisions. This group was composed of the President, Mr A.L. Williams and two Senior Vice-Presidents, Vin Learson and A.K. Watson, as well as a Chief of Staff, Dick Bullen. Over the years, this committee was to evolve, change its name and its membership, but the concept remained much the same: a collegiate directorship with of course one predominant voice, that of the Chairman.

Each member of this management committee had operational responsibilities in addition to those of general management. Mr A.K. Watson, for example, was in charge of the subsidiary, IBM World Trade Corporation. The second level of the company, as far as business outside the United States is concerned, is the World Trade Corporation, whose head office is 821 United Nations' Plaza in New York.

In 1964 Mr G.E. Jones was President of the IBM World Trade

Corporation, Senior Vice-President of the IBM Corporation and my immediate boss. He was supported by an executive staff composed of the vice-presidents in charge of all the important functions within the firm. At this period, there were already a great many non-Americans, especially Europeans, holding responsible positions at the international HQ.

Finally, the European subsidiaries were 'advised' by a European headquarters – IBM Europe – located in Paris. They carried out the same functions as those of the World Trade Corporation.

When I returned to Paris I tried to understand more clearly how the company was structured in Europe for I noticed, as I had already noticed in my previous post in New York, that it was so complex that many people within the company, as well as those outside it, had difficulty understanding the relations between the various executive groups. I became the champion of a doctrine of decentralization, which had been launched by Tom and Dick Watson. It was fairly easy to define, but not so easy to apply. We had to organize ourselves in such a way that as many decisions as possible were taken in the field by the very people who would have to put them into practice.

My friend Julius Sandorfi, Director of Organization for Europe, and I came to the conclusion that one should not speak of centralization or decentralization in general, but rather of variable degrees of decentralization according to the activities or functions involved. We defined a three-dimensional system of organization: world-wide – continental – national.

On the world-wide level

IBM's strength has always lain in having several principles which are clearly understood by the entire personnel in all countries (respect for the individual, the best possible service to clients, a very 'Puritan' ethic in business), as well as policies which are applicable everywhere. For instance, in spite of profound cultural differences between countries and the laws in force in individual nations that must always be respected, we have succeeded in developing universal methods of managing our human resources: no sexual, racial or religious discrimination; promotions based on merit; in all countries where it is legally possible salary increases are based on performance and not on any kind of index whatever; the possibility for everyone to express himself without necessarily having to go through the 'usual channels' of the hierarchy; the development of a very sophisticated system of continuous staff training.

We were trying therefore to evolve new policies for the whole of the group. In this respect the personnel management at the world head office at Armonk was very influential. A considerable degree of centralization was present as that office had a world-wide mandate. This did not lead, however, to dictates issuing from Armonk, but to a great many discussions between Armonk and those in charge at the HQ of the World Trade Corporation in New York, at the European head office and in the various countries. More and more often a new policy or a new method originated in one of the subsidiaries.

Research and development also operated world-wide. Since we had taken the decision to have a single line of products that could be used throughout the world – with the exception of modifications due to unique local needs such as the use of Kanji in Japan – we had to have a strategic development plan approved at a central level. It was, moreover, necessary to co-ordinate the work of the laboratories developing new products since these would have to be connected to the products of other laboratories.

As soon as I returned I was closely involved in this co-ordination. The 360 computers included many systems that were compatible between themselves; they had common hardware and software which could be used on any computer from the smallest to the largest. Two of the machines in this group had been developed in Europe: the 360–20 in Germany and the 360–40 in England. The other models had been developed in the United States. It was therefore necessary for the systems engineers who were in charge of the overall project to be absolutely up-to-date with what was being done in each laboratory, to dictate the approach, and to ensure that all these machines would be able to work together.

Here again, this approach to development does not mean that the Europeans, the Japanese or the Canadians in IBM laboratories act simply as sub-contractors. They create, innovate and develop with objectives that are identical to those of the Americans.

On the continental scale

I have already described the organization of European production at some length. The European factories manufacture almost all the equipment delivered within Europe, to the Middle East, and to Africa. Each one manufactures part of the range for the whole of this vast market.

It is therefore once again indispensable to co-ordinate everything on a European scale. The man in charge of manufacturing for Europe and his team are the only ones who have a total, overall view of the market. In addition there are many cases in which several companies in the group have had to resolve problems for a small number of clients — too few to justify having study teams in each country.

From 1964 on, I had to face the difficulties caused by the first installations of teleprocessing; these installations were complex systems comprising terminals with a telephone link-up to central computers. The first installations were made in airline companies, banks, insurance companies and large mail-order firms. The clients which taxed our expertise the most were the airline companies. In each European country there are one or two major airline companies. From the early sixties on, they had all been experiencing a greater and greater problem with seat reservations. In the USA, Remington Rand (UNIVAC) and IBM had already placed some computer systems. We had had to bring together skilled teams of systems engineers to study their requirements, write the programmes, and sometimes modify the machines. In Europe it was not possible to make up such teams in each country and so offer a made-to-measure solution to Air France, SAS,

144

Swissair, Lufthansa, Alitalia, KLM, Sabena, Iberia, British Airways, TAP, etc. Instead, for the first time, we created a European centre for study and technical support in which systems engineers from various countries were called upon to work together on a single problem. European support centres were also instrumental in aiding other sophisticated customers such as the banks.

In 1960 I had also hit upon the idea of asking two specialists in telecommunications, Mr A. Henry and Mr M. Tassaert, to join us. At that time we did not have many engineers who were familiar with the telecommunications system's technical and tariff-related problems, so for the first time I decided to offer important positions to executives from outside the company. These two men successfully got us out of a difficult situation.

Training for the upper levels of management posed the same kind of problem. While each important subsidiary could guarantee basic training, none of them could assemble the 'faculty' necessary for the high-level training of ten to fifteen people per year. The choice was simple: either send the executives to centres outside the company or create our own European centre. The latter was done: several schools, or 'institutes' as we called them, were created. At the beginning we had a centre at Blaricum in Holland for management training, and another in Geneva for the higher training of systems engineers. It was our search for the economies of scale, but above all the possibility of finding instructors of the very highest calibre that led us to opt for a European solution to this problem.

On the national level

We have seen that for an international group to be effective, the managing directors of each national branch must *delegate* certain decisions to a supranational authority so as to optimize the utilization of the whole group's human and financial resources. As long as they understand the best interests of their own company, their intervention won't give managing directors an inferiority complex.

145

There are some activities, however, which remain totally national:

1. The execution of research and development programmes and also manufacturing;

2. The responsibility for recruiting men and women of ability who will make the subsidiary competitive with the other companies in the group and with rival companies;

3. Sales and after-sales service;

4. The controller's and the treasurer's functions;

5. The management of human resources;

6. Communications, internal and external;

7. Relations with the government.

The more directly an activity of the company has to deal with the public, customers, governments and the universities, the more decentralized it should be. Total responsibility should remain in the hands of the managing director of the subsidiary.

From 1964 to 1967, during the years of my presidency of IBM Europe, I tried to develop a staunch *esprit de corps* between the European HQ executives and the directors of the subsidiaries. The managing directors began to understand that they were part of an ensemble; they began to help one another and to work towards common objectives. I had tough battles with some of them, but never any serious conflict. My successors were to follow in my footsteps and achieve more than I had done.

In the mid-sixties the executive staff of IBM Europe, housed in the *cité du Retiro*, was growing — a little too fast in my opinion. I tried to explain to my colleagues that after a certain point a headquarters can operate without actually producing anything. Its members can spend so much time contacting each other that they no longer have the opportunity to do what they should be doing, that is assisting operatives in other countries who are bringing in turnover and profits for the group. Rapid growth has another inconvenience: there are posts that must be filled quickly, and it is much easier to obtain the transfer of American executives than it is of Europeans. This is because Americans are more mobile and also because the managing directors of European subsidiaries have a tendency to say that they cannot do without the man earmarked for a job at HQ. This reluctance on the part of managers to send their best executives out of their own country has perhaps been the most difficult problem I've confronted. It was resolved later when I proposed that nobody could be promoted to an important post in a subsidiary unless he had served at least two years abroad.

In spite of this difficulty, we continued to internationalize the IBM World Trade Europe Corporation. During this period thirty-two different nationalities worked there. At the end of 1964 the twenty-seven top posts were occupied by: 11 Americans; 7 Frenchmen; 3 Swiss; 2 Englishmen; 1 Canadian; 1 Spaniard; 1 Hungarian and 1 Italian. At the end of 1966 the thirty top posts were occupied by: 12 Americans; 5 Frenchmen; 3 Englishmen; 3 Swiss; 2 Germans; 2 Canadians; 1 Spaniard; 1 Hungarian and 1 Italian.

Seeing these figures again, I am astonished that the number of Frenchmen should have diminished during my first two years as President of IBM Europe! It is proof of my objectivity, but still more of the President of IBM France's resistance to the expatriation of his executives.

I maintained very amicable relations and mutual trust with Gilbert Jones, President of the World Trade Corporation in New York. He went out of his way to give me a long rein, and I did my best to keep him informed about what was happening in Europe. He came to Europe regularly, three or four times a year, and I went to New York rather more often for meetings organized well in advance. There were very few crises. Gil Jones was a strong partisan of delegating without losing control, and I was convinced of the need for communication in each and every direction. Above all I understand that there is nothing more disagreeable for a boss than to have surprises sprung on him, so that he's landed with situations that by the time he is informed of them are already so close to disaster that he can do nothing about it. But at the time I did not realize that Gil Jones, like other bosses I have had during my career, must have found me difficult to control.

He has criticized me sometimes – and others before and after him have done the same thing – for being too sensitive. The reproach is well-founded. When those who work with me are criticized, or when someone makes what I consider to be an unjust criticism of myself, I explode. When defending ideas I believe in I fight vehemently, perhaps too vehemently. This attracts the sympathy of my subordinates who are perhaps a little amused by it and just waiting for the moment when I shall go too far. When I left Europe at the end of 1967 to take up a new post in the United States, they gave me a statuette of Don Quixote by way of a farewell present!

On 5 January 1965 we held a meeting in Paris of all the top European management. Gil Jones was present and, as always, made a statement that was dynamic, brilliant, informative and full of humour. The meeting was timed to the minute. I was allotted twelve minutes for my speech and took fourteen. At the end of the meeting Gil Jones said to me sharply: 'You went over the time allotted to you.' He was right, but I had had so much to say!

Here are a few extracts:

While it is true that Europeans have a lot to learn from the States about management methods, the Americans must realize that in certain domains they too can be criticized.

In his book, *The Americanisation of Europe*, McCreary writes: 'The American businessman dare not take decisions, he follows the instruction manual and telephones New York constantly to ask for advice.'

Naturally, any resemblance between this situation and our own is purely coincidental . . .

I believe we have a great deal of progress to make and I suggest that, in our policies, we should strive for the pre-eminence of three qualities: understanding, courage, imagination.

One way of progressing is by being totally aware of the differences that exist between the different markets we serve. Differences in management methods, in ethical standards and in the psychology of the citizens are gradually disappearing, but they still exist. We must recognize them, and without making the slightest compromise whatever where our principles are concerned, we must adapt ourselves. . . .

We must constantly invent the means to improve our effectiveness and give our great company the same response time as that of a small business. . . . To create a state of mind receptive to change, we must understand what is going on out in the field.

A meeting like this can be extremely helpful to us for the extrapolation of what we have learned in our own countries into other markets will not, of itself, be enough to bring us recognition as respected experts; we must also express a real interest in, and empathy with, the others.

Gil Jones is an internationalist. At the time he criticized me for my overlong speech, but not for its message.

In 1965 business was going well. The 360s were selling in great numbers, their quality was good, the clients were satisfied with the equipment but complained about the software so our laboratories were working very hard on schemes to improve it. IBM continued to grow. Not by acquiring other companies, but simply by virtue of the unsparing efforts of the men and women who worked for the company.

I visited the subsidiaries one after the other: I visited the factories and the laboratories. Everywhere I met with enthusiasm, the will to grow, and an awareness of individual responsibility. The amount of time I spent travelling began to affect my family life, but long ago my wife and I had decided that what little free time there was would be devoted to the family. We still went every weekend with our children to see our parents. We entertained a great many friends at home – friends of our childhood or youth, new friends met within the company, foreign visitors to whom we wanted to show that the French are not so unwelcoming as people say.

I took part in more and more activities outside my professional life: parent-teacher associations at the *Lycée Racine* and the school on the rue Ampère that my children attended, the American Chamber of Commerce in Paris, the alumni association of the *Ecole Centrale*. I had noticed that a great many French employers took no part in outside activities other than professional meetings. They did not explain their organization to outsiders; they were afraid of journalists, financial analysts, and the public. I did the opposite and began speaking in public whenever I was invited to do so, to explain micro-economy and the system of free enterprise. Every time I visited a foreign country, particularly in the Middle East or Africa, our local management organized meetings at which I could explain what a multinational enterprise really is.

In December 1965 I enjoyed an enthralling experience – I went to Nigeria to present diplomas in data processing to students from Nigeria, Kenya and Zambia who had taken a year's course in an IBM education centre created in co-operation with the University of Ibadan. This was my first visit to Lagos. During the drive from the airport to the city, I was saddened by the sight of all the run-down houses without proper roofs that bordered the road. I discussed this with my local colleagues and learned that badly-maintained houses are a hallmark of underdevelopment.

As the road from Lagos to Ibadan was very dangerous on account of guerrillas, Jack Fahey, our director for English-speaking Africa, another colleague and I hired a small aircraft. It was piloted by a Dutchman who was the worse for drink and I sat in the co-pilot's seat so as to be prepared for any eventuality. . . .

At the university I was struck by the impressive ceremony and the great contrasts of the occasion. While I was presenting the diplomas to young men who had learned programming and how to use computers, their wives were sitting in the auditorium wearing native dress, and in most cases with a baby on their backs.

On our return to Lagos, I visited the 'authorities' and several clients. In some cases I found the computers were being used just as efficiently here as in Europe.

On 24 February 1966, I took part in a conference in Paris organized by the *Ecole Supérieure des Sciences Economiques et*

150

Commerciales. The session was presided over by M. de Chambrun, the Minister of Foreign Trade. M. Schlogel, President of Crédit Lyonnais, the second largest French bank, introduced the lecturers. He read out my *curriculum vitae,* added that I was a representative of an American industry and stated, 'It is a pity that people like Monsieur Maisonrouge work for the Americans.' I was a little shocked. I quote here an extract from my reply, which was published in the conference report.

> *Monsieur le Ministre, Monsieur le Président, Mesdames, Messieurs . . .*
> I am a little disturbed by what M. Schlogel has just said, for, although I am the President of a company which is a subsidiary of an American corporation, I consider myself not as a representative of American industry, but as that of a multinational industry in which it is my wish to see many Frenchmen taking top positions which is as good a way as any of expressing a certain sense of grandeur.

Applause from the floor (mentioned in the report), long faces from the Minister and M. Schlogel (not mentioned in the report).

That was the start – from 1964 on – of the period of antagonism to foreign investment in France. The technocrats had refused to let Ford and Philips Petroleum set up in Bordeaux. This was absurd since the Common Market was expanding and these companies already had installations in Belgium and Holland. France lost the opportunity to create employment, and our industry was not 'protected' from competition thereby because there was free movement of goods.

I think it would be useful to quote some more extracts from my speech as there are certain things which have not changed.

> There exists an aura of fear around the industry to which I belong: the fear of automation. One hears relatively little about it in France, Sweden, Germany or Switzerland, countries in which there is full employment, but there has been a great deal

of talk about it in England, and nowadays they are saying quite a lot in the United States. . . .

There is a need to correct false ideas, since during the last fifteen years in the USA the population employed on administrative tasks has increased by 40 per cent, while the labour force has increased by only 10 per cent, and at the same time the use of punch-card machines and computers has been growing. . . .

For two or three years now a great deal has been said about the need for Europe to push ahead with research so as not to lag behind the United States. It is an indisputable fact that to be an industrial nation one must have solid technological back-up, but this is extremely costly and I believe that the problem facing us is still one of planning together, particularly when it comes to choosing subjects for research since we must aim at avoiding considerable expenditure on inventing things which have already been invented elsewhere.

The term 'multinational corporation' was invented in 1965. Many people, including myself, invented it. Louis Armand spoke of transnational enterprises, a name adopted by the United Nations. During a speech given on 5 March 1965 I explained to my salesmen colleagues, members of the 100% Club [the men who had reached their sales targets], what a *good* multinational is.

I spent practically all my weekends preparing speeches and writing articles on the subject. It became a family joke. My daughters, when I told them I was going to make a speech in Brussels, teased me, 'You're going to talk about the multinationals again.' And, in fact, on 7 October 1966 I did speak about them again at a dinner given by the American and Common Market Club in Brussels. Here is another extract:

One major phenomenon conditions the economic development of all countries: global markets. (This was before Peter Drucker used the term 'Global Supermarket'.) I believe that at last it is recognized today that research and development represent one of the essential ingredients of economic power . . . moreover the effectiveness of research in Europe is very poor, since it is very compartmentalized and there is considerable duplication of effort.

I remember 1966 as a year of hard battles.

The CII, the Compagnie Internationale d'Informatique [International Data Processing Company], was born and from that moment on our business in France suffered because this company was given preference for all purchases made in the public sector. Nevertheless we continued to invest in France, and the Montpellier factory continued to produce the large computers destined for the whole of Europe.

IBM was growing and so was my family. On 24 June 1966 my wife set out once more along the road to the American Hospital in Neuilly. Dr Ravina came out of the labour room, announced the birth of a little girl, and disappeared immediately. A little later I saw my wife; she was crying with joy not only because Anne-Sophie was a beautiful baby, but also because she was our fourth daughter. I was happy that all had gone well. I love girls. Here in any case was a child who would be warmly surrounded with maternal affection; our older daughters were now seventeen, fifteen and fourteen. The eldest, Christine, was just finishing her first year at medical school.

In 1967, a fashionable subject for discussion was the 'technological gap' separating Europe from America. I was among those who pointed out that there was no scientific gap nor any lack of inventions in Europe. In 1964, for example, 38,410 patents were registered in the United States; 13,673 in France; 12,081 in Germany; 10,810 in England; 6,100 in Italy; i.e., for the four countries combined, 42,664 patents – more than were taken out in the United States. I drew two conclusions from this:

1. If we take Europe as a whole, which gives us an area comparable to the USA, no scientific shortfall exists.

2. The real gap is not a technological one; it is a backwardness in management methods.

I wrote a leading article for the April 1967 issue of the magazine, *Gestion* [Management]. I would like to quote one passage:

In Europe, we failed to perceive in time that we were living through a new industrial revolution, that of handling information. A large part of economic activity nowadays goes toward producing information and no longer to producing energy. . . .

If we prove capable of closing the gap in management methods, I am convinced that the technological gap – supposing it actually exists – will disappear for we shall then be in a position to alter the structure of businesses and markets, and to make optimum use of our resources.

On July 5th M.H. Roy from *L'Express* came to see me to discuss M. Jean-Jacques Servan-Schreiber's forthcoming book. There were many points with which I did not agree. At the end of the month he telephoned to ask me to reply to three questions. I dictated my answers rapidly, sent them to him and went off on holiday. Shortly after my return, on 23 August, M. Jean-Jacques Servan-Schreiber invited me to lunch. He talked about his book, told me that he had found my answers interesting and that he would publish them in the form of an appendix. I explained to him that I would like to have another look at them so as to improve the wording, but he answered, 'Too late, the book is already at the printers.'

On Tuesday 26 September during the afternoon Dick Watson called me up to ask me to be in New York the next day. I tried to postpone it; impossible, and not a word of explanation. I was all the more annoyed because the marriage of my cousin, Alain Cazas, was to take place on Thursday the 28th.

The following morning I took an Air France flight and arrived in the New York office at about 3 p.m. Dick Watson greeted me very cordially and came straight to the point. 'Gil Jones is to be appointed Senior Vice-President of the Corporation. I would like you to become President of World Trade.' For my part I first felt astonishment and had little time for reflection before giving an affirmative answer. How could I refuse such a position? I did not even consult my wife. I flew home that evening reaching Paris on Thursday morning in time for the wedding. I kept my important news to myself because I did not want to ruin the day for my parents and my parents-in-law.

The official announcement was made at the beginning of October. The article in the December 1967 issue of *L'Expansion* amused me . . . a little: 'At the age of forty-three this head of a French business company, almost unknown in his own country, accedes to the highest post ever entrusted to a foreigner by *Big Business*. . . . The Frenchman who is taking up this key position *is not even a graduate of the Ecole Polytechnique . . .*'

My first duty in my new post was a trip to South America for a meeting of the Boards of Directors of the IBM Corporation and the IBM World Trade Corporation, held in Rio de Janeiro. Then, in one week, I made visits to the subsidiaries in Sâo Paolo, Buenos Aires, Santiago and Lima. Françoise came with me and we both felt how warmly the South Americans welcome the French.

On November 13th my farewell luncheon took place. My successor as President of IBM Europe was Billy Christensen who had been my right arm for a number of years. This was the occasion on which I was presented with the statuette of Don Quixote and also a lithograph of the Pont-Neuf on the back of which my colleagues had written: 'Good luck to the best builder of bridges between Europe and the United States.' They could not have known that my youthful ambition was to be an engineer of bridges and highways.

The years 1964–7 had been a wonderful training period for me. In the first place because I had carried out important responsibilities, but also because, more so than in my previous positions, I had learned to work in several European countries, and because this was the time during which I decided to be an executive who explained things in public. I had also learned how important it is for managing directors to meet the men and women in the company.

I do not want to give here a detailed chronology of all my activities, but briefly in the course of three years I visited all the IBM laboratories in Europe at least once, some of them several times; I visited all the factories and a great many offices as well as the head offices of the subsidiaries in every country in Europe, plus Iran and Israel. By attending all the important meetings held within the company, I was able to contact thousands of my associates. I paid visits to more than thirty of our clients each year. I also took part in numerous international gatherings and gave some lectures.

During 1964–7 in addition to visiting other countries and having frequent meetings with local management, I got much more involved in some of our subsidiaries by joining several of their boards of directors: IBM Germany, IBM Italy and IBM UK in September 1964; IBM France in October 1964; IBM South Africa in 1967. On 4 October 1965 I had the pleasure of announcing the appointment of Mr Edwin Nixon as Managing Director of IBM United Kingdom Limited.

Modern leaders must undertake such activities, but they demand an almost constant availability and I must admit that they require personal sacrifices. I am pleased that my wife has such an outstanding ability to adapt, and that she was capable of taking on, almost single-handedly, the task of bringing up five children. I owe a debt of gratitude to all six of them.

On 20 November 1967 I arrived in New York and was given the famous green card – the immigration visa that permits one to work without restriction in the United States . . . and to pay taxes there. My transfer from Paris to New York, however, happened to come at an awkward moment. The children had just started their new academic year: Christine was in the second year of her medical studies at the Saint-Antoine Teaching Hospital; Florence was in her last year and Sylvie in her next-to-last at the *Lycée Racine*. It would have been neither reasonable nor possible to ask Christine to leave at once for the USA. We decided that they should all continue to study for the remainder of the school year in Paris and thus my wife would have to remain there, too.

I was very unhappy about this because I detest being separated from my loved ones, and the eight months I was to spend at the Beckman Towers Hotel, at the corner of 1st Avenue and 50th Street, were not to become part of my happy memories. My associates must also have found this period rather trying, as I consoled myself by working very hard.

I settled into the office that Dick Watson and Gil Jones had occupied before me. It is a very pleasant place with a view over the United Nations building. From my windows I could see the flags of all the member states, and as I looked at them I felt a little dizzy because there were very few nations represented which had neither an IBM subsidiary nor an office. However, I modestly refrained from making it my aim to install IBM machines in all the countries represented!

At that date I did not believe that multinational corporations had power, but I must confess that I thought the proximity of IBM World Trade Corporation's HQ to the United Nations had something symbolic about it. Dick Watson, who had chosen the location, had had a stroke of genius.

I wonder how many of my friends can comprehend the terror that gripped the bowels of this 43-year-old Frenchman on becoming head of all activities, external to the USA, in a multinational that led the field in its own industrial sector? The biggest question for me was: How will the vice-presidents who are all Americans accept me? The French were not very highly thought-of in the United States in 1967. This was particularly true in New York where France's stance on the Israeli-Egyptian conflict had not been understood because nobody had explained it clearly.

Fortunately I had already worked with all those who were now my immediate associates. They gave me a warm welcome. The fact of my being a foreigner mattered little to them; they knew that I was first and foremost a colleague who had adhered strictly to the company's principles. Sometimes during this period of initiation I tried to imagine what the attitude would be of the upper echelon of executives in a French multinational if a German, an Englishman or an American became their boss. Like all young people who have spent some time in the United States, I have admired this country ever since my first stay there in 1948-9, but the kindness, co-operative spirit, and the devotion of the Americans around me made me more pro-American than ever.

I have only one thing to reproach them with, and I must say I did not understand what was happening until many years later I read an editorial by the humorist, Art Buckwald, entitled: 'Not

157

for lunch'. We were all perfect colleagues and we worked well together; they loyally carried out all the programmes we had agreed upon, but outside of work we had very little contact. Those who invited me for brunch, dinner or a tennis party during one of those wretched weekends when I was all alone in New York can be counted on the fingers of one hand. Perhaps I am not a very engaging man; perhaps in the United States it is not 'done' to invite one's boss, but I was hurt by it. Obviously I am not going to mention the names of those who did invite me to their homes, but if they read these pages I would like them to know that they have a very special place in my heart and I remember each and every one of them. The list of names is in any case so short that it does not need a computer to keep it up-to-date.

The working environment was very pleasant. The HQ was sufficiently small for all who worked there to get to know each other well. The top team was closely welded together. Bert Witham, who had already worked in Europe, was the Vice-President of Finances, Dick Warren was the Vice-President in charge of Marketing, Manufacturing and several other functions. Todd Groo, who had been my boss in Paris in 1962, was the Vice-President with responsibility for Personnel. Harold Christensen was the Secretary of the company, Bill Ketcham our lawyer. We met together very frequently and I proposed the organization of a management committee. From the beginning of 1968 on, we had a collegiate management.

In January 1968 I paid my first visit to Japan accompanied by Joe Beard, responsible for IBM World Trade in Asia and Australia. For the first time I experienced the real meaning of vast cultural difference, but it did not come as a shock because I had already met so many Japanese. Communications were much more difficult than in any other country I had ever visited before, be it in the Americas, Africa, the Middle East or Europe.

Our Managing Director, Mr Inagaki, asked me to pay several visits to clients and each time we employed an interpreter. Nowhere else have the heads of businesses asked me so many questions about Europe, the United States, modern technology and IBM. They listened attentively and their assistants took copious notes. Humility, curiosity and the desire to learn were the dominant attitudes of the Japanese, but an Under-Secretary at the Ministry of Industry and Technology (MITI) spoke to me of the 'knowledge industry'. I did not manage to make any headway when discussing the problems of added value networks with the manager of Nippon Telegraph and Telephones because Japan had already set herself a specific aim by 1968 of dedicating part of her resources to high technology, and more particularly to the information industry.

IBM Japan organized a grand reception in my honour and I was pleased to see that representatives of the government including some from MITI attended and stayed for a considerable time. They expressed no hostility whatsoever toward American multinationals. M. de Guiringaud, the French Ambassador, came to the reception and met the American Ambassador, Mr U. Alexis Johnson, for the first time. Franco-American relations were rather poor in 1967–8. When he shook my hand the American Ambassador said (not very diplomatically) to me, 'IBM is really a weird company; I'm surprised they didn't appoint a Chinese from the People's Republic of China to head their international operations!'

From Tokyo, I went to Osaka and met Mr Matsuchita, head and founder of the most important electronics business in the country. Naturally he received me in his Japanese garden, and I took part in my first tea ceremony. He talked to me about his business and about his employees with extraordinary emotion. He told me that he had made a close study of the methods and policies of IBM and of the life of Mr T. J. Watson Sr. He had taken them for his model and had gone a long way towards imitating them in a manner adapted to the local culture. While it is some time now since IBM employees engaged in training programmes have gathered together on Friday mornings to sing, all his employees still do so, and amongst their songs, as I noted before, there is one to the glory of Mr Matsuchita.

I came back from this trip feeling very much impressed; I had not yet acquired the 'fear' of Japan some people experience. I had moreover met many IBM employees whose enthusiasm at work impressed me, and been struck by the professionalism and sense of responsibility I met with in clients and members of the government. Even after a few days' visit, it is easy to understand how the Japanese people and their leaders have managed to make their country into a great power. The Japanese miracle follows the German miracle, and they both spring from common causes. During the war there was a great deal of destruction and so their factories and machine-tools today are new; neither Japan nor Germany had colonies thus unlike France, England and Holland, they did not have to expend the considerable sums involved in bringing about decolonization; they work hard; their defence budget is very low in comparison to their total budget; in spite of some rather violent demonstrations which have received press coverage in the West, relations between social partners in both countries are good; the system of consensus between the unions, the employers and the government is already in existence; and modernization is progressing rapidly.

The IBM World Trade Corporation's neighbour on United Nations' Square in New York is the International Institute of Education. This Institute administers the Fulbright grants which every year allow hundreds of students from every country to study in American universities, and organizes the exchange of young people, particularly artists, between the USA and other countries. The President of the Institute at that time was Ken Holland, a French-speaking, francophile American academic. I do not know how he found out that a Frenchman had just been appointed to head the World Trade Corporation, but he came to see me. He told me about his annual sojourns in the South of France and asked me to join the Institute's board of trustees. I accepted with pleasure and found myself, once again, the only foreigner amongst a group of Americans.

In March 1968 Mr Holland organized a joint meeting between rectors from some French universities and the presidents of various American ones. Amongst the Frenchmen was Rector Roche from the University of Paris, and amongst the Americans, Grayson Kirk, President of Columbia University. I was the only 'non-academic' to attend the two-day conference. I listened, I observed, and I was amazed. At no moment during the entire discussion did any of them mention what seemed to me a crucial question: What must the universities do to ensure their students are prepared for a swift and effective entry into professional life? At the end of the conference Ken Holland asked me if I had anything to say. That is the kind of invitation I never refuse! I expressed my astonishment, and my fear that students would rebel, out of impatience for a change in their courses and worry over their futures. After all they could not all become teachers. A discussion ensued and it was clear that these gentlemen regarded me as a 'barbarian'. Rector Roche and the President of Columbia both affirmed, with equal conviction, that there was nothing to fear; the students thought of nothing but their work. I wonder whether Grayson Kirk, later to be trapped in his office in Columbia for several days by angry students, has ever thought back to our discussion?

I was in New York when the 'events' of May 1968 exploded in France. Few people had foreseen what would happen; I remember one of the French trade union leaders confessing, 'It exploded in our faces.'

When one is far away events seem even more tragic. I was worried about my family, about my children who were students, and about IBM France, since strikes were now adding to the student revolution. Fortunately the international telephones were working and my wife was able to reassure me. I decided, however, to return to Paris as soon as possible, but had to wait as the airports were closed. I rang up Raymond Pailloux, Assistant General Manager of IBM France, in charge of factories and the laboratory. No strikes at IBM! I expressed to him my fear that our employees at Corbeil-Essonnes who were working regularly would be molested by strikers from other companies in the region. He did not think this would happen, but suggested taking a vote as to whether or not the factory should be temporarily closed. An overwhelming majority decided to carry on working.

All the same there was a serious problem. Because transport was not running other IBM factories could not get the spare parts and electronic components manufactured in France, which they needed for assembling the machines they themselves produced.

Our European production system in which each factory depended on the others had one weak point – the stoppage of one factory blocked the functioning of several others once the stocks of parts were exhausted. But there was another centre making the same components as those made at Essonnes – the factory at Fishkill in the United States. The European director of manufacturing immediately arranged for output in the US to be increased; components reached Germany, Italy and England in time and the delivery of machines to the various countries was kept going.

I managed to get a seat on the first Pan-Am flight to France, which landed at the military airport at Brétigny-sur-Orge. I was joyfully reunited with my wife and children, parents and friends, all of whom had so much to tell me. They had experienced no serious problems, just minor difficulties in obtaining food supplies. Next day I went to the HQ of IBM Europe.

Billy Christensen, the President, and Gordon Williamson, the Assistant Managing Director, had responded to this crisis calmly and efficiently. Gordon, who spoke little French, announced proudly that he had mastered the phrase 'I am Swiss,' without an accent, and this allowed him to go everywhere without trouble.

In early June I visited the United States Ambassador to Paris, Mr R. Sargent Shriver Jr. We talked about the French situation and about IBM; he was called away to the telephone and returned ashen-faced. He had just learned of the attempted assassination of his brother-in-law, Senator Robert Kennedy. At that moment he knew only that he was gravely wounded; I offered to leave but he insisted I stay. Mr Averell Harriman and Mr Cyrus Vance, the two American representatives negotiating with the Vietnamese delegation, came in to offer their sympathy. The telephone rang constantly.

One of the calls was from his wife. I only heard him say, 'No, you must stay here, you have an appointment with Mme de Gaulle.' For him duties of state had to override family sentiment. During our conversation held in such dramatic circumstances, he said to me: 'What can we do to convince the French government that the decisions we have to take in the realm of world strategy are in no way directed against France?'

162

Senator Kennedy died. On June 7th I wrote to Mr Sargent Shriver to express my sorrow. I also wrote to M. Michel Debré, our Minister of Foreign Affairs, reporting the Ambassador's remarks to him and adding a few comments from a Gaullist and pro-American Frenchman. Below is printed an extract from this letter:

> After the great crisis of these recent days, we are going to have to make strenuous efforts to increase our exports. As Vice-President of the French Chamber of Commerce in the USA, I can assure you that the decisions you make on foreign policy will strongly influence American purchases of French products . . . On the whole, the Americans have retained that breadth of outlook and a certain *naïveté* which lead to idealism, and I believe that the great problems of the world will have to be resolved with them. If you present the facts to them, they listen, and they are prepared to change their opinions. It is through friendly dialogue that we can best influence them.

In July, I was back in the States. While I was away in Paris my first academic distinction had been conferred on me: an honorary doctorate in 'commercial sciences' at the College of the Assumption in Worcester, Massachusetts. In my absence my friend Georges Parisot, Director of Long-term Planning of the IBM World Trade Corporation, had attended the ceremony in my place.

My family was due to arrive at the end of August and I started apartment-hunting again. I rapidly came to the conclusion that we could not afford to live in New York. Apartments big enough to house a large family were much too expensive. After making a great many trips every weekend, I found a beautiful house in Bronxville, a lovely village, which was very airy, close to plenty of clubs, close to the sea and close to New York. I returned to Paris to bring back my whole family on board the *France*.

The day we moved in, Mrs Pastoriza, the wife of one of my colleagues who lived in Bronxville, came to see us bringing coffee, tea, cool drinks and little cakes – thank you, Nancy! The children were happy. Christine, the eldest, was accepted as a second-year student in one of American's most prestigious hospital training centres, Cornell Medical School, which is part of the New York Hospital. Florence, our second daughter, was accepted by Barnard College, one of the rare American colleges for girls. Sylvie and François were to go to the *Lycée Français de New York* and our littlest one, Anne-Sophie, to the nursery school in Bronxville; she was two years and three months old.

From the time of our return we led a somewhat extraordinary life. Every day unless I was travelling outside the United States I took the four eldest to their respective schools. We left at 7 a.m.; I would drop Florence at Barnard, Sylvie and François at the *Lycée Français* – in two different buildings – and Christine at the New York Hospital. In the afternoon my wife came to fetch two or three of them, one or two of the others went home by train. These daily drives gave me a chance for long talks with the children and we were very close.

Shortly after our arrival, Dean McKay, the IBM corporation's Vice-President of Communications, held a 'cocktail party' to introduce us to his friends in the village. There were at least a hundred and fifty people present, and from that moment on we could no longer go for a walk or an outing without someone we recognized, but whose name we did not remember, saying to us: 'Hi, Jack! Hi, Françoise!' We quickly made friends. The six years we lived at Bronxville remain a wonderful memory.

Our parents came to spend six weeks to two months with us every year and thoroughly enjoyed these visits. In 1971 my wife's sister and her husband, Jean Caste, settled in New York where Jean had been appointed President of Cosmair which represents l'Oréal in the USA. Our children were happy to see their cousins again and they often came to Bronxville. We now had a 'permanent' family in the United States.

I was concerned about the future of our medical student since her American degree would not be recognized in France. During each of my trips to Paris I carried out a systematic campaign to persuade the education authorities and officials at the Ministry of Health that the United States had some good medical schools, and that they could perhaps credit a graduate from one of them with a few years' equivalent study. I could say a great deal about the replies I received. One director of higher education said to me – without a trace of irony – that we had to protect the values of our medical profession; another person, whom I shall not name, accounced: 'The daughter of Monsieur Maisonrouge has no need to work!' I had learned what liberalism was by working in the United States; I now learned what rigid bureaucracy was by trying to resolve this problem.

Let us come back to my professional life. On re-reading my agenda for the years 1968 to 1974 I realize how much time I spent in meetings with my associates at the World Trade Corporation, and how little with the Management Committee of the parent company. We had great freedom of action. For example, throughout the whole of 1969 we had only sixteen meetings with the management committee, four of which were dedicated to presenting plans.

During the months preceding my departure from Paris, I had realized that we should make greater use of outside advisers. In New York at the IBM World Trade Corporation we had an excellent board of directors, but all its members except myself were Americans . . . Americans who knew the world, no doubt, and some of whom were heads of multinational businesses, but who did not see as clearly as the Europeans did the complexity of the socio-economic environment in various European countries. Our subsidiaries had local Boards of high quality, but I felt that it was necessary to add a European dimension. I discussed this with Dick Watson and Gil Jones and we decided to create a European Advisory Board. The idea was to gather together some eminent personalities three or four times a year, inform them of our operations and ask them to give us their reactions to certain of our projects, as well as advice about external relations. The creation of this committee was announced on 8 April 1968. The first members were: M. Louis Armand, Lord Cromer (former Governor of the Bank of England), M.P. Sette (President of the National Petroleum Company of Italy) and M.H. Nordhoff (former President of Volkswagen), then M.H. Schwarzenbach (former President of the Federation of Swiss Industries). The committee became more and more active, and its members through the years played a very important role in advising the Chairman of IBM Europe.

In drawing up plans we had always attached great importance to economic forecasts. Each of the large subsidiaries had a department of economic analysis, and in the parent establishment there were several talented economists such as Dr Grove. Once again, however, we decided some outside opinions would be useful and I suggested that M.R. Marjolin, former Vice-President of the Communities' Commission, should become our economic adviser. He accepted, took up his position on 29 April 1970, and remained a counsellor who was listened to and respected by the European management team and also the heads of the IBM corporation right up until he reached the age of retirement. We became good friends and I must say that his viewpoints, like his forecasts, were always remarkably clear and precise.

In analysing my activities during this period, I find that on average I spent ninety days in every year travelling outside the United States, and out of the total number of hours spent in the New York office, roughly one third were spent on problems of production (relations with the laboratories and factories) and the rest on all my other functions. The results were such that I passed relatively little time discussing financial problems, which in any case were handled by a vice-president of outstanding talent.

A few anecdotes are worth the telling. On 2 March 1970 a dinner was held at the Waldorf Astoria in honour of President Pompidou. M. and Mme Pompidou had had a very bad reception in Chicago where they had been two days previously. Some Jewish societies had organized anti-French demonstrations and the police, a little remiss in their duties, had allowed someone to spit at Mme Pompidou. The host at the dinner in New York was to have been the Vice-President, but to compensate for the disgraceful attitude of some of his compatriots it was President Nixon himself who came. He started his speech by saying, 'This is the first time that the vice-president of our country has delegated his duties to the president!' Next morning, there was a breakfast meeting for President Pompidou to which a lot of the top executives of corporate America came; our president looked rather

happier than when we had greeted him, with a group of Frenchmen, at the airport at White Plains.

That same evening I left on a trip to Asia: Hong Kong for a
meeting with the salesmen and some visits to clients, then a
meeting with our local managers; Taipei for a farewell to Mr Pong,
our manager in Taiwan, who was retiring, as well as visits to
customers and some members of the government; lastly, Tokyo.

During my sojourn in Japan I visited our factory at Fujisawa
and found a remarkably high calibre of personnel, a discipline
which I had seen in few other establishments, and, if the reaction
of all the employees to whom I was asked to make a speech was
anything to go by, a very good atmosphere.

The President of IBM Japan had asked me to visit the newest
cold rolling-mill in Japan, situated some thirty kilometres to the
southeast of Tokyo. This rolling-mill, which formed part of the
Yamata Steelworks, was 1,500 metres long. I saw only a dozen or
so employees during my visit. On the other hand, there were six
control computers of the IBM 1800 type and two 360–40s. This
was my first experience of a highly automated factory. The engineer who was showing me round explained how the introduction
of computers had increased productivity. I wanted to know more
and got him to explain to me, in detail, the performance of the
Japanese steelworks. I learned that the Japanese produce about
three times as many tonnes per man per year of work than the
Europeans and the Americans. I asked for a more detailed analysis
which showed that Arbed in Luxemburg was the most productive
of the European steelworks, that the English were at the bottom
of the list, and the Americans at the same level as France.

I realized at once what the utilization of modern technologies
– data processing and robotization – can bring by way of gains in
productivity, and thereby a reduction of costs in the traditional
industries. During my trip to Paris which took place soon afterwards I tried to explain this, but our steelmen told me that the
reason the Japanese were so competitive was the very low cost
of their manpower. Why will they not investigate, analyse costs,
and understand?

A little later, in August, I learned what life is like in an atmosphere of revolution. I paid a visit to Buenos Aires and to Montevideo where the Tupamaros had created a reign of terror. Our local managers lived under the constant threat of kidnapping and did not allow me to take a step without bodyguards. Business was difficult and I admired the courage of the employees who worked very well in spite of the danger. All the subsidiaries of American companies were subjected to daily harassment.

A little while after this trip, the daughter of our Managing Director in Argentine, Mr B. Esmerode, had both her hands blown off when she opened a box of flowers in which a bomb had been placed. Terrorism spreads very quickly. These were very eventful years in the world at large and within the company.

I would like now to speak about two of my 'discoveries': to begin with, the first contacts, for me at any rate, with the countries of Eastern Europe; then, the constant effort made by my expanding company to change in such a way that its organization and management systems remained sufficiently flexible to avoid being weighed down by bureaucracy.

RELATIONS WITH THE SOCIALIST COUNTRIES

From 1970 onward a debate took place within the company about the development of IBM's activities in the Soviet Union. We already had operations in the other 'Socialist' countries, and to our great surprise the IBM office in Budapest had never been closed. There were still some employees who had been there before the war. In Yugoslavia IBM was represented by an agent and I must say that, when visiting the exhibition in Ljubljana in August 1971, I was astonished to see that the salesmen had the classic look of IBM salesmen everywhere: white shirts and blue suits, and the same ability as their colleagues in Western Europe. Our base of operations was in Vienna because we already had an important organization there (IBM Austria), and because access to the Central European capitals was easy from there.

We began prospecting in East Germany, Czechoslovakia,

Hungary, Poland, Roumania and Bulgaria. It was pioneering work, very hard, and I pay due homage to the men who, for a long time, led the difficult lives of agents who leave their base on Monday morning, work all through the week in uncomfortable conditions, and return home on Friday evening. If we omit Budapest, which always stands out from amongst the other capitals, spending weeks in Prague, Sofia, Bucharest and East Berlin adds none of the joys of tourism to those of work.

Our business developed slowly since all these countries had serious balance of payments problems and were short of 'hard' currencies. Some of them had a great desire to open up to Western technology, and generally two forms of transaction were offered: a 'barter agreement' whereby the supplier of equipment undertook to purchase some local national products in exchange and sell them in the West, or the creation of a joint venture (at least 51 per cent of the capital to come from the Socialist country) to build a factory. Our manufacturing directors made numerous exploratory journeys but we never succeeded in finding a satisfactory solution.

During 1970 and and the early part of 1971 there were a great many meetings at Armonk to decide upon our approach to the Soviet market. The Soviet purchasing commission in New York, run by a very able and likeable Russian, George Shukine, had approached IBM and explained that there was a great need for computers in the USSR.

In the summer of 1971 an exhibition of data processing equipment was mounted in Leningrad and we decided, after many discussions amongst ourselves and consultations with the American government, to put a computer on show there. The Russians had imposed one condition: the equipment displayed had to remain in the country. Hence the decision was taken to begin selling our machines there.

This decision was facilitated by two things: several of our competitors, such as ICL of England, Bull of France, and the American NCR, Remington Rand and CDC, had already installed some computers there. Secondly, the Russians had launched a vast programme for the design and manufacture of computers, called

RIAD, which were to be a unified series. In their conception, these machines were similar to IBM 360s and were compatible with them – successfully compatible, moreover, since the programmes devised for the 360–50 could be utilized without problems in their top-range models.

They had organized their production system like ours: the entire range of products was manufactured for the market as a whole in the USSR and her satellites by factories in Russia, East Germany, Czechoslovakia, Hungary and Bulgaria, each of which specialized in the manufacture of one part of the total range. To start up production in this manner was a hard task.

I had occasion to visit the Bulgarian data processing factories with Paul Kofmehl who was then a Regional Director, and I must say I have never had a better reception in any country than I had in Bulgaria. The Deputy Prime Minister, Mr Ivan Popov, a former student of the Electrotechnical Institute in Toulouse, was quite surprised to find a Frenchman representing IBM, and he was happy to speak our language. On a visit to Sofia and the factory where the memory discs were manufactured, we were surprised to see so many workers employed to make such a limited quantity of products. Then we went to Plovdiv, flying in an aircraft belonging to the Bulgarian government. At the airport we crossed a real red carpet from the aircraft steps to the reception building, where we were greeted by a lady who was the head of the local Communist party, and we then got into a Ziss. It was about six miles from the airport to the factory and all the traffic had been stopped to allow our convoy of two cars and four motorcycles to pass. Even the cyclists were standing to attention holding their bikes with one hand and saluting with the other!

The manager of the factory welcomed us, but he did not take us in through the door Mr Popov had expected him to use. And so we went through a part of the factory that was completely empty, except for some women who with buckets and floorcloths were mopping up the water which had leaked in through the roof. Mr Popov was not too happy about this, and I understood from his tone of voice that what he said to the manager in Bulgarian was not very pleasant. We reached the bay where the magnetic tape units were assembled. Some ten of them were just being put together. The workers and the technicians were very enthusiastic, the machines they tested worked well. I recognized an exact copy of the IBM 727 tape unit and pointed this out to Mr Popov.

'Mr Prime Minister, these machines are very similar to the IBM 727 units.'

'Yes, in fact they are 727s.'

'Bulgaria has adhered to the Paris convention on patents. Aren't you afraid we shall come and ask you to pay patent rights?'

'Oh, I don't think you would do that, as we only sell these machines to communist countries!'

After these visits we had a long discussion on the evolution of Bulgaria which, Mr Popov said, would soon open up in the way that Hungary had already done. He suggested we should set up a factory on behalf of the government. This meeting was to be followed by many others in New York and Paris. The discussions did not lead to anything, for the Bulgarians' idea – like that put forward by other socialist countries – was that we should make the original investment and they should reimburse us by supplying us with the machines produced!

The exhibition of our equipment in Leningrad had been a great success. At every meeting the Russians explained that their market was enormous, and that they very much wanted to work with IBM. At this time, an American organization, the 'Young Americans for Freedom' mounted a very active campaign against trade exchanges between the United States and the USSR, in particular, against the export of technologically advanced products. They addressed hundreds of letters to our Chairman, and of course to the Senators and Congressmen in their own constituencies. It was at this moment that the Secretaries of both Defence and Trade began carefully studying the specifications for equipment eligible for export licences. They crossed large computers and their latest components off the list. IBM's position remained the same: it is not the job of a private company to determine 'foreign policy', that is the State's responsibility; this does not, however, prevent the company from making its viewpoint known.

Contacts were maintained and in May 1972 we received an important Russian delegation led by a member of the Academy of Sciences in Moscow, Professor Zhimerin, who was the Under-Secretary of Technology. There were a great many introductions, visits to factories and laboratories, and visits to some of our customers' installations. Two details struck me. On their arrival I was asked to explain IBM's structure to them. I spoke especially about the distribution of capital. In their minds, Mr T. J. Watson Jr, since he was the Chairman, must own at least 51 per cent of the shares. I have explained earlier what the true situation was.

On the following Sunday, we invited the entire delegation for drinks at our home in Bronxville. They were relaxed and friendly, toasts were proposed to scientific co-operation between the USSR and the USA – I reminded them that they were forgetting France! Mme K., who was rather an imposing figure, remarked to my wife that our children were too thin, and that our son after two years' study of Russian did not speak it fluently. They must be undernourished! She was astounded to see that my wife and I waited on them ourselves.

'I have a maid in my Moscow apartment.'

Then she asked if we had a house by the sea.

'No, we haven't.'

'Oh, I have a *dacha* on the Black Sea.'

This was our first encounter with 'one-upmanship'.

During the following months, several IBM managers went to Moscow for long discussions concerning methods of approaching the market. They sold a few computers; the first, a 360–50, was installed in the Ministry of Chemistry. In May 1973 I paid my first visit to Moscow. During the course of many working meetings I found the Russian officials much less relaxed than they had been in the United States.

Moscow is a beautiful city, but unfortunately I had no time to see it as a tourist. I was at the Intourist Hotel, where I could not find any French or American newspapers except *l'Humanité* [the French Communist party daily]; I was made very welcome and accompanied everywhere by an interpreter. During our meetings at the hotel my colleagues and I were extremely careful to communicate in writing, since we had noticed that everything we said aloud was known to our interlocutors the next day. I visited several Ministers and Under-Secretaries, including Professor Zhimerin and the Minister of Chemistry. They all told me more or less the same story: 'Our unified series of computers functions well, but our desire for modernization and for data processing is so pressing that our own factories cannot produce all the computers we need; we have no problems with the very powerful scientific computers, which we use for high energy physics and in our aerospace industry, but we must keep them for those purposes. What we want from you are commercial computers.' The Minister of Chemistry was very pleased with his IBM 360–50 and explained to me that memory discs must be added to it very quickly, because then, thanks to teleprocessing, he would be able to control the 30,000 chemical factories in the country. What a demonstration of bureaucratic centralization! At this moment, we were initiating discussions for the opening of an office in Moscow.

For me 1973 was the year in which I really explored the countries with 'planned economies'. On 29 June three of my colleagues and I left for Shanghai and Peking. In the group were Gordon Williamson, who knew Asia from having spent quite a long time in Japan; Joe Galante, who was an expert on our equipment; and a researcher from the Yorktown laboratory, Dr Tsu, a Chinese who had acquired American citizenship and was to act as both our interpreter and the scientist of the group. The Air France flight stopped at Shanghai and we went on to Peking via China Airlines. The aircraft was an old Ilyushin 62.

We stayed at the Hotel Friendship, built in 1954 by Russian technicians. It was an immense complex with offices, restaurants, and a club for billiards and ping-pong. The plumbing reminded me of old hotels in France. The temperature was 29°C, humidity was high and there was no air-conditioning.

From Monday 2 July to Friday the 7th (with the exception of Wednesday the 4th), we spent from 9 o'clock in the morning till 6 o'clock in the evening in a large room in which were assembled members of the Academy of Sciences, the Ministry of Trade, and the Import–Export Corporation. Our whole time was spent in presenting System 370 and System 3 and answering innumerable questions. Our Chinese friends were astonished when we gave them IBM brochures on these machines and considered we had done them a great favour in doing so. We explained that they were obtainable in any of our sales offices. All explanations were made in English and translated into Chinese.

Mr Hsien, from the Ministry of Trade, and Mr Liu, Managing Director of the Import–Export Corporation, welcomed us with great courtesy. They insisted on our staying longer than a week, and when we discovered that they had forgotten to declare our presence to the police authorities – a formality without which we would not be able to leave – we were a little uneasy. On Tuesday evening they told us that in celebration of the American Independence Day holiday we would be excused from meetings the next day. So, on Wednesday the 4th of July, they took us to see the Great Wall. I was in one car with Mr Tchang, the Managing Director of MACHIMPEX, the government office responsible for importing machinery. Our interpreter was Mr Han. I endeavoured not to ask embarassing questions, but for them even such simple questions as 'What is the percentage of girls in your schools?' present a problem.

During the two-hour drive conversation being rather sporadic, I tried to observe as much as I could. There were very few private vehicles, plenty of lorries (whose drivers had never heard of a straight line), plenty of heavily-laden bicycles, and carts pulled by horses, mules or asses. The road was good, the villages muddy. Men and women alike dressed in the same uniform. Military vehicles were everywhere.

The Great Wall was impressive and, every fifty metres, loud-speakers broadcast the thoughts of Chairman Mao. On the return journey, we drove along the Street of Stone Statues; then made a visit to the Forbidden City where there was an enormous crowd. Everyone stopped to look at us and smiled very sweetly. Foreign visitors were rather rare; I counted six in our entire visit, one of whom was an American woman in a skirt. The Chinese gathered round her at a respectful distance to look at what was for them an extraordinary garment, since all Chinese women wear trousers. We made our visit on the run which was a pity; however, we did have time to admire the water-clock, the stone boats and the Emperor's garden.

On the way back to the hotel, we passed some new three-storey buildings. I asked how apartments within them were allocated, since there is a severe shortage of housing in Peking. Mr Tchang explained to me that the employers discussed it with the Town Council and persuaded them to reserve them for the best workers. Questioning him more closely, I learned that it was the executives and managers who had priority. Salaries ranged from 100 to 400 yuans a month; rent for an apartment with three rooms, kitchen and w.c. was about 10 yuans, but a washing machine cost 400.

Thursday and Friday were spent in more presentations. At lunchtime I visited the French Ambassador. He confirmed what all the Chinese had told me: their dominant feelings were fear of the Russians and a desire for *rapprochement* with the West.

We also visited the computer factory in Peking. It was built in 1954 but looked older than its years. The machines manufactured there were twenty years behind those manufactured in the West. With 3,000 workers they produced only a hundred per year!

On Friday evening we had our final discussion. We had explained to our hosts that regulations governing exportation of strategic products prevented us from offering them our high range models. These, however, were the ones they were interested in; they were ready to order several. Was this perhaps a polite way of saying: 'We cannot buy anything from you?'

A farewell dinner took place on the Friday. It was very hot, a great many toasts were made to friendship between peoples, a succulent Peking duck was served . . . and we discovered that all the scientists and civil servants we had met during the week spoke perfect English. Some positive conclusions emerged: they wanted to buy two or three System 3's for the Bank of China; they also asked about the prices of all our systems and agreed that we should send some instructors to China to train programmers.

We left Peking very impressed on the whole. Obviously we had seen only one city, and it had been too short a visit for us to make any well-informed opinions but my own main conclusions were the following:

1. That this underdeveloped country (one must not be afraid of the word) contained some poor citizens, but they were not suffering the miseries I had seen in Africa and in the Indies.

2. The Cultural Revolution which caused them to lose half a generation of educated people was well and truly over. Chou En-Lai had taken matters in hand again.

3. The Chinese had a genuine desire to open up their country to the West.

4. They were very frightened of the Russians. The Peking subway system which was in the course of construction was also a network of atomic shelters.

5. Egalitarianism was beginning to be seen by certain leaders as a stumbling-block on the road to development.

6. They had a great respect for the Chinese of the diaspora and were ready to welcome back any who wanted to come and help them.

7. The only tricky point in the improvement of relations with the United States was the closeness between Taipei and Washington. They reiterated endlessly that Taiwan must be reintegrated into the People's Republic of China.

Most certainly, post-Cultural Revolution expansion was on its way; more and more teaching of foreign languages took place, the radio broadcast courses in English, and they wanted to send their students and their teachers abroad.

I returned via Paris where I met the man in charge of our operations in the USSR, Ray Fentriss, a young American who was already Vice-President of the IBM World Trade Corporation. He had been able to establish excellent relations with all the leaders in Russia who carried any weight in international trade. Every time delegations visited the USA, he managed to get them to come to IBM.

In February 1974 George Shukin, head of the Soviet purchasing commission in New York, telephoned me: 'Mr Ponomarev has arrived in the United States with several members of the Politburo. He wants to visit the IBM computer centre at White Plains next Monday.' I explained to him that Monday was a holiday, and that in our capitalist system we respected the workers too much to ask them, on a Friday, to give up their day off due on the following Monday. George was very insistent; he seemed to be in a bit of a panic. I ended up by telling him that we would organize a demonstration, and invite the delegation to lunch afterwards at the Rye Town Hilton which was very near our centre at White Plains.

Ray Fentriss managed to gather together a sufficient number of people to prevent the place from looking too empty. Mr Ponomarev saw for himself how much computers have done to improve communications between clients, and between the sales departments and the factories; he asked a lot of questions about the reliability of the systems which made us wonder whether the Soviets' unified series was really working as well as we had been led to believe.

I was approaching fifty and was the oldest of all the IBM managers present. Ray Fentriss, at forty, came next. Mr Ponomarev through the intermediary of George Shukin gave me to understand that he was astonished at not being received by somebody more senior! I could hardly have asked the Chairman of IBM to sacrifice a holiday after all, and . . . in any case he was only three years older than me.

During the luncheon we talked about China. I told Mr Ponomarev that I had not seen any wretched poverty there, and he replied that the real misery was to be found in the country, and that there were a great many Chinese in rehabilitation camps. He did not believe that China would change over the next ten or twenty years.

During the years that followed, I was to make several trips to Moscow and receive many Soviet leaders in New York and Paris. I built up friendly relations with a few of them. The USSR is an advanced industrial country which has administrators, scientists and engineers of the highest quality. But it makes me sad, as in other cases, to see a high potential for creativity and for production, badly utilized on account of a politico-economic system that gives rise to a flourishing centralized bureaucracy, bogged down in dogmatic attitudes. It is a well-known fact that Lysenko's theories seriously retarded the development of biology in the USSR. It was a similar case with data processing. Not until Kruschev visited the United States did the Soviet government come to recognize that data processing was not a demonic science, nor an expression of the capitalist oppressor!

When one knows what the Soviets have achieved in science and industry, in atomic energy, in the construction of missiles of all ranges, in the conquest of space, and in the realm of energy, one sees very clearly that they have the mathematicians, the physicists, the chemists and the engineers who would enable them to possess a world-class data processing industry. But the State alone decides which programmes are to be undertaken and what kind of training should be given to scientists and engineers for the general good. Priority was accorded to military research and certain heavy industries, therefore the funds allocated to data processing were totally inadequate. Since there are no business enterprises free to decide their own destiny, and since there is no competition, it means that if the technocrats make a mistake the entire country suffers the consequences. The failure of their agricultural plan is a well-known case in point; it was caused by a lack of both initiative and individual reward. The same applies to data processing. Good work is being done in some university laboratories, but it does not move on from research and development to mass production. The experts who draw up the Plan may declare 'We shall do it' during the next Five Year Plan, but there are some delays that can never be made up. It is not enough to obtain – by rather dishonest means – the designs of machines, or even the machines themselves, then to dismantle them in order to try to reproduce them. The country needs a technological infrastructure, and this is particularly true in the case of electronic components and integrated circuits.

The Japanese have already shown us that, if one has the foresight to grasp which industries will be the important ones of the future, business organizations in the country will, of themselves, make the necessary efforts to place themselves well-ahead in a competitive market.

THE NECESSARY REORGANIZATIONS

Tom Watson Jr has said: 'IBM is a company which is ready to change everything except its principles.' It is true that the period I spent in the States from the end of 1967 to August 1974 was one of change and reorganization in many ways. Change was launched in 1956 with the creation of six divisions in the United States and it has carried on ever since.

If a company's objectives are clearly defined, and if one of these is to respond very quickly to its customers' needs, it is vital the company should be ready to change its method of organization very frequently. I had already heard Dick Watson say that what made the company so strong was its 'constant rejection of the status quo'. Now I was actually experiencing change at a level which gave me a share in its preparation and in its practical application.

The World Trade Corporation changed even more quickly than IBM USA, and Bert Witham, Dick Warren, Paul Kofmehl, who was Director of Management Systems from 1968 to 1971, Jacques Lemmonier, who was Director of Organization, and I spent a considerable amount of time in meetings with our Chairman, Gil Jones, and the management committee of the corporation throughout all these years.

Rather than enumerate the various stages in chronological order, I would prefer to examine the factors which in my opinion must lead a management team to modify a company's structure. I will not place them in order of importance because each one of them becomes pre-eminent at a given moment.

The size of the company

Growth in terms of volume of business can lead to some bureaucratization, which slows down the speed of response, and in
certain cases makes the task of some higher executives impossible.
Here are some relevant figures concerning the IBM Group during
the period under consideration:

	Turnover in Billions of Dollars	Number of Employees
1967	5.4	221,800
1968	6.9	241,000
1969	7.2	258,000
1970	7.5	269,000
1971	8.3	265,000
1972	9.5	262,000
1973	11.0	274,000
1974	12.7	292,000

In seven years the turnover multiplied by 2.35, the number of
employees by 1.31. This meant there were numerous new clients,
that it had been possible to change methods of selling, that new
factories were needed and that a great many managers must have
been trained and promoted.

Further, for some years now, the World Trade Corporation,
which covers all IBM's activities outside the United States, has
had a higher growth rate than the American divisions. This growth
was particularly large in terms of manufacturing, for in 1958 a
new principle had been agreed: the American factories would
manufacture for the American market; the European factories for
Europe, Africa and the Middle East; the factories in Canada,
Japan, South America and India for the rest of the world. We
were trying to match production to the market.

New factories were built and put into production in the following places:

In 1971: Bromont in Canada, Sumare in Brazil, Yasu in Japan.
In 1972: Bordeaux.
In 1973: Berlin, and a laboratory in Yasu.

And every year an extension to one of the older factories or laboratories was also built.

Employment at IBM plants also developed as follows:

	Number of Employees		From 1962–74 multiplied by
	1962	1974	
USA	26,500	43,300	1.63 times
Outside USA	12,500	32,400	2.59 times

At our New York Headquarters we had a very good manufacturing team, but it soon emerged that their task was very difficult to accomplish. One of their objectives was to organize liaison – which had to be very close – between the labs and the factories, and between the American factories, and the laboratories and factories in the rest of the world. It is not very easy for an expert in one function to work in the same manner with the Fujisawa Plant in Japan, the one in Sumare in Brazil, and others in Montpellier, France and Jarfalls, Sweden. It seemed to me that for manufacturing, at least, we would have to cut our top executive team in two, one half to be responsible for Europe, the other for the rest of the world.

In 1969 we introduced new marketing approaches. Some of the activities of the systems engineers, many of the programmes, and almost all training would henceforth be at the clients' expense. This was not a simple change; its setting-up depended on how sophisticated the market was. And there again, the marketing specialists in New York found great difficulty in helping the sales services in countries as far away as New Zealand, Norway and the Argentine.

Technological evolution – the products

The change-over from electrical technology to electronics using transistors, and then miniaturized circuits with solid logic technology, and the change-over from batch data processing to teleprocessing had already provoked a good deal of change in manufacturing methods, sales, services and maintenance.

The period from 1964–74 saw the rapid development of teleprocessing. The two major consequences of this were the entry of IBM into telecommunications, and the exponential growth in the number of direct users of data processing in business through the intermediary of terminals. In this era we were beginning to speak of machines that were 'user friendly', and of the service that must be offered to the end user. For World Trade the consequences of this development were still more important than for IBM USA. At a time when large computers could be identical almost everywhere, the terminals themselves had to be adapted for clients in almost every country.

Differences in language became important – the creation of the Japanese laboratory demonstrated this point – and the programmes had to be in the native language of the country in which they were sold. Specific uses for the computers, such as were met with in the postal services, the banks, the hypermarkets and many others, necessitated the creation of departments to study more complex new products; above all they required very exact communication of the customers' needs to the laboratories developing these products.

I would like to mention here some products which were put on the market from 1967 on, which explain these developments and also demonstrate how innovative the company's laboratories were, and how harmoniously data processing developed (an * indicates a special product for teleprocessing).

1967 — *Quicktran 2, an improved version of the Quicktran

programme for organizing a network of terminals. *Binary-synchronous communications.

1968 — System 360 model 85. *Two visualization consoles: the 2265 and the 2760. The optical reader 1288. *Introduction of computer-assisted training in maintenance services.

1969 — System 3 for small businesses. System 360–195: the most powerful computer of the day. *Two terminals, the 2770 and the 2790.
Typewriters with magnetic cards.

1970 — System 370 (165–155–145). Model 145 was the first computer to utilize a logic circuit. System 3 model 6.
*System 7 (for use in factories and laboratories). Memory discs 3330 with 800 million characters. Floppy discs. Printer 3211, which can print 2000 lines a minute and 80 programme-products.

1971 — System 370 – models 135–195. *3270 – Visualization console. New magnetic tape unit, the 3410. *A system of communications for stockbrokers, the 3670. System 2730 for checking credit at the point of sale, and 125 application programmes.

1972 — System 370 – Models 125–158–168. Virtual memory. *Communications controller 3705. *Communications terminal 3780. *Ticket distributor 2984. Copier II. Blood-cell separator 2991.

1973 — The 370 115 (the smallest of the 370s). System 3, model 15. New memories for the 370s. *Banking system 3600. *System 3650 for retail shops. *Communications controller 3704. Magnetic disc unit 3340 (Winchester).

1974 — *Advanced functions for telecommunications with new terminals 3767–3770. Mass memory system 3850. Improvement of memories on the 370–115 and 145.

In addition during these years the La Gaude laboratory developed the first electronic telephone switching systems to be put on the market by IBM as well as modems (modulators–demodulators), which permit the linking-up of terminals to computers via telephone lines.

The environment

One of the aims of a multinational, conscious of its responsibilities towards the subsidiaries' host countries, is to conduct itself like a good citizen everywhere. Since 1965 we have experienced anti-multinational campaigns: economic nationalism; protectionist sentiment; pressure from certain States who want a share in the capital of local subsidiaries; subsidies allotted to some of our competitors; social demands expressed through violence; and intervention not only by the State in the form of industrial policies but also by supranational organizations such as the UN in the form of a Code of Conduct, and by the Common Market Commission in the form of directives. In order to be ready to respond to this environment, to create a good image for the company, to listen carefully to politico-economic reactions, a multinational must have capable men and women who are good spokesmen and at home in the outside world.

The men and women at the top

In a well-organized, long-established business, the principles, policies and objectives are well-known to everyone. A way of doing things has been created within the organization which will ensure that a change of president, or some other person at the top, will not cause a major disturbance. This is especially true if the company has developed an appropriate system of succession to all the most important posts. The hand-over of power is made smoothly, the new man, who was already occupying an important position, is not going to cause any culture shock.

In spite of this the personality of the president and his immediate associates can have an influence on the organization. Executives belonging to the same company will, after all, still have differences between them. One may attach special importance to external relations. One prefers discretion to open communication. Another is very interested in the international scene. One delegates a good deal, another does not, and so on.

During the period under consideration, IBM had three Chairmen:

T. J. Watson Jr.	up until June 1971
T. V. Learson	up until December 1973
F. J. Cary	since 1 January 1973

Each of them left his mark on the company.

Tom Watson launched us into computers; he had vigorously reaffirmed the principles declared by his father and added that the company had a general responsibility towards society. Very active in the outside world, it was he who created IBM's modern image.

Vin Learson did not hold the post for very long. He is remembered as the man who oversaw the launching of the 360. He was also a fanatic for Equal Opportunity and he set up a programme of promotion for women.

Frank Cary carried the anti-trust lawsuits through from A to Z, and it is greatly to his credit that he was able to convince all the executives that these trials should in no way affect the smooth running of all undertakings and all divisions. He was also the man who carried out major restructuring and played a very important part in the development of international operations.

The Chairman of the World Trade Corporation up until the end of 1970 was A.K. Watson. Gilbert E. Jones succeeded him on 6 November 1970.

It is interesting to note that T.V. Learson was the President when T.J. Watson was Chairman; Frank Cary was President when T.V. Learson was Chairman; John Opel (a future Chairman) was President under the Chairmanship of Frank Cary.

The same type of succession planning occurred in the IBM World Trade Corporation. Gil Jones was President, then I became President, while Dick Watson was Chairman. I remained President when Gil Jones was Chairman, and followed him as Chairman.

A difficult succession in an important post

It sometimes happens that the head of one undertaking or the president of a division leaves, and that there is no available successor. Unfortunately this situation arises rather frequently in business firms and provokes a good many crises. However, IBM has always attached so much importance to the good management of executive succession that this situation has not cropped up very often. In the higher ranks, I know of only three cases, one of which was Nick Katzenbach's entry into the company as head of the legal department. Sometimes, when a void appears, one can reorganize in such a way as to give extra responsibilities to an executive of higher rank or take a risk and give rapid promotion to a young man or woman.

Anticipating problems. The creation of new activities

Adapting or reacting not to existing problems, but to those which long-term planning allows one to forecast is an implicit cause of the four types of reorganization considered up to now. First, we have the case where a company decides to launch itself vigorously into new activities, but its old structure will not allow it to go ahead fast enough. A new department, which will take the project in hand, can be added to the existing structure; its director will be appointed at a very high level and will be allowed as much autonomy as possible. For example, in 1962 when we realized that a growing number of users were calling for 'telematics', we added a management team responsible for the market development of telematics to the existing marketing management at European HQ: we employed a manager there for industrial control systems (the beginning of robotics) and a manager for teleprocessing systems. This type or reorganization was to become common during the years that followed.

The second case is one in which it has been foreseen that a certain area will become more important, and that the management will have to devote a great deal of time to it; the man in charge is then given a different position in the hierarchy. When I arrived in New York in 1967, the director of planning was accountable to the vice-president of finance. I created the post of vice-president of planning, directly accountable to myself, and two other directorships: one for organization and one to be in charge of executive resources. In this way I grouped together all the managers who were concerned with the future.

Nearly all these factors were taken into consideration during all the reorganizations in which I played a part from 1968 to 1974, as well as those which I personally proposed and directed. I will speak here only about the World Trade Corporation. In 1970–1, after carrying out a study I had asked them to do at Gil Jones' request, Paul Kofmehl and Jacques Lemmonier proposed that our headquarters should be moved from New York to Paris. The corporation's management committee rejected our proposal for two reasons: it was essential to maintain good liaison with the parent company, and Canada and South America were too far from Paris; the United States was going through a period when companies were cutting down on staff and it would have been difficult to find posts in the USA for those American executives who were not to be transferred to Paris.

We set to work once more and proposed that the World Trade Corporation should be reorganized in two groups: IBM Europe/Africa/Middle East and IBM Americas/Far East. Frank Cummiskey took charge of the first and Dick Warren of the second. We maintained a top management in New York but a great many heads of department were transferred into one or other of the two groups.

In 1972 I was put in charge of quite a small Task Force to study an eventual reorganization of the corporation in greater detail. As I was eager for my partners – all Americans – to gain a better understanding of the environment overseas, we spent a week in Europe meeting the directors of our subsidiaries and some important people outside the corporation. One visit was particularly instructive: we spent two hours with Mr Spinelli, who was then one of the commissioners in the Common Market

Commission in Brussels. After we had explained to him the organization and the European objectives of IBM, I asked him:

'What can we do to make ourselves more acceptable?'

He pondered for a moment then replied:

'You should put your subsidiaries' shares on the national financial markets.'

'What percentage do you think would be satisfactory?'

'20 to 30 per cent.'

'*Monsieur le commissaire*, that would represent a call on capital of roughly 3 billion dollars.'

'That is obviously a lot for the European market.'

I also explained that the shares of the parent company are quoted in London, Paris, Brussels, Amsterdam and Zürich, and he acknowledged that this was not a bad solution. As we were leaving, I asked him for the last time: 'What can we do?' and he answered, 'Nothing. You are too big, and you are too efficient.' I then asked Mr Spinelli if I should direct our salesmen to stop persuading clients to buy our maintenance services and to leave machines broken-down, and should I ask our factories to produce poor quality machines and our engineers to stop inventing anything. He laughed and reminded me that 'Small is beautiful.'

One outcome of the Task Force's work was the creation of three divisions in the computer group (development and manufacturing). This system of management enhanced World Trade's influence. We also achieved a better understanding of the pressures of the environment, and later created two marketing divisions, one for the large systems, the other for the smaller ones.

In 1974 after numerous studies and meetings, IBM World Trade Corporation emerged as a totally restructured enterprise. The size of its operations and their dispersal led to the two groups being transformed into subsidiary companies which were each profit centres: IBM Europe/Middle East/Africa and IBM Americas/Far East. I became Chairman of the first and Ralph Pfeiffer of the second. For me this meant a return to Paris. Ralph and his associates decided to remain in the USA, which was perfectly reasonable considering the importance of Canada and Latin America.

The World Trade Corporation, of which I was still President, became a holding company and regrouped the service departments which could be useful to the two new companies. For example, the international sales office staff were responsible for receiving clients who came to the United States and organizing visits to factories, laboratories, and clients' installations for them. Other departments retained their importance, such as the centre for testing new applications and programmes, the distribution centre responsible for shipping all the products made in the USA to the rest of the world, and a personnel department which assisted the eight hundred or so 'foreigners' who found themselves working for IBM in the United States every year. In February 1974, Gil Jones became Vice-Chairman of the IBM Corporation.

After the reorganization of the World Trade Corporation, my family and I were, once again, ready to depart for the other side of the ocean. During these seven years so many things happened in the personal as well as in the professional sphere of my life that I have eliminated many events. I am not writing a diary, only noting some episodes from the life of a family and the life of a company. Some I have already described, but I would like to add a few more experiences that made an impression on us and try to deduce some general comments from them.

I learned during these years the extent to which the head of a business or a top executive has to take part in the life of the community! There are conflicting views on this, but I am absolutely convinced that a low profile is a bad thing. If businesses in several European countries do not play their due part, it is very often because their top executives lack the courage to express themselves. . . .

Participation in the life of the community, the country and the company demands personal sacrifices, for the simple reason that it takes up time, and time outside normal working hours. During these seven years, I launched myself into 'external relations'; my bosses, Vin Learson and Gil Jones, often criticized me for doing too much. Nevertheless my conscience was clear because I always prepared my articles or speeches for these 'outside' occasions on Saturdays and Sundays.

189

I made a lot of speeches, a score or so every year within IBM, a score or so outside. The universities were my favourite stamping-ground. Each time I felt I was also doing useful work for France. This earned me the job of 'trustee', that is to say director, of the International Institute of Education, membership of MIT's Visiting Committee, trusteeship of Barnard College in New York, and INSEAD in France and of the *Lycée français* in New York. I also got to know the American universities – Harvard, Berkeley, Columbia, Northwestern, Stanford, Cornell, Notre Dame and many others. I was able to exchange viewpoints with students at the *Polytechnique*, Sciences-Po, HEC (*Ecole des hautes études commerciales*), the *Centrale*, the *Polytechnicum* in Zürich, the University of Saint-Gall and the Management Centre at Oxford.

It was during this period that I joined the boards of directors of various companies, and also left some of these: Air Liquide; Philip Morris; Bankers' Trust; Sogen (a subsidiary of the Société Générale in New York); French-American Banking Corporation (a subsidiary of the BNP).

I remember my first encounter with M. Jean Delorme, the Chairman of Air Liquide. I was sitting beside him at a luncheon given by Baron Hottinguer in honour of Dick Watson who was at that time President of the International Chamber of Commerce.

'What do you do?' M. Delorme asked me.

'I work for IBM in the United States.'

During the conversation, I talked to him about the attacks made against the multinationals and the necessity for them to explain more fully what they did. I told him, for example, that Air Liquide, one of the very front-ranking French multinationals, should be better known. M. Delorme was a little annoyed at this slight criticism.

'What is your function at IBM?'

'I am President of the World Trade Corporation.'

Next day, M. Delorme telephoned to offer me a place on the Board of Directors of Air Liquide Canada and I accepted at once.

I cannot mention all the other organizations with which I was associated, but from them I garnered a rather exceptional range of experience through making contacts with people from very different walks of life. What they all had in common was that they taught me a lot, and reinforced my optimism regarding the possibilities of amicable understanding between people. I visited many countries and came to know some of their citizens. And, if I cannot claim to know the world well, I know it a great deal better than most of my compatriots and most citizens of other countries. Believe me, human resources in every country are badly utilized. This is what makes me sad: I have met with goodness, with warm human qualities everywhere, but I have observed that many political systems fail to get the most out of them.

I do not want to give too many figures here but, during our stay, I received — my wife and I received — hundreds of managers of French companies. Many of them seemed to me excellent, a few very bad. I feel no bitterness towards the bad ones, only a certain compassion for the people who have to work under their direction. Many of the visitors who came from Europe were particularly interested in our system of long-term planning. We were constantly seeking to improve the system, and at the end of 1968 and the beginning of 1969 an interesting experiment was carried out by the corporation. It was a study for very long-term planning — ten to twenty years — worked out on the Delphi method. This consisted of interviewing a large number of managers, asking questions such as, 'At what date do you think 25 per cent of American homes will be equipped with a computer terminal linked to the data banks?', or 'In what year do you suppose that 50 per cent of agricultural production will be influenced by the use of computers for planning and control?' Once all the replies were gathered together, we were able to make the analysis which showed the date the majority considered probable; we then had to modify, or maintain, our previous response. I was very surprised to find that I was amongst those who gave the earliest dates. I had more confidence in the possibilities of technology than did many of my colleagues. They had understood, better than I had, that the utilization of new technologies takes a long time to reach the general public.

Living in Bronxville, working in New York and travelling all over the country gave Françoise and I the chance to know America and the Americans well. Our conclusion: we liked them very much, we admired them, and this did not detract in any way from our love of France. In 1974, American morale was not good. After the Vietnam war, the Watergate scandal, the resignation of President Nixon, the Americans entered into their period of *mea culpa*. Still something of the Boy Scout, I decided to try and raise their morale by choosing as my theme, each time I was invited to speak: 'What's right with America!' The older the audience, the greater my success, but the message went down well everywhere. This nation was ready to listen to a message of hope.

10

A Defence and Illustration of the Multinationals

The power of words never ceases to amaze me! It is probable (although it has occurred to me rather late in the day) that if certain people including myself had not invented the words 'multinational' or 'transnational', the debate which has been going on for more than twenty years, and which crops up everywhere, might have been a lot calmer.

Because novelty and change are disturbing, every innovation, every new human organization which is created, gives rise to a group of adversaries who express themselves more or less passionately. The 'anti-multinationals' debate is, however, curious in that the organizations labelled in this way have existed for several centuries. It seems to me that the enemies of the multinationals only discovered their existence when they were baptized with this name, and that they have fully exploited the hostile reaction a mere word can create in the minds of an ill-informed public.

Faced with these attacks, the very people who should have sprung to the defence of multinationals and clearly explained their role have often recoiled. They found it easier to avoid the word, rather than make other people understand the benefits these companies have brought to the countries in which they have subsidiaries. I recall a discussion in the large lecture hall of the *Ecole Centrale* in Paris on the occasion of an international meeting organized by the student committee entitled 'International Week'. The subject for debate was 'The Multinationals'. To warm up the atmosphere, a group of students had handed out leaflets with the title, 'Exploiters' Week'. I had the honour to be portrayed in caricature on it; naturally I was wearing a top hat and smoking a cigar, rather old-fashioned symbols of the capitalist. One member of the panel, the chairman of a great French enterprise, began his speech by saying: 'I manage an important French company that has subsidiaries abroad.' He declined to use the word 'multinational', hoping thereby to lower the tension.

I have sometimes had disagreements with my management, who were afraid that a frontal attack and a frank explanation of the role of multinationals would provoke negative reactions. During a meeting of top management Frank Cary, who was President of IBM at the time, suggested we should stop using the word multinational, and I replied – with that lack of diplomacy which has all too often been a handicap to me – 'If you call an elephant a bird, he won't be any lighter if he sits on your lap!'

In France the most violent verbal attacks against the multinationals came from M. Georges Marchais, the Secretary General of the Communist party. For him, the multinationals were, and still are, the most modern expression of capitalism and of 'wild' liberalism. What annoys him all the more is that many of these companies have set up very progressive systems to handle their human resources, and these have made it clear – to their employees at least – that there exists a social liberalism which is the outcome of capitalism and not of the class struggle.

Many books have been written on this subject. It is important to recognize that very often the writers, whether amateur or professional, fail to present any original ideas which are likely to upset public opinion; on the contrary all they succeed in doing, since they have a certain talent for synthesis, is to express the public opinion of the moment more lucidly than others have done, flattering it and finding apt words. One of these books, which has become famous for its hostile attitude of the multinationals, is *Global Reach*, sub-titled *The Power of the Multinational Corporations*. This book, published at the end of 1974, was signed by two American Professors, Richard J. Barnet and Ronald E. Müller. Checking the index, I found that there were more quotes from my lectures and speeches than from anybody else's. It was an honour I would willingly have forgone, for several of the extracts had been cut by the authors or been taken out of context in order to demonstrate that I was defending 'evil'. During the years that followed the publication of this book I spent a lot of time criticizing it, which was quite easy since the authors did not know how to avoid 'going over the top'.

Events since 1974 have proved the falsity of certain theories it elaborated, and, moreover, that the 'facts' examined in it were very often totally unrelated to the actual organization of the corporations. The most interesting point, however, is that at least one of the authors has changed his mind.

Late in 1976, I was invited to take part in a conference on the multinationals in Geneva. The programme announced that I would speak at the end of the morning after Professor Müller. In expectation of a vigorous attack from the latter, I prepared a speech criticizing, point by point, what he and his co-author had written. I arrived too late to hear Mr Müller because of fog at Geneva Airport, but in good time for my speech. Fortunately the organizer of the session warned me in time that Professor Müller had made a very mild speech with virtually no attack on the multinationals, so I had to modify my speech as I went along, and found the solution by simply saying, 'Two years ago, Mr Barnet and Mr Müller wrote . . .'. At the end of the conference, I had a chance to talk to Mr Müller for a moment and ask him why he had changed his mind. He replied, 'I have learned a lot in two years.' I regretted then that he had not waited a while before publishing his book!

I cannot deal with this subject exhaustively in the space of a single chapter, and will confine myself to a résumé of the experience I have acquired through direct participation in the management of two multinationals: IBM and Air Liquide, and through my presence at the deliberations of the boards of directors of some other multinationals of which I was or still am a member: Moet Hennessy, Philip Morris, Bankers' Trust, French-American Banking Corporation, Chase Manhattan Investment Corporation and N.M. Rothschild; also through my participation in organizations such as the International Institute of Education, the INSEAD, and the International Chamber of Commerce.

I am not enumerating all these institutions in order to brag about my activities and give proof of my experience, but to bring my first statement about the multinationals into sharp focus. If I said 'the multinationals don't exist', nobody would take me seriously. But I do say that it is dangerous and perhaps not entirely honest intellectually – although I am the first to fall into this error – to group together under a common name companies which have:

— totally different activities
— totally dissimilar export or investment policies
— different dimensions
— styles of management and objectives which have nothing in common
— different 'nationalities' from the parent company.

In the organizations with which I have been or still am associated, all of which engage in important international activities, there are:

— four banks, two of which are American, one French (French–American Corporation is a subsidiary of the BNP) and one English
— two educational institutions
— two American industrial companies involved in totally different fields: data processing and tobacco
— two French companies whose industrial activities have nothing in common.

When speaking of French companies one rarely says French companies are like this or like that; one makes distinctions between them. True or false? True certainly, therefore I too am guilty of gross generalization by referring in the title of this chapter to 'the multinationals'. However, ever since the United Nations created a centre for studying transnational companies, it seems to me impossible to avoid the subject.

In a great many States and also in many international organizations it is a typical contemporary reaction to regulate the activities of any newly-emerging organization. Over the last twenty years

196

the transmission of data has become increasingly easy between computers, between terminals and computers, and now between micro-computers. From the moment when several companies placed terminals beyond the frontiers of the country where their central computer was installed, the idea of regulation and control was born. Several countries have already promulgated laws for the control of data transmission across frontiers. As fast as electronic data banks develop, proposals for laws for the defence of individual liberty multiply.

I am not opposed to this reaction, however. In the case of the multinationals, we see the same phenomenon. A legislative solution is difficult because so many countries are involved, hence the idea came up of appealing to the UN to develop a code of conduct acceptable to the various governments and companies concerned. Since 1972 many people have been working on it, but the code has still not been approved even after at least thirty international meetings.

There have been a great many economic studies on the multi-nationals but not very many world-wide juridical studies. This lacuna is particularly regrettable at a time when there is an attempt being made to regulate their activities. Amongst the receiving countries, rare indeed are those States which do not have current legislation which allows them to control foreign investments. The most extreme cases have been in the petroleum sector, where the initiative henceforth belongs to the producer-States which negotiate directly with the consumer-States without passing through the intermediary of the great petroleum companies.

Not only are restrictions imposed by the receiving States, but the country of origin intervenes as well. For example, the American government through the intermediary of a number of agencies – the Federal Trade Commission, the Department of Justice, the Food and Drug Administration – keeps a very tight control over the activities of American multinationals. In the same way some European businesses are subject to 'surveillance' by the Common Market Commission. Lastly, we are now seeing some attempts at internationally-concerted action regulating the multinational companies. The initiative for this came in some cases from international or regional bodies.

One such important action was conducted by the Economic and Social Council of the United Nations. Forty-eight nations were represented at the plenary meetings, and in addition to the national delegates there were some VIPs chosen for their expertise in international trade. I had suggested to Mr P. de Seynes, who was at that time in charge of the Economic and Social Council, that he should organize hearings with industrialists, trade unionists, and officials with responsibility for the regulations. The aim was to bring all the representatives up to the same level of knowledge and awareness. At the time of the first hearing in 1972 Mr G.E. Jones and I, along with five or six others, were invited to make speeches. Amongst other things I proposed an international system of negotiations regarding investments. It had become apparent to me that GATT, which is essentially concerned only with trading exchanges, had become totally inadequate now that direct investment in foreign countries was growing faster than trade. It would have been a good thing, in fact, to extend the functions of GATT and to call it General Agreement on Tariffs, Trade *and Investments*. The death of President Allende was announced during the session, and I believe that this event had an effect on the work done during the next few years.

ECOSOC later created the centre for studying transnational companies. For a long time the International Chamber of Commerce was one of the interlocutors for the Centre, whose essential aim was to define a 'code of conduct'. Mr Wilfrid Baumgartner, ex-Governor of the Bank of France and Minister of Finance, was the first President of the commission on multinationals, I was the second and Mr H. Van den Hoven (Chairman of Unilever NV) followed me.

Unfortunately political questions all too often predominated over economic questions. Countries on the road to development did not want to consider anything except the 'duties' of the multinationals, not those of the receiving nations: the Soviet bloc did not want State-owned industries – which is what all theirs are – to be subject to the code.

This convergence of efforts on the part of the receiving countries, the countries of origin, and international organizations bears witness to a cautious attitude towards the multinationals, which may seem paradoxical in a context of ever-expanding international trade. An explanation for this can be found in the fact that the multinational corporations, who have made it possible for international exchanges to grow very rapidly, have set up an effective system for the gathering of information and for decision-making at an international level.

Some believed that they saw in this a 'power' that menaced the sovereignty of individual States. Rather than re-examining this belief to seek to discover the real reasons for the existence of multinationals and to draw the logical conclusions, they first ignored the multinationals, then distrusted them often in spite of reality, and finally they created myths about them. This is why before I examine the origin and development of the multinational companies I think it would be useful to know the reality of the international trading environment today.

WHAT IS THE REALITY OF THE COMMERCIAL AND INDUSTRIAL ENVIRONMENT TODAY?

In 1984 the number of non-American businesses with a turnover exceeding one billion dollars was estimated at 143, and those whose parent establishment was in the USA at 301. The structure of international trade itself has changed: the developing countries are now demanding a readjustment of exchange rates to their advantage. First Japan then Europe have become serious competitors of the United States. The countries with planned economies and China intend to take a greater part in international trade.

In 1983, out of the $1,665 billion which represented world exports, the ten EEC countries accounted for 575 billion (34.6%), Japan for 147 billion (9%), and the developing countries for 495 billion dollars (29.7%). In 1983, the exporting countries were ranked as follows: 1) the United States; 2) West Germany; 3) Japan; 4) England; 5) France.

In 1966, the United States accounted for 23% of world exports, Europe for 50%. In 1973, the figure for the USA reached only 19% while the European share rose to 56%, that is, three times that of the United States. In 1983 the USA stood at 12%, Europe at 59.3%. (European exports include trade between members of the EEC.)

In 1966, the United States manufactured 45% of the world automobile production (in 1953, it was 75%), France, Germany and Italy 16%. In 1983 the United States produced 28% of the total, France, Germany and Italy 34.5%.

The international economy has not become Americanized, it has become globalized. The reality today is that we have an international economic order at the heart of which established trading exchanges are becoming ever more widespread and varied in origin. International exchanges have developed at a faster pace than industrial growth: the volume of world-wide production doubled between 1960 and 1974 while that of exports tripled. In 1982 exports had increased by 73 per cent in relation to figures for 1974; industrial production had increased during the same period by only 8 per cent.

It is in the evolutionary context of the liberalization of exchanges, the global nature of the economy, and the fact of international inter-dependence that for more than twenty-five years new companies – called multinationals – have been created and continue to develop. Accused, applauded, brought to account – according to some, they are the *enfants terribles* of economic life because they are uncontrollable giants with secret and elusive powers. According to others, they represent a means of economic progress because they are effective, rational and useful. Thus the multinationals belong to modern mythology. Only they are not a myth. They exist. They develop. They act.

I would like, now, to try to explain how and why.

WHAT IS A MULTINATIONAL?

I have already spoken of the hotch-potch of ideas connected to multinationals, but here are some other things one reads and hears about them:

'The multinationals are American.'

'The multinationals are too powerful.'

'The multinationals are the power of money.'

'The multinationals represent the ultimate creation of capitalism.'

'The multinationals are stateless.'

'The multinationals are instruments in the service of an ideology.'

'The multinationals are speculators.'

Any serious analysis, carried out scientifically, will show that none of these statements means anything. The difficulty of defining the multinationals demonstrates this very well, for, if they all behaved in as homogeneous a fashion as the above statements would have us believe, there would be no difficulty in finding a definition for the multinational company.

Let us examine the facts. I have already said that the multinationals differ greatly from one another. These differences result from:

1. The industry to which they belong. The problems faced by, and created by, the mining industries are different from those of manufacturing industries, and these in turn are totally different from the problems of service industries.

2. Their volume of business. The Radial Company which has fewer than 2,000 employees is different from Air Liquide which is different again from General Motors.

3. Methods and general policies which vary from one to another.

4. Legislation in the country where the parent company is located.

201

5. The fact that the capital of some of them belongs to the private sector, others are nationalized industries and still others are, for the State, instruments of industrial policy.

Given these differences, it seems to me very difficult to speak of the multinationals in general terms and to suppose that they will all behave in an identical manner. Their only common characteristics are:

1. They operate in many countries.

2. Several of their subsidiaries have a complete range of industrial activities, research and development, manufacturing and other services.

3. They have men and women of different nationalities in positions of responsibility.

4. Lastly, in the case of private enterprises, their capital is multinational.

While American companies were among the first after the war to develop according to these criteria, the end of the sixties marked the beginning of a significant growth in direct investments abroad by the other industrialized countries. In 1973, the EEC Commission enumerated 9,481 multinational enterprises. The total number of multinational enterprises originating within the EEC (4,532) was already greater than that of companies originating in America (2,567).

In the United States, the importance of direct foreign investments has increased since the beginning of the 1970s.

According to a report issued by the Department of Trade, foreign investments in the United States rose to 26.4 billion dollars at the end of 1974. In 1978 they were over 40 billion dollars, an increase of 18 per cent in comparison to the year 1977. In 1983 European countries as a whole accounted for more than two-thirds of the total and the EEC for more than half (60 per cent). In 1984 the Japanese alone invested 47 billion dollars in the USA. The great change in the direction of the flow of investments dates from

1980. From 1974 on, European investments in the United States were greater than American investments in Europe.

The Group of Thirty (a group of economists, bankers, directors of central banks and industrialists from several countries, set up by the Rockefeller Foundation under the Presidency up until the start of 1985, of Mr H.J. Witteveen, former President of the International Monetary Fund) conducted a study of international investments from the end of 1983 to the beginning of 1984. I do not want to quote too many figures, but a serious analysis of the facts helps us to understand the problems, and sometimes leads to solutions.

Without going too far back into the past, I will quote the net flow of direct investments, i.e., the difference between foreign investments at home and investments abroad (in billions of dollars) for each country or group of countries under consideration.

	United States	Europe	Japan	Developing Countries
1978	− 8.5	− 3.4	− 2.4	+ 7.3
1979	−14.6	− 8.3	− 2.9	+ 8.9
1980	− 5.6	− 6.7	− 2.1	+10.1
1981	+12.6	−24.0	− 4.7	+13.9
1982	+12.2	−13.0	− 4.9	+11.4

Source: Group of Thirty report on foreign investments.

I do not have the corresponding figures for 1983 and 1984, but it is certain that European and Japanese investments have continued to grow and that the United States will have a positive balance; in other words, foreigners have invested more in the USA than the Americans have invested abroad during these two years.

I would also like to show relevant figures for 1964–6:

203

	in billions of dollars	
	USA	Europe
1964	− 3.4	+ 0.8
1965	− 4.6	+ 0.7
1966	− 5.0	+ 1.0

One can see that even at that time the excess of foreign invest-ments in Europe over European investments abroad was very small. It is true that this positive balance essentially results from American investments, but it is so low that a scientific study of the facts should not lead to talk of the Americanization of Europe.

It is interesting to note that many European governments are worried this year by the fall in American investments in Europe; moreover, after a meeting of the Council of Ministers held in June 1985 the spokesman for the French government announced that a scheme would be set up to study means of increasing foreign investment in France. It was M. Deferre, the Minister of Planning, who had proposed this action. I am absolutely in favour of foreign investment in France since it can and must create employment, but it affords me a certain amount of amusement to see how economic thinking has come round in fifteen years. In 1965 I was publicly criticized for suggesting that we should accept American investment in France, and in 1967 I was castigated by the French Consul-General in New York when I had the audacity to propose that the French should invest in the United States. I derive some satisfaction from knowing that I was right all along, although I am sure there will still be some people who will contradict me and say I was wrong. I shall confidently leave the future to judge.

To finish, I should add that gross investments, that is total investments in one country or in a region, have also changed considerably. In 1965 and 1966 foreign investments in Europe were about six times greater than foreign investments in the USA.

In 1979 foreign investments in the United States rose to 9,730 million dollars, and foreign investments in Europe to $9,403 million. This turn-around in the trend was scarcely noticed.

HOW TO EXPLAIN THE DEVELOPMENT
OF MULTINATIONAL COMPANIES

Amongst the economic explanations given, I will put forward two:

1. The one given by R. Vernon who links international investment to the life of a product internationally. It is no longer exact in an epoch when technology is spreading very rapidly.

2. The one given by Professor Michalet for whom a system of world economy takes the place of an ensemble of international relations, generally defined in terms of the circulation of merchandise. The multinational would be the product of such a system of world economy since it causes delocalization, but it would also be its agent since its activities represent its real practical application.

For my part I am more receptive to a thesis, promulgated by modern economic theory, which is founded on an explanation of the origins of the company. This thesis, expressed notably by Ronald Coase in 1947 (and it seems to me important to quote an economist who was a 'free marketeer' then), is as follows:

> If it was necessary to satisfy every individual demand by a series of elementary transactions then one would have to be ceaselessly negotiating, and to this end travelling about gathering information on the quality and the prices offered by the various suppliers of goods and services.
>
> Such activities are costly and the more complex the economy becomes the more complex they become, too. This is why it is necessary to form companies. The company appears as an organizing element in the market, indispensable to the production of complex goods: those whose cost would be too high if one had to have recourse to individual transactions at each

stage of production. The company then becomes the means of making savings for society as a whole.

At the level of the international market characterized by an increase in the number of exchanges, the multinational enterprise is the result of the same necessity. Its organization and its structure tend to reduce the cost of transactions, but *it must not be forgotten that the creation of multinational companies is not a recent phenomenon.*

Ever since the development of communications and transport, companies have emerged which sought the raw materials they needed beyond their own frontiers, and who to reduce costs or increase efficiency decided to participate in the extraction and development of natural resources and raw materials. Without going back to the sixteenth and seventeenth centuries, let us examine the factors that since the nineteenth century have caused certain companies to become multinational:

1. Knowledge of the markets. The company discovers that its goods and services are useful to foreign consumers. It therefore begins to export.

2. It then comes up against obstacles to the importation of its products and discovers that transport costs, added to customs duty, make it difficult for its products to compete on a foreign market. It therefore sets up the means to produce them within the foreign country.

3. The management of the company wants it to grow. Its national market is too small; hence its only possible source of growth is implantation abroad.

I know there are some who would reply to this by saying that, first, one must conquer the home market. Let us not forget, however, that given present demography some of these markets are saturated; moreover, this policy will lead to a protectionist attitude which is totally unrealistic nowadays.

4. To fight against competition from foreign goods on one's own national ground, one must operate on their terrain of origin.

5. Certain goods and services cannot be exported. They must be supplied on the spot. This is the case with industrial gases, banks and many other industries.

There are other reasons for the creation of multinationals, but the above already demonstrate that it is a question of a natural phenomenon and not of who-knows-what greed for power on the part of the company management. The multinational form of a company constitutes an extension of its pre-existing international dimension, which may be due either to the volume of its exports or to an international demand for the product manufactured. This natural development can be explained by the *liberalizing of foreign exchanges and the necessity for an international redeployment of industry*. It is a fact that, as international trade liberated itself through the action of common markets and negotiations on tariffs, more and more multinationals came into being.

It is also a fact that the multinationals are present in the developing countries and that they contribute to a new international distribution of work. But as they develop the multinationals shake up, disturb and call into question traditional structures. If one finds it difficult to see what benefits they have brought, it is easy to blame them for everything that goes wrong. The myths about their behaviour persist.

THE BEHAVIOUR OF THE
MULTINATIONAL COMPANIES

For example, in the industrialized countries as a whole the number of people who believe that the profits made by multinational companies are excessive has doubled since the early seventies: (1971: 26%; 1979: 51%). Further examples – according to a survey carried out by a French public opinion survey company in 1978, the French cited multinational companies as the principal cause of unemployment. (Employers and bankers came at the bottom of the list!) According to an important French daily newspaper, the multinationals are responsible for the traffic in blood in Brazil. The multinationals are also said to extract profits from speculative movements which in many cases they themselves have helped to create. The multinationals are a threat to national sovereignty. . . .

I would like to end this section by giving you briefly my opinion on some of these points.

Profits

First, like all businesses, multinational companies with private capital *must* make profits in order to survive. Profits are vital if the company wants to invest so as to remain competitive, retain the confidence of its shareholders and clients, and maintain employment levels. The volume of its transactions and profits are in proportion to the size of the company, but they are too often measured against those of companies whose activities are limited to their own national territories.

One of the most erroneous ideas current is that the multinationals try to make maximum profits in those countries where taxes on company profits are lowest. I have heard even very intelligent men say this. They were simply ignorant of economic realities, for there is no possibility of making profits unless one produces and sells. This is the reason why the bulk of investments are made where the markets are large.

The study carried out by the Group of Thirty, which I mentioned above, shows that 89.7 per cent of direct investments by industrial firms have been made in the countries where these businesses originated and in the other industrialized countries. Now it is a well-known fact that in all the industrialized countries, there are taxes of between 35 and 52 per cent on profits from industry and commerce.

Speculation

I am always surprised to hear people talking about speculation. There is risk, but most often it is the multinationals who run the risk of loss through changes in exchange rates. The running of a multinational company in no way resembles a series of manoeuvres on the Stock Exchange: funds are not raised from one day to the next. What is true, however, is that the size and spread of the company enables it to withstand currency fluctuations better than the small companies can. It may make gains, but it also suffers losses. It is stability, not fluctuation of currencies, that the heads of multinational enterprises desire.

Since the end of 1980 we have been living through a period in which exchange rates have changed too swiftly, and this has served as a clear example. The rise of the dollar has had a serious impact on the American multinationals. Consolidated accounting is done in the currency of the parent company's country. In the case of the American companies the turnover and profits of the subsidiaries, converted into dollars, are very much below real economic performance. I was particularly struck by the fact that while the turnover of IBM Italy, when quoted in lire, grew by 26 per cent in 1983 as compared to 1982, the same turnover, converted into dollars, gave a zero growth rate. By contrast, over the last two or three years the results of European multinationals which have major subsidiaries in the USA look good when expressed in French francs, Swiss francs or even German marks.

One must realize, nevertheless, that the companies can do nothing to adjust the calculation of their turnover as expressed in the currency of the country where Head Office is sited. In the IBM group's consolidated results, the turnover for IBM France expressed in dollars equals the turnover in francs divided by the average current rate of the dollar, just as the turnover for Saint-Gobain's American subsidiary, Certain Teed, is X number of dollars multiplied by the average rate of the franc for the year.

It is true that as far as their funds are concerned, the multinationals can advance or delay certain payments between

INSIDE IBM

subsidiaries or between the parent company and the subsidiaries, and that one of the responsibilities of the treasurer's department is to avoid losses through exchange. What is too often forgotten is that these advances or delays can only be done on real transactions in which products or loans are transferred, and the sum total of these represents only a very small part of the movement of international funds.

Responsible firms do not speculate; they do not profit from variations in the exchange rate unless they are banks or central banks for whom this is a normal part of their professional dealings.

Employment

Implanting a multinational in a new country immediately creates employment. It also creates it indirectly by the practice of subcontracting, or by giving a boost to the rest of the economy. A study carried out by G. Hawkins in the United States underlines such positive effects; thus from 1965 to 1973, the multinationals had an employment growth rate which was 75 per cent higher than that of the other American companies.

In addition multinationals generate a substantial trading surplus and so contribute to achieving an equilibrium in external trade. The study also emphasizes the difficulty of knowing whether or not the multinationals reduce employment in their countries of origin. At worse, a balance is established, which leads me to agree with Professor Galbraith's opinion when he says that we must look elsewhere for the causes of unemployment.

On a micro-economic level, it is easy to demonstrate that an American company whose cost prices are too high to compete with foreign firms selling identical products in the USA, and which therefore decides to manufacture in Hong Kong or Taiwan goods which will subsequently be imported into the United States, creates unemployment in its own country. I am not in favour of export platforms and I believe that it is possible to achieve competitive cost prices on condition that one makes the investments necessary to obtain higher productivity. However, in the extreme case of manufacturing abroad to sell locally, what are the choices?

1. To be competitive by manufacturing abroad and still selling on the home market, which will wipe out jobs in manufacturing but maintain a marketing network, all the administrative posts, all the company's services, and allow dividends to be paid to shareholders.

2. Not to be competitive, which leads to failure, destroys the marketing network, penalizes the shareholders and damages the company's image.

3. To be modern. That is to say: automate, robotize, increase productivity by reducing the proportion of labour costs in the total expenditure so as to compete with products coming from countries where labour costs are low.

4. Lastly, appeal to the government to protect local industries by raising customs barriers or by introducing controls which will prevent the import of foreign goods. This is protectionism, whose harmful long-term effects are apparent to anyone who has studied trading exchanges over the last eighty-five years.

The best solution is obvious. It is the third. It is by making considerable investments in modernizing production that companies such as IBM, Chrysler and Philip Morris succeed in resisting foreign competition in the United States. I do not choose the United States on account of my close links with that country, but because, with the present dollar exchange rate, it is the country which has the highest average hourly salary in the industrial world. When a company also has very advanced social policy and social practices and when one of them is full employment as in the case of IBM, it is easy to imagine the extent to which the management must make long-term forecasts and take risks.

The closure of a textile or an automobile factory is at once spectacular and dramatic. I know the misery of men and women who are unemployed and would really like to work. But we have long ago entered the post-industrial era, and the proportion of the population active in the service sector is growing constantly. The service industries are less susceptible than others to foreign competition, perhaps not at the level of remuneration on capital but certainly as far as employment is concerned. A shop situated in the United States may belong to a French or a German company, but the staff with the possible exception of the manager will be American. We find the same situation in banks, insurance companies and many other firms. In the long term, therefore, we need not be as uneasy as we are now about the international redistribution of work.

I know that what I am broaching here is not an easy or a popular viewpoint, because unemployed men and women are suffering now, today. What I am trying to say is that, knowing the problem will disappear one day, we must have sufficient imagination to prepare as from today (it should have been yesterday, but when I spoke about this ten years ago, nobody would listen) for society's adaptation to the future. Above all this demands an inventory made up by businesses of the jobs that will require filling in five or six years' time, and a considerable effort to set up training, which they must undertake on behalf of their employees whose jobs have disappeared, so as to give them a chance to retrain for the new tasks.

In suggesting this approach, I am not just airing theories. For thirty-six years, I have worked in a company that knew how to move on from the manufacture of mechanical parts and electric circuits to making the most sophisticated electronic components. The lathe-workers, millers, toolmakers and unskilled workers whom I knew in my early working years, are today operating ion implanters, using electronic microscopes, controlling robots and utilizing computers to control production. In 1984 IBM France spent 11.2 per cent of its total salary expenses on permanent training!

Relations between multinationals and national governments

The multinationals have power but it is a power to manage, to be enterprising in business, and to invest or disinvest. Their power cannot be compared to the power of the State. The State alone decides the conditions under which a national or multinational company can operate within its territory. The success of a multi-national company depends on its capacity to adapt to a diversity of economic, political, social, linguistic and cultural climates. It must be integrated into the national environment and respond positively, as long as its own equilibrium is not threatened, to the imperatives of national industrial policies.

There is no lack of examples to show how far the multinational companies have co-operated with efforts at decentralization, industrial restructuring or the correcting of geographical imbalances. The fact that more and more heads of subsidiaries are nationals of the country concerned only serves to confirm this.

It is false to say that the multinational company threatens the sovereignty of the State because it will do away with the notion of frontiers: the activities of its subsidiaries are subject to the laws of the countries in which they are implanted, and the circulation of trade which they stimulate is carried on in accordance with international trading regulations.

The host country can intervene in the multinational's exploitation. It can expropriate; it can insist on nationals being appointed to managerial positions, arbitrarily fix prices, demand discriminatory taxes on profits, ban the repatriation of capital. On the other hand, like all other exporting businesses, the multinational benefits from the relative disappearance of economic frontiers, which have nothing whatever to do with political frontiers.

You, too, will often have heard the absurd argument I have heard in which the power of the multinationals is compared to that of governments. This argument takes different forms. One of them is that given the fact General Motors' turnover is higher than the gross national product of Portugal, therefore General Motors must be more powerful than the Portuguese government. Absurd! One cannot compare the power of a State to that of a business company, especially when its turnover is largely achieved beyond the frontiers of this State. At the least one should compare it to the sum of revenues in all the countries in which it is active, and even then this would be a specious argument. When the governments of Cuba, Vietnam and Iran decided to seize all IBM's property, what could we do? Ask politely that they should pay us some compensation, and above all allow all those employees who so desired to leave the country. The only real power a multinational has is to decide to stop further investments or – which is more serious and very difficult – to start pulling out investments.

Another form of the same argument is: look what ITT has done in Chile. I have had to answer this question every time I have lectured on the multinationals. Quite simply, this was a matter concerning *one* multinational in *one* country. I could cite purely national companies, in France or elsewhere which have behaved in the same way – and with what result? In Chile the ITT subsidiary was nationalized. Simultaneously, Mr Allende himself signed an agreement with IBM allowing the company to continue operating as in the past, to import spare parts, and send dividends to the parent company.

The third form is the distortion of one item of information. For example, Nestlé supplied powdered milk to the underdeveloped countries. They were perhaps 'developing', but at the time when the incidents occurred they were really underdeveloped. This was perhaps the fault of the West, of the old colonial powers, but was a fact nonetheless. Mothers of families used water to convert the powder into milk and this water was not always clean. Some children died. Nothing is more tragic than the deaths of children but how many would have died without the powdered milk? How many are dying this year in Ethiopia or in the Sudan? It is no longer the fault of Nestlé but of the drought (though it is true that the drought in Africa is multinational). Here again a group of enemies banded together to attack Nestlé. Nestlé took the initiative and brought an action against them. At the end of my lectures people have frequently said to me: 'How can you defend the multinationals, when a group of Swiss – and therefore reasonable, democratic people – are bringing a lawsuit against Nestlé?' Now, in that wonderful country of Switzerland, there is the usual distribution of reasonable and unreasonable people; as for the lawsuit, it is the other way round.

214

The transfer of knowledge

The process of development demands a transfer of knowledge. If you consider technological transfers alone, you are leaving aside a large part of what makes the acceptance of new technologies possible. There are several reasons for the somewhat mediocre results obtained by international aid programmes. One of these is that funds are often handed over to the heads of developing countries who do not always make optimum use of them. Even supposing there is not much corruption, there is sometimes conflict between good economic utilization of outside aid and the country's political objectives.

Ways to aid development can begin by reducing the suffering of the people: medical care and food can be given and perhaps both will be indispensable. But as the Chinese proverb says: 'Give a man a fish and he will make a meal of it; teach him to fish and you will nourish him for life.' To my mind the really indispensable aid which should take priority is the development of education and whatever material infrastructure is necessary to facilitate it. It requires a great deal of diplomacy to help the countries which receive aid to decide on their priorities because their civil service and their governments believe they know better than anyone else what they need, and they often allow themselves to be seduced by the allure of advanced technologies which seem to them prestigious, but which will not improve the people's standard of living.

Installing a factory, even in a traditional industry such as iron and steel or petrochemicals, must begin with the training of personnel. If the country has no engineers, technicians and well-trained skilled workers, such a factory will always remain dependent on foreign executives. Now in order to have employees with the relevant qualifications, one must begin with a sound system of primary and secondary education. The 'take-off' of many African countries has been held back by their high illiteracy rates; the difficulty of promoting Blacks in South Africa springs from the fact that very few of them can follow higher courses of study.

After education, the transfer of knowledge must take the form of transfer of 'know-how'. It is here that the multinationals can, and must, play an important role. Even if they have invested solely in commercial activities, they must teach their local employees modern management methods and the trades involved in maintenance, and they must establish permanent opportunities for further education.

If, in addition, they are conscious of their responsibilities towards 'society', they will play an active role in improving the environment. In this domain, too, certain enemies of the multinationals put up a specious argument, saying: 'The multinationals introduce inequalities among the population, for their employees are treated better than those of local companies.' This is a refrain to do with inequality in poverty; I believe, by contrast, that it is a good thing to have spurs forward, and that development requires the creation of a 'middle class'. The transfer of technology comes later. Is it not reasonable to suppose that successful multinationals have good products or offer good services? As soon as they set up business in a new country they want to put the same products or services, adapted to local needs, on the market. One cannot ask them to develop what is sometimes called 'adequate technology' unless the number of products to be sold is very large. In cases where the products are the same as in the country of origin, the technological level of the people who are to manufacture them locally must be the same as that of employees in the parent establishment. If the company also has laboratories abroad, and their product research is to be utilized throughout the world, it would be impossible to have a technological gap existing between them and the labs of the parent company.

In modern science and technology we speak more and more of centres of excellence. The multinationals contribute to the creation of such centres. From the outset, they send engineers and scientists to a host country to transmit their own knowledge to their colleagues there, and immediately create a 'snowball' effect, culminating in the happy moment when the pupils equal and then overtake their teachers and go on to help the parent company to progress. This is the fastest way to overcome technological backwardness, and it is the principal reason why – except in very rare cases – I do not believe in the much touted theory of 'adequate technology'.

To conclude these few remarks I would like to say that experience shows clearly that reprehensible acts do not benefit a multinational company, and that it takes time to shake off the bad image and all the consequent ill-effects such acts create. What must be admitted is that the multinationals have always been ahead of their time. They open the way to new economic and social relations, and by virtue of these pose problems of adaptation.

My anxiety: protectionism

I do not know whether anyone has yet written a book on 'Protectionism from Antiquity to the Present Day' (after all, protectionism has existed for a very long time), but it would make a very good subject. It is curious to note, moreover, that people generally talk about *protectionism in other countries.*

Since World War I the world economy has been unhealthy. The first great crisis was the Wall Street Crash at the beginning of the thirties. One of the legislators' reactions to the rise in unemployment was simple and classic: 'We shall cease to import and so we shall make work for our fellow countrymen.' And it was the consequent Smoot Hawley Act which, as even the most isolationist Americans agree today, aggravated the disaster. The European nations reacted briskly by setting up all sorts of barriers to prevent American products from crossing their frontiers and there was a significant drop in world trade.

Europe went through its period of protectionism after World War II but the Marshall Plan prevented it from becoming too serious. In France we had the famous 1945 rulings on the control of export–import; the IMEX agreements compelled businesses to export twice as much as they imported. The growth we experienced during the years 1950 to 1973, when Europe was going through a period of full employment, enabled us to forget them.

The American recession of 1971 provoked a reaction from the unions, and the proposed Hartke-Burke Bill – a series of measures to reduce imports and reduce American investments abroad – was laid before the US Congress in September 1972. This proposed law was not passed, thanks partly to the action of ECAT (Economic Committee of American Trade). In spite of the absence of such a law, the net flow of foreign investments in Europe became negative for the first time in 1973. That of the United States rose from −8.6 billion dollars in 1973 to −4.3 in 1974. What provoked this proposed law was obvious; the increase in unemployment. The powerful American trade union, the AFL–CIO, had organized its lobbying well.

Every country has at some point or another taken up a protectionist stance. It is not an economic doctrine; it is a defensive reaction:

1. Up until the present day, when the balance of payments is negative, this has always entailed a weakening of the currency. There has been one exception to this rule – since 1980, the American trade balance has deteriorated more and more, while the dollar rose to its peak in February 1985.

2. A negative balance of trade means the country is importing more than it exports. Internal consumption continues to rise, unemployment increases, and some industries find themselves in trouble.

The years 1983 to 1985 have witnessed such a phenomenon accompanied by another, namely, the extraordinary growth in Japanese exports. Nor must we overlook the actions of consumer organizations. Being better-informed, consumers now demand the best products if not at rock-bottom prices then at least at prices offering a better performance/price ratio than available national products. The penetration of Japanese goods into numerous countries cannot be explained otherwise. The performances of some American and European industries, if we add high-quality marketing and sometimes uniqueness of product, can also be explained in this way.

Lastly, there is the problem of certain national industries which are not competitive as against other countries, because their cost structures have failed to adapt to the new conditions at work in international markets. When a country has a negative balance of payments, or a negative trading balance, the actions that can be taken immediately are limited:

1. Impose higher customs duties. This is not compatible with the GATT (General Agreement on Trade and Tariffs) and will provoke identical reactions from other countries.

2. Impose rulings and standards which will slow down imports. This was the case in Japan when they decided that American baseball bats represented a hazard to the players. Certain European food products cannot be imported into the United States either because they do not conform to norms established by the Food and Drug Administration, nor can French mustard be exported to Germany because it does not meet local standards!

3. Decide on a substantial devaluation. This is a dangerous weapon which gives only a temporary advantage, since the economy of each country depends on its imports. Lowering the exchange rate of the currency makes the national products competitive, but imports become more expensive, internal prices rise, inflation goes up, and at the end of two or three years the same problem reappears as before. It is difficult to solve anything by devaluing!

4. Negotiate import quotas with the exporting countries. This is a little like the safeguard clauses in the Common Market. This method has been applied to Japanese car manufacturers and to European steelmen, who accepted a limitation on their exports to the USA because the American iron and steel industries were at risk. But such a solution cannot be favourable to consumers.

When certain industries disappear, close their factories, or go bankrupt, unemployment rises. When American farmers do not sell successfully overseas or even within the United States, thousands of farms are compelled to cease growing crops and again unemployment rises. The same situation exists in Europe, and this leads one to conclude that the intensity of protectionist feeling is in direct proportion to the level of unemployment.

219

However, in the long term the opposite may be true. It is protectionism itself which can lead to a higher rate of unemployment, because it reduces consumption on the home market and this is harmful to the service industries which nowadays employ more than 55 per cent of the working population in all the industrialized countries.

When it comes to economic warfare protectionists are behind the times. The more important the services which create local employment are in terms of percentage of the gross national product, the less important the trade balance becomes in the life of the citizen. Let me make myself perfectly clear: I am a firm believer in exporting and investing abroad, and in putting on the market goods which can be sold everywhere. But I also believe, and for the moment it is no more than a strong intuition, that current econometric models do not sufficiently take into account changes in the distribution of the working population between the primary, secondary and tertiary sectors, and that the birth of the fourth – the information industry – has not been taken into account at all.

Since 1983 the United States has had a budget deficit of more than 190 billion dollars, a substantial negative trading balance, powerful lobbies seeking government protection for their industries, and a strong dollar which renders some of their products uncompetitive; but the rate of inflation is low, and unemployment has dropped since 1983, reaching 7.3 per cent in May 1985 which is a fairly low figure for this country. I do not know of any economic theory that could totally explain this situation. What has happened?

Taxes have been reduced and this has increased purchasing power and enabled leaders to explain to workers that they must be reasonable in their wage demands, since in any case their standard of living has improved. Interest rates have been reduced and this has made it possible for the building trade to construct 1,700,000 dwelling units in 1983 as against 800,000 in 1982.

Massive foreign investments in the United States have rendered the current balance of payments 'less negative' than the trading balance. Also there have been constant efforts on the part of the government to make the Japanese understand that they must open their frontiers. These efforts would be more effective, in my opinion, if they were multilateral, as Europe has the same problem with Japan.

The creation of employment in the service sector has accelerated. But, above all – and this is still not fully grasped in Europe – there has been a very advanced restructuring of American industry. Increased productivity has become fashionable. Employers, executives and employees have come to realize that manufacturing costs must be brought down. Wage agreements are now related to the rate of inflation during the previous year, being either equal to it or lower. Mechanization, automatization and robotization of all business and government functions are under way. The civil expenditure of the administration reached a ceiling in 1983. The proportion of government expenditure in the gross national product is 38 per cent as against 52.5 per cent in France. The striving for quality is beginning to bear fruit: in three years the maintenance costs on a Chrysler car after 20,000 miles have been cut by half; 90 per cent of the large computers delivered to clients by IBM were counted as having 'zero default' at the time of installation.

All this leads me to hope that protectionism will not become a dominant feature in American economic life. While some American senators and congressmen have allowed themselves to be swayed by the electorate – the farmers' lobby, for example – the President, himself, has taken up a very clear anti-protectionist position.

Europeans and the Japanese should be aware, nevertheless, that the Americans are struggling to safeguard certain industries, and that their most urgent concern is agriculture. They should also be aware that the industries whose output is only 60 or 70 per cent of their capacity on account of export difficulties (occasioned by high costs which make their products non-competitive against foreign goods) are making great efforts to win over public opinion. Advertisements in the press, on television, and in New York even on buses carry slogans like this: 'Buy clothes made by American trade unionists'. Candidates for election to

221

the Senate or the House of Representatives are influenced by the opinions of their electorate.

An opinion poll carried out by the *New York Times* and CBS television from 29 May to 2 June 1985 on the basis of a sample of 1,509 people, gave the following results:

> 47% think that international trade is damaging to the American economy.
>
> 74% believe that imports create unemployment.
>
> 76% think it is a good idea to limit imports.

Is it not desirable therefore that the European Commission and industries in European countries mount a massive campaign to explain themselves? For many years, and even in 1983, the USA's trading balance with countries in the Community was positive. This is not, however, because the USA had a deficit in 1984, because the dollar rate was too high for the Americans to take protectionist measures just at a time when the dollar fell!

And where do the multinationals come into all this? American multinationals involved in manufacturing industries are penalized by the rise of the dollar, which makes their consolidated results less good. In the case of protectionist measures, which would be unpleasant for both Japan and Europe, they know that their subsidiaries would suffer from the counter-measures which would be taken. Although they are 'patriots', they want to increase the size of their markets and they resent embargoes on certain sales. They are, in effect, the unbiased allies of the Europeans.

My hope: knowledge

The development of communications and of data processing have transformed the world. There is even a saturation of data and information. I am convinced that a rapid if not instantaneous look at economic results can at least lead to a serious analysis of the facts. One can always disagree over the interpretation of facts, but the more there are the more scientific analysis will take the place of emotionalism.

It is still possible to manipulate public opinion by selecting only those facts which support a pre-established thesis, while ignoring the facts which demolish it, but this is becoming less and less feasible. Perhaps this is why critics of the multinationals are becoming increasingly rare.

Slowly but surely, economic knowledge is progressing. In France one can observe how our citizens are becoming fonder and fonder of those business firms which create the riches that allow them to maintain or improve their standard of living. They now know that the heads of companies are responsible men and women. During my entire career the only problems that ever stopped me sleeping were human problems which I had to solve alone. The executive, who decides to reduce his staff and lay off his workers in order to save a firm, must also spend some pretty terrible nights. He has a difficult choice to make: to cause the suffering and unhappiness of 1,000 people so as to ensure the continued employment of 5,000 others or to do nothing, and two or three years later be forced to lay off 6,000 people because his business has gone bankrupt. But those who like to say 'I told you so' can always point out that he should have foreseen this earlier, and that there are ways of organizing one's work force in order to avoid such dramas.

A second reason for hope is that in all countries in the industrialized world the idea of profit is now better understood. It was an English Labour Prime Minister, Mr Callaghan, who was the first to say: 'No profits, no investments – no investments, no job-creation.' Chancellor Schmidt, a Social Democrat, said the same thing a little later.

Finally the imperative need to export and to invest abroad is better understood. The majority of French people realize that in order to improve our balance of payments we must export more and welcome foreign investments. Large scale exports and major investments are essentially due to multinational companies. One cannot rationally be *pro* exports and investments and *anti* the multinationals, unless one is prepared to choose a schizophrenic economic doctrine.

The 95,000 Europeans who work in the IBM subsidiaries in Europe demonstrate every day that they are in no way inferior to the Americans or the Japanese. The working methods and the style of management inspired by the mother-company in the United States have helped to achieve excellent results. American investments have made them possible.

Europe holds many trump cards. We must play them well and take care not to let our hands be idle. The multinationals have known better than other companies how to make use of these trump cards. At a time when the French government is putting forward the Eureka project, I think of all the efforts I have made over thirty-six years to get my European colleagues to demonstrate every day that they have no complexes. But while I am a French patriot (and not a chauvinist) and a confirmed European, I am also convinced that any important project which is not 'world-wide' in scope is bound to fail. Being strong consists not in rejecting others, but in working with them as equal partners.

11

The Joy of Leadership

The decision to reorganize the IBM World Trade Corporation was taken in April 1974. The subsidiaries were then employing 150,000 people, 32,400 of them in the factories. We had achieved two goals which were very close to my heart: in 1970 profits outside the United States had reached those of the parent company, and in 1974 the consolidated turnover of the World Trade Corporation caught up with that of IBM in the United States. It was necessary to set up the new organization as quickly as possible, but our major worry was finding satisfactory posts for all those who worked in the headquarters at 821 UN Plaza, where the staff was to be very rapidly reduced. The most difficult problem was placing the Americans; the Europeans, South Americans and Japanese could re-enter the IBM companies in their own countries without much difficulty.

A Task Force was formed whose sole mission was to find a job for each man or woman which would not create too many problems for their families, but this group did not have the authority to say to anyone, 'You will go to such and such a place and work at such and such a job.' Every week the organizing committee together with the president of our Americas–Far East Company reviewed suggestions. Some of our discussions were rather abrasive since in the redistribution everyone wanted the best men and women to join his own organization. Some precise rules were laid down. As some of my colleagues put it, we developed an 'algorithm of repartition':

1. The 'foreigners' had to return to their own countries or work in HQ near that country. For example, the French could return to IBM France or to IBM Europe (in Paris).

2. The non-executive Americans had to be placed in jobs in the US. This may not seem very democratic, but there were two reasons for proceeding in this way. In a sophisticated system of remuneration, there are all sorts of bonuses for expatriation – the lower the salary, the higher the percentage of the bonus or living expenses – there was therefore a problem of how much reorganization would cost. Secondly, the more willing the higher-ranking staff of a subsidiary are to accept foreign executives and specialists being integrated into the structure (whether it be a local company or HQ outside the United States), the more the office staff and the secretaries think – and with good cause – that there are people on the spot, within the company or outside it, who could equally well do the work.

3. The most difficult to redeploy were the talented men and women who held responsible positions. Ralph Pfeiffer and I fought to keep them with us and several times we had to call in our Chairman, Gil Jones, to arbitrate. I had one small advantage – many of the executives were very eager to spend a few years in Paris.

If I am rather insistent about the question of redeployment within an existing organization – and it was an established fact that we were committed to finding a satisfactory post for everyone – it is because this type of experience has been and continues to be a trauma for many companies. The rigidity enforced by our principle of never laying anyone off on economic grounds or on account of reorganization put a heavy constraint on the team who had to redistribute jobs, and on those of us who had to make drastic cuts. Also, on such occasions, one perceives that some employees who have settled into a rut and gone to sleep find few 'takers'. One can fight to keep someone; one can also fight to 'pass somebody on' to a neighbour within the company.

This activity lasted until June and in the end there remained only some fifteen difficult cases in which the Chairman had to make the decision. There were no dismissals, not even if someone had been offered a new job and turned it down.

I was happy with the outcome and I was very touched to see

that the employees as a whole were satisfied. Frank Cary and Gil Jones had had the idea of gathering all the personnel together to explain our deliberations to them, and at the same time say *au revoir* to me. I was extremely moved when I delivered my farewell message to the friends with whom I had worked for seven years, and I was happy to be able to thank them. At the end of my speech everyone stood up and applauded. I was bowled over by this, but I knew then that the operation had been successful.

It may seem a little childish or naïve of me to record this 'ovation', but the heads of business enterprises are very rarely rewarded for their dedication by such positive displays of affection. Nevertheless they need them; most of us need human warmth. Good results are gratifying, but if there are smiles as well and even appreciation it is much better.

Out of HQ staff, 185 Americans were preparing for the move to Paris. I will not speak about the workload this massive transfer imposed on our European HQ as well as the one in the US, for it was understood from the beginning that their assignments would last from two to four years and that we had to be as fair as possible with them. This was the time when what we called the 'mentor programme' was created. One manager in the corporation was put in charge of the careers of from one to three people sent overseas. He had to follow their progress, see them at least once a year, and find them a satisfactory job on their return. There were some hitches, but only a few given the number of people transferred. The main difficulty came from the dynamic nature of the company itself: the mentor assigned would be promoted or transferred and the new mentor would not know the people he was made responsible for.

I was part of the Paris group. At the end of July an appalling accident occurred. Dick Watson fell down a staircase and landed on his head on a marble floor. He was in a coma for several days before he died. I grieved deeply; from the first day I met him at Endicott in 1949, he had never ceased to offer me his very warm friendship. We often spoke French together, he loved our country, and those who worked closely with him knew what ambitions he had for the IBM World Trade Corporation. He was its creator and its inspiration.

At the end of July we moved out of Bronxville and sold the house where we had spent six marvellous years. My wife and I were somewhat saddened at the thought of leaving our daughter, Florence, in America; she had just married a young American doctor. We consoled ourselves with the thought that we would return often and that now we were going to be reunited with our parents, our eldest daughter, her husband, and our first granddaughter in France. We had decided to take a holiday in the Rockies, but this time we had neither the time nor the courage to do the whole trip by car. With Sylvie, François and Anne-Sophie, we took the plane to Denver, Colorado and remembered the happy times we'd enjoyed when we had travelled West with all five of our children. The three who were with us this time were happy to be making the trip, especially Sylvie and François, who were about to see again the landscapes they had loved so much during our first journey.

We hired a car and went first to Jenny Lake in Wyoming then up towards Montana. At Helena, the state capital, we read in the *Billings Gazette* next day that President Nixon had resigned. The article on this historic event was very short and I amused myself by counting the pages dedicated to Washington, the East, and the rest of the world. Out of thirty-two pages, I found only one and a half pages on anything happening outside Montana. And yet, like all the States in America, Montana has two senators. Once again, we understood why isolationism could be such a strong feeling in the United States, although the senators from States which have small populations are often among the best.

We continued driving North, crossing the Canadian border to visit the region around Lake Louise, the national park at Banff, then Calgary from where we caught the plane to New York. Two or three days later, we embarked on the *France*. The director of 'the French Line' delighted us by giving us the 'Ile-de-France' suite which had not been booked.

The voyage was far from being as pleasant as those we had made in past years. The French government, and perhaps the manage-

THE JOY OF LEADERSHIP

ment of the French Line, had decided to take the *France* out of
service because the increase in oil prices had made it unprofitable
to run her. We arrived at Le Havre, sad to think that our seventh
voyage on this magnificent liner would also be the last. Moreover, it
seemed to me that this situation was yet another proof that without
careful control of costs any business will go to the wall, and that
technocratic intervention will not save it.

Once more we set up house in our apartment on the rue
Alphonse-de-Neuville. Life resumed its normal course. Sylvie
began her professional career and made her debut at McKinzey,
François was enrolled for the final year at the *Lycée Louis-le-Grand*,
and Anne-Sophie found herself at the public school on rue Ampère where her brother and her three sisters had been before her.

I once again made my familiar way from the rue Alphonse-de-
Neuville to the *Cité du Retiro*. My new office was ready. Marilyn
Theisen who had been a wonderful secretary throughout my stay
in New York had arrived in Paris a few days earlier, and now as
my staff assistant already had everything organized. Her competence, her unfailing good humour, her feeling for human
relations had already convinced all those who would need to see
me that they would be very well-received.

From April to August there were a great many changes in top
management at IBM Europe. But once again at IBM, it was change
without revolution. No heads rolled. Frank Cummiskey was
President of IBM Europe and Kap Cassani Vice-President and
Managing Director. My return placed them under my authority,
but there was no difficulty. As President of IBM World Trade, I
already held 'a higher rank'; we knew and liked each other and, as
I believe in the value of a collegiate management, I reorganized –
once again. Frank became Administrator–Managing Director. Kap
became Managing Director, and we created the European Management Committee. We shared our responsibilities and the supervision of the various countries in which we operated. Functions
directly accountable to me were external relations; legal services;
organization and management of executive resources; the vice-
president of finances; the vice-president of operations in the
USSR; the vice-president of planning; and the scientific director.

It seemed to me that the chairman of a company had to occupy himself with everything which concerned the future, with development in the broadest sense of the term. External relations were the only function that did not come into this, but as we were in France and I was the only Frenchman in a team of three it seemed right for me to take this on.

It may seem rather odd that legal services were included in my personal brief. But it was not a question of a litigation service in the sense in which this was understood in the majority of French businesses. In 1973 the General Directorate IV of the Brussels Commission, the directorate responsible for applying the anti-trust laws of the Treaty of Rome (Articles 85 and 86), launched an enquiry into the activities and commercial practices of IBM in Europe. The American government for its part had started a lawsuit in 1969. The Commission did not want to lag behind and from the outset had frequent contact with the American Department of Justice. I felt that it was very important for Bartow Farr, our Vice-President in charge of legal matters, to be very close to me. I had to keep myself up-to-date on many of the details and I often visited Brussels.

We were a homogeneous organization which functioned well; since there was no longer an intermediary between IBM Europe and the corporation at Armonk, we had to prove we had the necessary competence. My boss was still Gil Jones who was Vice-Chairman (not to be confused with Vice-President). John Opel had been elected as President of the IBM Corporation.

In an earlier chapter I amused myself by listing the number of executives in terms of their nationality. At the time of this reorganization the 23 top posts in IBM Europe were occupied by: 8 Americans; 3 Frenchmen; 3 Swiss; 4 Germans; 2 Englishmen; 2 Italians and 1 Hungarian. One might react to these figures by saying there were a lot of Americans. I would reply that there were more Europeans, that this was a company of American origin and that the offices run by the Americans who had worked with me in New York had been transferred to Paris, and that it was at my request that they came. And I will ask the same question again: how many companies are there in the world which have a senior management responsible for almost $6 billion turnover in which only one-third are nationals of the country where the parent company is situated?

In our business we began to feel the harsh effects of the 1973 oil crisis. Just when our factories were in full production on the 370 systems, we began to notice a slight falling-off of orders. The European director of manufacturing, who made a daily appraisal of the orders received by the factories, warned me in time. In fact, every Friday when I was ready to leave for home, he would poke his rather sorrowful head round my door, but his eyes were sparkling all the same for he had found a solution. John Ciovacco was one of those great managers who notice problems in time, roll up their sleeves and search until they find one or more answers, and immediately go to see the boss if they consider that he can be of help.

In 1975 I had learned by experience what industrial redeployment meant, and now I profoundly felt how my instinctive hostility to the partisans of zero growth was justified. They were a little less loudmouthed than they had been in 1972.

Our plans showed that we were going to have a surplus of 2,000 people in our European factories caused by a fall in demand, but there could be no question of dismissing them. Our sub-contractors and suppliers were feeling the backlash. Nevertheless we had a very strict policy towards them: the orders we gave them were never meant to exceed 25 per cent of their total workload. (This was so that a drop in our own volume would not create too many problems for them.) But we did not have enough people in the purchasing departments to verify that this ratio of 25 per cent was regularly adhered to. They lost orders from other companies but did not tell us, and we discovered rather late that for some of them work for IBM represented 60 to 70 per cent of their total workload. Everything possible was done to warn them in time and let them reduce production slowly, but there were some painful situations of which I was kept informed every month.

We had recourse to the classic methods for finding jobs for the 2,000 factory employees we no longer needed. The American factories were having the same problem, but it was easier for them to resolve it thanks to the homogeneity of a huge market and the physical mobility of Americans. For us in Europe, languages and frontiers were obstacles, therefore we had to resolve the problem within each country. The measures taken were:

1. Total halt to staff recruitment, with the exception of what we call 'vitality hiring', i.e. taking on some young people every year, whatever the circumstances, so as to avoid a hiatus in the 'age-pyramid';

2. Non-replacement of personnel leaving the company, their jobs being filled by others from within the organization (but with a few exceptions, however, for what we call 'critical qualifications');

3. Reinforcement of the sales services;

4. Acceleration of certain internal data processing programmes which were dragging behind a little owing to a lack of sufficient numbers of programmers and analysts;

5. Acceleration of educational programmes, on the one hand to overcome some deficiencies, on the other to provide new qualifications for those who found themselves without specific jobs.

The difficulty in putting such programmes into effect are manifold. For example, if you have to redeploy a factory worker whose usual job has been testing a machine, and there is now a job as a sales engineer available, it is hard to offer him such a complete change of activity. To find a new job for each person in a redundant post therefore creates a succession of job redeployments: the tester becomes a maintenance engineer, the maintenance engineer becomes a systems engineer, the systems engineer becomes a salesman. To reintegrate 400 surplus workers in our French factories, 2,000 changes of job were necessary. That is to say, in one year more than 11 per cent of the workforce changed their activity and very often their place of work as well.

In any case we demonstrated that redeployment is possible. There were some tears and some gnashing of teeth, but the results were good; the morale survey made in 1976 was the best to date and in the numerous conversations I had with my associates in the factories, I noted with appreciation that they were grateful to the company in spite of all the difficulties they had undergone, especially those caused by changes in work locations. For me, this was yet another proof of the fact that liberalism is not 'wild'.

At the end of 1975 the total manpower of IBM was 288,000 as against 292,000 in 1974. In spite of the crisis, turnover had risen from 12.7 billion dollars in 1974 to 14.4 billion in 1975. Our engineers kept up their performance, and in particular announced the laser 3800 printer, capable of printing 13,360 lines per minute.

I have avoided saying too much about the performance of our equipment. Perhaps this is the moment to mention it for there is no other industry which has seen such rapid progress in the price–performance ratio. Furthermore, such progress was one of IBM's best defences in its anti-trust trials since constantly giving more, at a lower price, is not exactly the attitude of a monopoly! Without going back to 1948 and the early days of electronics, the following table will give a good idea of the truly enormous leap forward that had been made.

The table shows the time and cost of execution of a set number of operations in data processing. It involves a combination of 1,700 typical operations which call upon millions of instructions in a sample of applications. (Costs given are those of the period without adjustment for inflation.)

	1955	1960	1965	1975
Time of execution	375 seconds	47 seconds	29 seconds	4 seconds
Cost	14.54 dollars	2.48 dollars	0.47 dollars	0.20 dollars
Technology	Electronic tubes	Transistors	Microcircuits	Monolithic memories and logic circuits
	Magnetic cores	Channels	Memory discs	
	Magnetic tapes	More rapid cores and tapes	More rapid cores and tapes	Virtual machines
	Magnetic drums			More rapid memory discs

Control programmes can be shown to have developed almost as fast. In twenty years the speed of execution of the same operations was multiplied by ninety-four, the cost divided by about seventy.

The new reorganization altered my travelling schedules considerably. Frank Cummiskey and Kap Cassani, and their regional directors, spent a lot of time visiting the subsidiaries; I spent more time in the United States: seventy-three days in 1975 as against fifty-nine in the other countries in my territory (France excluded).

In March 1975 my wife accompanied me on a journey to the Middle East. There had been no 'family dinners' held in these countries for a long time and four were now organized in Cairo, Jeddah, Dhahran and Kuwait. We were thus able to meet all IBM's employees and their husbands and wives. I must admit that the dinner organized in Cairo in an immense tent set up at the foot of the pyramids and with magnificent entertainment laid on – I strained my back trying to imitate the whirling dervishes – made a great impression on both of us. So did the povery in this country. Even the IBM office in Cairo had a poverty-stricken look; I spent quite a time with the manager, who was a Frenchman, explaining to him that a lick of paint would improve the working environment. For me this was still further confirmation of the need for visits to local offices from outsiders who are not influenced by the local situation. A fresh eye sees things the accustomed eye misses. He replied that our offices were better kept than those of other companies and I explained that they had to be not merely better than the others, but up to, or at the very least approaching, the standards we had set throughout the world.

We also visited Beirut where the war was just beginning. I admired the courage of our Lebanese associates, not one of whom asked me to find him a post elsewhere. Later, at Jeddah, we were invited to lunch by IBM's agent, Sheik Ahmed Juffali. This was the first time this 'great lord' had ever invited women to a meal arranged at his home. I sat next to Mme Juffali who spoke faultless French.

During this trip I met a great many representatives of the government, the press and big business; I came home rather

234

depressed because I could see no early solution to the problems of the Middle East, although Iran was calm at the time. We returned from Beirut to Paris on 11 March. On our arrival at the airport, we learned that our second granddaughter, Marion, had been born the previous night. Our daughter, Christine, had waited until her mother came home!

In June the IBM education centre at la Hulpe, near Waterloo, was inaugurated. It was to be called the Arthur K. Watson Education centre. Our colleagues had a tactful idea: the day chosen for the inauguration was 18 June, the anniversary of the battle of Waterloo. A week later I went back there for a second inauguration held for the press and general public; at dinner, the main dish was *beef Wellington*! Well, really . . .! We had grouped together on one campus all the educational institutes we had in Europe. It was an instant success and because of this centre – and the EEC Commission – Brussels became a very busy place for us.

From 8–22 February 1976 Françoise and I enjoyed the most pleasant business trip I can remember in Africa. Frank Cary, Gil Jones, Nick Katzenbach and their wives asked us, together with Gérard Lefort (Managing Director for the Middle East and English-speaking Africa) and his wife, to accompany them. First stage: Paris–Abidjan–Freetown–Lusaka. We met all the staff at these IBM offices. Nick Katzenbach, who had been the most active US Attorney General in the cause of desegregation, was delighted to see that our local branch offices were staffed mainly by Blacks.

During a meeting at Abidjan on the Ivory Coast Frank Cary made a speech to the staff in English. He asked me to translate. This made me realize the degree of skill required by interpreters at international meetings. I remembered the Italian phrase *Tradutore, Traditore* – the translator is a traitor – and I was more aware than Frank was as to how these French-educated employees might react. When I translated they laughed several times. After the meeting Frank said to me, half in jest, half in earnest, 'I think you must have added something, because I didn't say anything funny.'

Our manager in Lusaka (Zambia) was the former governor of the central bank, and I found it rather amusing to use banknotes signed by the manager of one of IBM's smallest offices. We had lunch with President Kaunda and attended a reception with members of the government, during which my Gaullist wife was outraged at the ignorance or prejudice of these officials in regard to France. We spent the weekend in President Kaunda's house in the bush which he had opened specially for us, and enjoyed a two day photo-safari – a marvellous experience.

Then we flew over the Victoria Falls and went to Cape Town, Johannesburg and Pretoria. One half of our group also went to Durban. We visited the black township of Soweto and met some Chiefs of the Homelands, including Chief Buthelezy. Gérard Lefort and I had spent some time in South Africa before this trip and so knew what to expect but, for our American friends, it was a great shock. Our manager in South Africa, Jack Clarke, was remarkably calm and courageous. It is a culture shock for a Westerner to spend several days in South Africa, and to meet plenty of important people there, including the Prime Minister. Almost all the members of our group arrived with the firm intention of telling members of the government that, if the policy of apartheid was not abandoned, relations with the United States would become very difficult. We met several black chiefs who explained to us that a halt to new American investment, or disinvestment, would be disastrous for the black population.

We left the country with the conviction that a company such as ours must do everything in its power to promote the welfare of the Blacks, the Coloureds and the Indians, to drive apartheid into a corner, adhere to the principles of the Reverend Sullivan and be an example to others. Already at that time our black employees were receiving the same salary for the same job as the Whites, which was not a common thing in the country. In 1976 IBM South Africa had already given considerable support to many educational projects for Blacks: a Centre for Technical Studies in Soweto, a secretarial school, the preparation of a vast aid programme for science teachers, and a supply of videoscopes to enable experiments to be shown to the pupils. We were also drawing up a project aimed at creating a commercial school in co-operation with the US Chamber of Commerce. We left, however, with feelings of great sorrow and anxiety. Improvements would come very slowly, and the ability of any company to change things is limited.

We returned via Windhoek (Namibia) and Douala (Cameroun), then spent two days in Marrakesh which seemed to us a haven of peace. While mentioning Douala, I cannot resist recounting an incident that happened there in 1975. I have already explained how we had to fill all vacant posts from within the company to ensure the redeployment of surplus personnel in manufacturing. A 'manpower committee' had been created at Armonk and we had to submit to them all applications for the employment of staff from outside the company. (In periods of crisis, companies have a tendency to recentralize.) I sent a telegram to the president of the committee: 'Request authority to employ a secretary from outside the company to fill vacancy in Douala office.' The reply arrived three days later: 'With the surplus staff you have at Montpellier, you must transfer a secretary from there to Douala.' I should add, by the way, that the offices in the majority of French-speaking African countries form part of IBM France, and that in our company yearbook offices are classified according to their subsidiaries (in this case IBM France) and in alphabetical order. I telephoned Armonk again and immediately obtained the authority I desired. A few days later, I questioned all the members of the committee. The only one who knew where Douala was, was the man I had telephoned!

I became more interested than ever in defending the 'good' multinationals. The more I learned about new countries, the more I realized how much multinationals could benefit them. I was particularly aware of this in South Africa. I had just replaced Mr Wilfrid Baumgartner as President of the Committee of Multinationals in the International Chamber of Commerce (ICC). I made some slight changes in the methods of the ICC Committee and tried to organize short and to the point meetings. Few heads of French-origin multinationals attended. How sad to see a country in which the representatives of free enterprise, warped by decades of a planned economy, are ready to rearrange their timetables to hang on to the coat-tails – or (with due respect) the skirts – of a minister who can open doors for them, but who will not make the slightest effort to attend a meeting of their peers from other countries, even if this meeting has been planned well in advance.

Autumn 1976 was very sad for us. My parents-in-law returned from a holiday spent in the Dordogne at the home of their friends, the Seilers (Hans is a great painter). Papy, my father-in-law, was not well. On Thursday October 1st, he dined with us on the rue Alphonse-de-Neuville. The following weekend we went to our house in the country. On the Sunday morning my brother-in-law, André Feron, telephoned: 'Papy is dead.' We rushed to Chennevières. My mother-in-law was distraught. Fifty-three years of marriage and a very happy life had been cut off for her at one blow. We were all deeply distressed. My father-in-law had always been extremely affectionate towards me and we had had a great many very frank discussions; he was a man from northern France who spoke simply and to the point.

My father-in-law was the first of our four parents to leave us and it was a painful shock. For the first time it was our generation, my brother-in-law André Feron and myself, who had to take on the sad responsibilities that follow a bereavement in the family.

1976 was also the year of the bicentenary of the founding of the United States. IBM presented an exhibition called 'The world of Franklin and Jefferson'. Many Franco-American events took place and the Franco-American Chamber of Commerce played an important part in them. Its President, Maurice Blin, hit on the idea of sending some of its members to lecture on modern France in several cities in the USA. I was responsible for a meeting in Philadelphia; the theme of my lecture was 'Modern France' and Franco-American ties. At that particular moment the French government and the management of Air France were fighting for landing rights for Concorde at Kennedy Airport in New York. I ended my talk with a quotation from Emerson, 'Good Americans, when they die, go to Paris,' and then added, 'I hope you will come and visit us *before* you die, and that you will make the flight in three hours and thirty-five minutes' — the time it took Concorde to make the New York–Paris crossing.

It was also in 1976 that the *Enterprise*, the first space shuttle, made its debut. It was equipped with IBM computers. It was not the first time special products had been manufactured by IBM for NASA or other American government agencies. The control rooms for the launching of NASA rockets had long been equipped with IBM computers, as had air traffic control. Amongst other special products were the System/4 Pi, a small computer of great reliability developed in 1966, which has been fitted in the space shuttle and also in some aircraft of the American Air Force; a digital sonar system for the Navy's submarines; the French air defence system, STRIDA, developed and constructed, as far as the data processing equipment is concerned, by the military division of IBM France.

The Federal Systems Division, responsible for answering calls for tenders from the US Administration, developed the products and also the software for civil and military use. It should be said, however, that this division was only responsible for a small percentage of the group's total activities. Those who have explained IBM's success as being the result of technological spin-offs from work done for the American defence establishment are very wide of the mark.

Business had picked up. New models of the 370 were announced; our first word processor was introduced on to the market. Our lawyers had not been idle and several private lawsuits were successfully terminated.

It had been two years since we had had a major reorganization. Well, never mind, a new International Division was now created for the small systems; its HQ was at White Plains, New York. I had fought for over a year against this type of organization being applied to IBM Europe. Our operations were organized geographically by countries and I was convinced that the top management in France, in Germany, in the UK, in Italy and in other countries should be in charge of all operations. In relation to sales it was a good thing for our clients to deal with only one face. Our Chairman, however, was convinced that the example of General Motors with its various divisions – Chevrolet, Pontiac, Buick, Oldsmobile and Cadillac – was a good model.

I fought vehemently and gained some concessions: the treasury, personnel, relations with governments, would still be controlled by the president of the subsidiary. In the field this type of organization created a lot of problems since clients found it hard to understand how two IBM salesmen could propose different technical solutions to the same problem. However, thanks to good will all round, assisted by several high-level arbitrations, it did not work out too badly. Frank Cummiskey returned to the United States to take on the presidency of the new division and was replaced on our European Board of Management by Michel Faucon.

This experience nevertheless confirmed the risks of bureaucracy, and more particularly the risk of a breakdown in communications from the bottom up in very large organizations. When we visited provincial branches in France or in other European countries, we swapped 'war stories'. Such and such a client had chosen the competitor's equipment because he couldn't make up his mind which of the two IBM solutions to go for. I told Frank Cary about this and he assured me that the problem did not exist in the US. I then paid several visits to sales offices in the States, in Nashville, Tennessee for example, and found the same problem. But Nashville is a long way from Armonk and the intermediate echelons had either found a solution to the problem or swept it under the carpet. I must acknowledge all the same that this kind of organization allowed a section of management to concentrate on the products at the lower end of the range; in spite of some hitches the total number of orders, and the growth in the number of new clients, were higher than they would have been with the old organization.

I felt very much at ease in my work; the years followed one after another punctuated by the announcement of new products. 1977 saw the birth of a new family of computers, the 3031–3032–3033, which were even quicker and had larger memory capacities, denser integrated circuits, and a better price–performance ratio than their predecessors. The Typewriter Division, which had become the Office Machines Division, introduced System 6. We had entered the field of office automation. IBM won some new lawsuits. And for the first time in the company's history, we stopped operations in one country. This happened in India where government demands were deemed unacceptable.

Each year was also marked by improvements in our personnel policies. In 1977, for example, a plan for the reinvestment of dividends was set up.

On 30 March 1978, Frank Cary and John Opel asked me to return to the United States to join the management committee. What an astounding offer, but I asked for time to reflect. I was very keen to accept, because it would have meant a non-American joining the group at the summit for the first time, and this would be a demonstration of IBM's total multinationalism. Françoise and I talked it over for a long time. We had family problems: my mother-in-law was a widow; my parents were 78 years old; three of our children would in any case have to remain in Paris. We had very close friends in Paris and we loved our life in France, especially during the last two years since our country house was finished, and we had spent some very pleasant weekends there with all our loved ones. I was happy in my work and enjoyed great independence. Of all the posts I had held up till now, this was the one in which I could exert the greatest operational influence, and I was surrounded by an excellent team. However, this good team was an argument in favour of leaving. Kap Cassani was ready to step into my shoes, and since we had different styles of management he would no doubt do better than I had. Our children would prefer us to stay in Paris. By the evening we had still not reached a decision. Next morning my mother rang up. My father had had an infarct during the night which fortunately was not serious, but his ill-health tipped the balance. I telephoned John Opel to tell him of my refusal. He asked me to reflect on it until my next trip to the States. A few days later I was at Armonk. I explained my decision, which the extra time to think it over had done nothing to change. They were disappointed, and although they did not say so straight out I sensed they were thinking: 'These Frenchmen are not mobile! How can he turn down a promotion like this?'

Throughout the following years, I suffered a little each time one of my American colleagues joined the management committee. It was certainly not jealousy, but I could not tell anyone of the offer that had been made to me so I could say nothing to those Europeans, within IBM as well as outside, who said to me: 'You can see perfectly well that even IBM isn't really multinational!'

These years were marked by great technological advances. In 1978 System 38 was announced, as well as the first memory chip with 64,000 positions; in 1979 the thin film head which was to give IBM an incontestable lead in memory discs was manufactured and the first deliveries of the middle of the range, Systems 4300, the colour video screen 3279, new modems, and new dictation machines were made. The telephone electronic switch 1750 was announced in five European countries.

In 1980 John Opel became Chief Executive Officer. Frank Cary remained Chairman of the Board and after the retirement of Gil Jones, Dean McKay, a member of the Board of Directors, became my immediate boss. New products continued to appear on the market and a new family made its debut, the 3081–3082–3083. The 3081 had twice the internal speed of the 3033 and took up much less space. It was more powerful and smaller, thanks to new technology called the Thermo Conduction Module, which allowed 750,000 logic circuits to be assembled in the space of about one-tenth of a cubic metre.

In 1979–80 the division of information products (General Business Group) began a fundamental alteration in its methods of access to the market. IBM traditionally had always had salesmen and systems engineers in direct contact with clients. They studied the problems and the organization of data processing, then sent in their proposals; the maintenance engineers installed the equipment and the sales engineers helped the clients to set up programmes to use it.

For the equipment at the lower end of the range, this was a

costly method of selling, and, as there were never enough salesmen to explain our products to all their potential users, we missed a lot of sales. Advertising was very quickly developed, but it was inadequate for the very expensive products. Product centres were therefore opened, first in the USA, then in Europe. Twenty opened in 1979 alone where 'small' products could be demonstrated; in a lecture hall, one salesman could explain to fifteen or twenty potential customers what our equipment could do for them. This was the start of retail selling. This development in our marketing methods was not clearly understood by the outside world until the announcement of the PC micro-computer in 1981.

This was a great event in the world of data processing. The success of micro-computers, whether for use at home or in the office, for electronic games or serious work, was already great. The Atari and Apple machines were sold in great quantities, and the number of MIPS they represented became an important part of the power of the data processing installed. MIPS stands for a 'million instructions per second' and serves as a unit of measurement in comparing the machines against one another, and also for evaluating the processing power of the total number of computers installed. This rapid growth had been made possible by Motorola and Intel's production of micro-processors, which were the arithmetical and logical units of all these machines.

IBM had succeeded in presenting users with a very complete range of equipment, from the Systems 3 and 38 at the bottom of the range right through the 3031–3032 and 3033 to the series 3080 at the top of the range, and the corresponding software. The development laboratories had very full work schedules. Every time they drew up their development plans, a list of projects was presented in decreasing order of priority. The projects at the bottom of the list were not launched. This was the case with the micro-computer for some time.

Several of our executives, and I was among them, believed that we could not stand aside from a market which was developing so swiftly. However, the management committee came to the conclusion that we could not announce a micro-computer quickly if we used the normal process of development with all its stages of reviews and approvals. It was decided to create a new group charged with the development of a micro-computer, and with devising new methods for manufacturing and marketing it. Don Estridge, a talented engineer, was given this responsibility. He was told in so many words: 'We need a personal computer within one year; you have complete freedom to use the IBM components and sub-assemblies, or to buy from outside whatever will best suit the needs of the architecture you choose. You will not be subject to the normal rules of project reviews. You will have to prepare the initial manufacturing and suggest ways of marketing a product which is to be sold on a massive scale.' A year later in 1981 the PC was announced; the production line was ready and distribution outlets had been selected. It was a great success.

In the case of the World Trade Corporation, responsibility for studying the commercialization of the PC by the subsidiaries had been entrusted to the 'General Business Group International'. Frank Cummiskey, the President, had had the necessary studies carried out, but his conclusions were as follows:

1. This product, which has been developed very rapidly for the American market, cannot be sold in its present form in the majority of countries.

2. It would not be profitable.

3. We do not have retail distributors in every country *ergo* we cannot announce it.

I found these conclusions unacceptable since Europe at least needed the product just as much as the United States did. My colleagues on the European Management Committee and I began a series of lively discussions with Frank, and finally the company President, John Opel, arbitrated in our favour. After it was announced in the USA, we formed a group to launch the PC in Europe and begin its manufacture. And it was a success.

This demonstrated yet again that the data processing market is a world-wide market, and that the specific needs of each country must be taken into account from the very beginning of the development of a product or a programme. At the start this process takes time, it can delay the announcement of a product for a little while, but this delay is largely compensated for by the greater total volume sales achieved after two or three years.

The case of the PC also demonstrated that, to fight against bureaucratization which is to be feared in all very large enterprises, one must form what I call 'creativity cells' from time to time. If IBM has managed to remain agile (so agile a magazine article in America was headed: 'The elephant that can tap-dance'), it is because the general management has understood for some years now that it is necessary sometimes to create departments which are independent of the large divisions and exist like small businesses, under a boss who is directly responsible to someone on the management committee. Their structure must be flexible, the overall requirement must allow for variations from one unit to another.

The creation of specialized units had already begun long ago when divisions were first formed. In 1955, for example, the Typewriter Division was created, as well as the division for military products, which was later to become the Federal Systems Division, whose task is to develop, manufacture and sell special systems to the Federal government.

These divisions, these 'business units', have a common characteristic: they are profit centres with their own board of directors. They are, basically, smaller companies within the heart of the group. When one of these units has accomplished the assignment entrusted to it, it may be dissolved and absorbed into one of the divisions; when one of them continually loses money, beyond the date forecast for it to pay its way, or keeps asking the parent company for further investments, it is shut down. In such a case the personnel are redeployed in other company divisions.

In fact the IBM Group reproduces what happens in a regional or national economy. Entrepreneurs (directors) have new ideas: an enterprise is set up. Some grow very fast and are then 'acquired' by the Group and inserted into existing divisions, for their size will allow them to follow the normal procedures in future. Some will never get off the ground and will disappear. Others develop a useful product, but one which cannot be sold profitably by a company with high overheads and high salary costs; this product is then offered to another company for whom it may be a useful addition to their range and who will make it profitable because it will not add to their overheads or their marketing costs.

During the years 1974–81, top management in the United States, as in Europe, spent a lot of time embroiled with lawyers and judges. The case brought against IBM by the anti-trust division of the US Department of Justice had given some of our American competitors ideas; they thought they could prove that certain commercial or industrial actions on the part of IBM had reduced their own turnover or profits. In such cases the court can award the plaintiff three times the amount of damages suffered. As lawyers for the plaintiff can be remunerated in proportion to the sum the court decides to award, it may easily be imagined how intense and even brutal the counsels' pleading was. While the government's case was based on 'IBM's intention to monopolize the market', an allegation we never ceased to refute, the private suits were generally phrased as follows: 'IBM has launched a new product which makes ours obsolete, therefore IBM, by its actions, has affected our profits.' All these lawsuits ended with a victory for IBM or an agreement between the two parties.

In 1973: agreement with Control Data Corporation. For a limited period, we agreed to stop our service bureau activities and sell the Service Bureau Corporation to CDC.

1975: the telex case was settled without payment on either side. The hearing of the government case began in a New York court.

1976: the presentation of the government's complaint went on throughout the year. Lawsuits brought by Data Research Corporation, Memory Technology Inc., Reynolds Computer Corporation and VIP Systems Corporation were settled. A judge rejected the allegations of Symbolic Control Inc.

1977: the presentation of the government's case continued. One judge rejected the California Computer Products' complaint.

Another rejected that of Forro Precision Inc. A new judgement was called for in the Greyhound case.

1978: Xerox and IBM agreed to stop litigation, which eliminated twelve separate lawsuits in the USA and Canada. The Federal judge, Samuel Conti, decided in IBM's favour in the Memorex case. Memorex appealed.

1979: the government's lawsuit entered its tenth year. A federal judge, R.H. Schnacke, decided in IBM's favour in the Transamerica case. Calcomp lost on appeal. The Ninth Circuit Court of Appeal confirmed Judge Conti's decision in IBM's favour in the Memorex case.

I have mentioned only a few cases, but these are enough to show that in the United States one can do nothing without good lawyers. Our position was sound, but the qualities and experience of our Chief Lawyer and Vice-President, Nicholas de Belleville Katzenbach (I give him his full name here for he is a descendant of the Dr de Belleville who accompanied Napoleon to St Helena), his team, and the outside lawyer, Tom Barr, from the law firm Cravath Swaine and Moore, played a determining role, just as Frank Cary did from the point of view of management. Hundreds of people – lawyers, engineers, salesmen – helped them prepare the defence; millions of pages of diverse documents were gathered together and fed into computer memories. IBM developed the most sophisticated system of information retrieval that could be imagined.

On 19 December 1979 Dr Schlieder, Director of Competition at the Commission in Brussels, telephoned me to announce that he was sending a 'Statement of Objections'. In spite of the long discussions we had with the Commission's investigators, the demonstrations we gave showing the development of the equipment, the visits I paid to all the Commissioners and to two successive presidents of the Commission, we could not convince them that the complaints made to the Commission by two of our competitors, Amdahl and Memorex, were unfounded. We achieved only a small result from these efforts: at the beginning there had been four complaints, now only two remained. Ed Buhl and Chet

MacLaughlin, who succeeded one another as our European top lawyers, were going to have a slight surfeit of work. We organized a series of explanatory visits to the Commission and to the Common Market countries, whose representatives on the consultative committee were to explain their views to the Commission.

The Under-Secretary for Justice in the USA stopped the Department of Justice's case against IBM by declaring that the accusations were without foundation. The Commission in Brussels went ahead and did not come to a decision until August 1984: IBM undertook to change two of the marketing practices for which it had been taken to task.

The Statement of Objections altered my working schedule and I had to devote a great deal of energy to it. I felt that I was to blame, that I should have prevented its ever being issued, and, although he never said so, I had the distinct impression that Frank Cary was not very pleased at my failure.

Our relations with the subsidiaries were very good, thanks to the quality of their presidents, but also because almost all of them had spent several years in our HQ in the USA or in Paris. We formed a united group, aiming at common objectives. Like my colleagues, I applied the good old method of personal contact and I paid visits to a dozen countries regularly each year, as well as to five or six factories and laboratories. One or other of us attended every event that brought together a large number of the company's employees. The annual reunion in January, when we assemble all the employees from European HQ at the *Palais des Congrès* to present the results of the preceding year, speak about our objectives for the current year and reply to their questions, became a tradition.

However, IBM's growth provoked hostile reactions in several quarters. An English minister had this to say: 'IBM is marching through Europe like Napoleon,' to which I replied that there would be no Waterloo. Nonetheless it was important for us to improve our image. This task was entrusted to the 'communications' directors in the various countries and at HQ. Themes were chosen, the company's advertising was considerably stepped up, and I asked all the managers to make people understand what IBM was by attending international meetings and by giving as many lectures as possible to large audiences. I played a considerable part in this activity by accepting external duties, which meant that I spent a lot of weekends working – surrounded by my family who gathered together in our house in the country – and had to reduce my holiday-time annually.

At the end of each year we drew up a retrospective list of our various external activities, including our visits to foreign countries, with the aim of eliminating mistakes during the following year. In 1978, for example, I was travelling for 112 days, visited a dozen countries and eight factories and laboratories. I took part in five meetings of the International Chamber of Commerce and in thirty-seven conferences outside IBM. I chaired five IBM conventions, three employees' meetings and five programmes of internal education. I attended twenty-eight IBM meetings, made twenty-one speeches outside and twenty within the organization. I was interviewed four times and took part in three press conferences. I met the heads of sixty client companies and ninety-seven personalities from the world of politics. Anne-Sophie, who was fourteen, began to reproach me for my frequent absences and my wife continued to be the real head of the family.

I must quote the itineraries for this same year of some of my colleagues who also accepted the need for a 'higher visibility'. Paul Kofmehl logged up 101 days travelling time, ahead of Kap Cassani with ninety-seven. Kap Cassani visited two more countries than I did; Michel Faucon led the field by visiting fifteen countries. Kap visited ten factories and laboratories and gave eight lectures externally, thirteen to IBM colleagues. This is what it takes to change or create an image. One day during a meeting of managers John Opel said, 'You must become visible.' I could not resist adding a word to the résumé of our activities in 1978 which I sent him, 'Have we been visible enough?'

This effort to make ourselves understood bore fruit, and in the studies of large companies in which we regularly figured knowledge of IBM on the part of the general public, the decision-makers and members of parliament improved year by year. We tried to apply the golden rule of public relations – 'Do well, and let it be known.'

Attaining all our objectives in terms of growth, which we regularly categorized as tough but achievable; promoting men and women of merit; gathering together a competent team; fighting against economic nationalism; improving the company's image; explaining what benefits the multinationals can bring; fighting our battles in Brussels; struggling against the preferential treatment certain governments gave to our competitors; participating in social life, while at the same time maintaining family stability, were our principal concerns during this period. On the whole the results were good, thanks to the intelligence and hard work of all my colleagues.

But I had another worry, and I must admit that in this case I asserted my position as *primus inter pares*. From 1967 to 1974, during my stay in the United States, I had become very sensitive to the problems of equal opportunity, that is to say the avoidance of discrimination based on sex, race or nationality. IBM was committed to a big programme aimed at employing competent women, Blacks and Hispanics, and also to a dynamic promotion programme. Vin Learson, during his time as Chairman, had championed it and I had stuck closely to its objectives. Much as I am against egalitarianism, I am for equal opportunities, and my old hatred of racism reinforced this. Moreover, the fact I have four daughters out of my five children, three nieces out of five nephews and nieces, makes it easier for me to understand the problems women encounter in their professional lives.

On returning to Europe in 1974, however, I observed that while the laws were respected – equal pay for equal work – there was no large-scale effort to promote equal opportunities, especially where women were concerned. The racial problem scarcely existed in European countries. In the African countries the movement towards Africanization in our offices and subsidiaries was making good progress; in South Africa we were clearly the leaders in industry. In the United States I had seen that there were some women already holding important positions, such as Jane Cahill, who was Vice-President in charge of Communications. I had also noticed that there was a growing percentage of women in the sales force.

I therefore asked Michel Faucon, who amongst other things was in charge of Personnel, to appoint a manager who would be responsible for keeping an eye on the employment, training and promotion of women in all the subsidiaries. Mlle Diamant Calbour, who had been my assistant from 1964–7, took up this post in May 1975. Extremely competent, and with the healthy attitude that consists in helping women without being a rabid feminist, she was able to analyse the situation within a few months and make recommendations for plans of action.

It became apparent that the only countries where the percentage of women managers was high were those which some years earlier had found difficulty in recruiting systems engineers or salesmen, and had therefore 'condescended' to hire women graduates from good universities. This was the case in Italy, England and Finland. In other countries women were mainly engaged as factory employees, clerical workers and secretaries, and in general they did not have the necessary basic education to enable them to rise high in the hierarchy.

I very quickly realized that it would take time to catch up with the Americans, and that we would have to start by taking on women who had the same degrees that we insisted on with men. Therefore I decided to impose on each country a hiring quota for taking on women in the sales force. If, for example, Germany had a programme designed for one hundred student sales people, only seventy men could be employed, the other thirty students had to be women.

A number of programmes were developed to make male managers aware of this necessity. Every time a post fell vacant, I enquired which woman was ready or even 'almost' ready to take it. The system of replacement tables was revised to include women. The list identifying men of high potential was also extended to include women. Palpable progress was made and Kap Cassani, when he succeeded me, carried on and improved the system. But much remains to be done.

At the end of the summer during one of my trips to the United States, John Opel told me of the coming departure of Dean McKay, a member of the Board of Directors and my immediate boss, who was retiring. He suggested I think over the possibility of replacing him. Once again my family was faced with a difficult decision, but circumstances were now a little different. I knew that if we left for the United States it would only be for three years, since like all executives in the company I had to retire at sixty. The children were grown up and the eldest and her husband, both doctors, were living in Paris; François was about to go to the French Embassy in Washington to do his 'civil service', which for some young Frenchmen is an alternative to military service; Sylvie and her husband were in Paris; my father had made an excellent recovery. Our parents would be surrounded by their grand-children who were now responsible adults, by my mother's brother and his wife, and by very good friends. Could I once again say no?

I also realized that seven years in the same job is rather unusual at IBM, and that I was blocking the promotion of Kap Cassani who was my obvious successor. However, I did not want to make myself out to be better than I am; I would not have made a considerable personal sacrifice for the sole purpose of allowing a colleague, or even a very dear friend, to be promoted. It was my pride which led me to decide to go. I wanted to prove that it was possible for a European, a Frenchman, to reach the summit of an American multinational. And I must say that the hundreds of letters I received when my appointment was announced from colleagues and friends in Europe, Japan, Canada and Latin America, proved to me that my nomination to the management committee had pleased them immensely, and ... Kap Cassani was beaming.

By the time I left, the HQ of IBM Europe had grown. I am not particularly proud of the increase in manpower, but the dimensions of IBM Europe had changed from 1974 to 1981, and new activities had been started to take care of clients' needs and fulfil the exigencies of governments and the EEC Commission. In November 1981, among the thirty-four highest-ranking executives at IBM Europe, there were: 11 Frenchmen; 7 Americans; 4 Germans; 4 Englishmen; 3 Italians; 3 Swiss; 1 Canadian and 1 Dutchman.

The proportion of Europeans had therefore increased noticeably since 1974. Frank Cary and John Opel had been very helpful to me in bringing about this evolution. John went almost too far in his desire to entrust the management of IBM Europe to Europeans, and for some positions I had a lot of trouble arranging the transfer to Paris of Americans who in their own field were ahead of us. Nonetheless, we did employ a markedly higher percentage of French men and women and of 'locals' (people of various nationalities who had been engaged on the spot under French conditions of employment), as opposed to what the multinationals call the 'expatriates', who form a permanent part of the subsidiary of origin and spend only a short time abroad. We had reached our target: 50 per cent of the total workforce were either French or locals.

On 30 November my appointment to Armonk was announced; we flew to New York the same evening and the announcement was made in Paris on 1 December. The new team was set up without the slightest difficulty. For me it was easy to integrate myself into a management committee whose members I knew very well.

There was the usual ritual of departure; my wife had to see to everything! We had to leave Anne-Sophie behind as she was in the top class at her school and would have to wait until the end of the academic year to join us. As we prepared to move out, we decided to give up the lease on our flat in the rue Alphonse-de-Neuville where we had been very happy for nineteen years. We looked for an apartment in the New York area. Françoise found it hard to accept this new upheaval, but, as always, once the decision was made she put her whole heart into making it work. All the same she insisted that we live in New York itself rather

than in the suburbs. Her sadness, however, would be softened by
the joy of being once again close to her sister, to our second
daughter, Florence and our American son-in-law and their three
children, and to our son. We also promised our parents that we
would visit Paris very often, and we kept our word.

12

The Entry of Women into Professional Life

On 11 March 1672, the first performance of *Les Femmes Savantes* [Learned Women] was given at the Théâtre du Palais-Royal. Molière played the part of Chrysale. In a scene in Act II, he said:

> If she knoweth not the laws of Vaugelas, what matter,
> As long as she can cook and make good batter?
> What care I if, while chopping up her herbs,
> She muddles all the nouns up with the verbs?
> I'd rather far that she to vulgar words should stoop
> Than burn my meat or make too salt the soup.
> 'Tis good soup that I live on, not fair speech,
> And 'tis not to cook that Vaugelas doth teach,
> While Balzac and Malherbe, so clever with fine words,
> Were no doubt fools with pastries, pies and curds.

More than three hundred years later there are still a lot of men who look only for these same housewifely virtues in a woman; but they may be three centuries behind the times. In fact, the twentieth century may well be the age of the 'decolonization' of women. Nowadays there is a tendency to laugh at the suffragettes who were active in the early 1900s; they were, however, demanding a fundamental right, the right to vote and take part in political life. In many countries, they have acquired that right by now. In the same way women are entering more and more fully into the world of business, to such an extent that some people attribute the high rates of unemployment in Western countries to the rapid rise in the female working population. After centuries of subjugation, discrimination and injustice, we have reached a turning-point. Progress could continue but that is still far from being securely established.

If you study the question of women in society you will observe that male chauvinism has always existed. The first thing to ask yourself is why? We are no longer living in the age of the caveman, and today we can hardly claim that the muscular superiority of men justifies the superior nature of their position in society. But physical strength was certainly fundamental in primitive societies. And weapons, a typically masculine obsession, carried things a stage further. Armed with such elementary symbols of greater strength, men were able to ensure their mastery of all real power be it religious, judicial, economic or military.

Since the nineteenth century the predominant image of women has been one held by the middle classes, who assign to woman the essential domestic responsibilities – the care and upbringing of children, washing and ironing, cooking and housework. Today the depressing fact remains that since women gained access to the world of business, such stereotypes have followed them there, too. There are bosses or executives who treat their secretaries like servants, expecting them to bring them their coffee and be attentive to their 'little comforts'. A good many attitudes still need changing. Sometimes I wonder if any of us are truly liberated from these outdated notions and enduring stereotypes. The past continues to weigh us down. Why is it so difficult for us to have a healthy attitude and to recognize that women and men are equal and complementary?

There has of course been some change. Our image of love, for instance, has been transformed over the centuries. We smile nowadays at the sentimental dandies with slicked-down hair and their old-fashioned seductresses in films made in the twenties and thirties. Such change of outlook has primarily affected the world of work. In the industrially advanced countries it has manifested itself in the increase in the number of people working in and through automation, which renders physical strength unnecessary. Today we are in the era of the industries of knowledge.

It has been abundantly demonstrated – and it needed to be! – that women are the equals of men intellectually. Scientific studies of intelligence quotients show identical statistical distribution between men and women. The same applies to almost all psychological tests (aptitude tests, general knowledge, creativity, memory tests, etc.). This being so we must frankly ask ourselves why there is such a low percentage of women occupying managerial positions in both the private and public sectors?

The first reason, no doubt, relates to a well-known phenomenon: a group in power tries to protect its own position. This is what men have been doing for centuries. They want to keep the advantages they have acquired and consolidate their position of power. Inside every man Molière's Chrysale lies dormant. Thus the men who hold the reins of power invent a multitude of reasons why women are unfit for certain jobs. They say women are frequently absent from work owing to their fragility and to maternity leave. The truth is that the rate of absenteeism for any reason whatever in the USA (a country which produces good statistics) from May 1977 to May 1979 was, on average, 3 per cent for men and 4.3 per cent for women (and only 3.4 per cent for unmarried women). Such differences are negligible.

They also say that the company has to make a substantial investment to train women and once they get married or have a child, they end up leaving their jobs. Statistics seem to confirm this point of view. The table below shows the time spent in the same company by civilian employees over the age of twenty-five out of all those who were in work in January 1983.

Time spent in the same company	Men	Women
1 year at least	3,487,000	3,157,000
2 to 4 years	8,564,000	8,241,000
5 to 9 years	9,464,000	8,121,000
10 years or more	20,833,000	11,030,000

(Extract from a Department of Labor document)

One sees from this that from zero to nine years the figures are more or less the same for men and women. The difference becomes significant only after ten years of service. This is partly because some women give up work to look after their children, but there are also those who take part-time work, work at home, or leave their employer because their husbands who often have more important jobs are transferred to another city.

Lastly, and this is perhaps the most important factor, the arrival of very large numbers of women on the labour market is a fairly recent phenomenon. In the United States in 1979 there were 12 million more women in the working population than in 1970. With a change of this magnitude, it is self-evident that the number of women with ten to fifteen years seniority in one company must be lower than the number of men.

Another male chauvinist attitude maintains that certain jobs necessitate mobility and that one cannot ask a married woman to travel. Yet travelling affects a couple just as much whether it is the husband or the wife who travels. My eldest daughter, Christine, who co-ordinates the international development of a new drug for a pharmaceutical company, knows all about this. In 1985 my third daughter, Sylvie, who works for IBM, attended three three-week courses which were held nearly 1,000 miles from her home.

Some men say there are fewer problems at meetings if all the people are of the same sex. I, on the contrary, think that women bring complementary and very necessary points of view to any business meeting. And one must recognize that the 'male club' atmosphere of certain business meetings is often deplorable. Not only is the mingling of the sexes healthy, but so is their equality and this is true both in schools and in business. It is segregation which is unhealthy.

They also say that male employees will not agree to work for a woman; one might as well say that whenever they meet a woman they are incapable of recognizing her intelligence and her professional capacities. The list of arguments, in which ignorance goes hand-in-hand with bad faith, could be extended still further.

But the worst of it is that a great many women subscribe to

these specious arguments, just as they conform to the image that society — in other words men — have imposed on them, and which they absorb and internalize. A study of women's magazines would be very revealing in this respect. In business this often takes the form of women hesitating to accept certain positions; they are paralysed by the above-mentioned objections.

Many qualities are considered without any proof whatsoever to be typically masculine, and at the same time vital in the world of business. However, in a great many jobs, a woman can do the work as well as a man by showing qualities that may be different but are equally outstanding. Our prejudices spring from the 'model' that prevails in the world of business, which is a masculine model. One must be self-assured, strong, aggressive — in a word *male*. We speak of businessmen, but rarely of businesswomen. This gives rise to another danger: that to succeed, a woman will feel it necessary to adopt the type of behaviour that is acceptable to men. It is much harder for a woman to remain herself in a job traditionally held by men, than it is to get herself noticed by aping masculine behaviour. Nevertheless it is desirable for a woman to be wholly herself, and wholly a woman in her work as well as in her private life.

Not long ago, socio-cultural prejudices were particularly noticeable in the realm of education. Young girls were taught dressmaking or 'domestic arts'; we tried to turn them into good little housewives. The gap between the sexes has narrowed considerably, and today girls follow almost the same studies as boys even in the universities. But the tendency to steer girls towards areas of study leading into professions where women have long been accepted remains strong. The professions frequently adopted by women are the following: school-teacher, secretary, nurse, salesgirl, social worker, hostess, university lecturer, research assistant, journalist. But it must be said that these professions are often undervalued: the fact that such jobs are available to women is counterbalanced by a lowering of their value — in the matter of salaries as much as in social status. (I am thinking particularly of the teaching profession and the paramedical sector.)

But above all there are very few women who attain really high-ranking positions: there are very few who are chairmen of businesses, rectors of universities, ministers or members of parliament.

Throughout the world, however, women represent a larger and larger proportion of the working population (50 per cent in the USSR, 38 per cent in France, 43 per cent in the USA in 1983). Being so numerous, they are becoming aware of their strength, and moreover that they have a range of talents which can no longer be ignored. In many countries, the law demands that women have equal rights with men, particularly the right to work and equal pay for equal work. In the USA penalties for infractions are severe – in two years $70 million was paid out in fines by companies who were sued by female employees. In spite of this female graduates from American colleges earn an average of $5,000 per annum less than their male counterparts. Recent statistics from the Department of Labor in the US show that in 1983 the average salary for women was 63.6 per cent of the average salary for men (as against 58.8 per cent in 1975). This is partly explained by the differences in qualifications between men and women and therefore in jobs.

A survey carried out early in 1985 gives the following results for manufacturing industries in the United States and at IBM (American classifications are used in this table).

	Overall percentage of women	IBM percentage of women
Higher executives and managers	7.8	14.0
Professionals	16.5	19.3
Technicians	15.0	10.6
Salesforce	11.5	29.4
Secretaries/clerical workers	78.6	66.9
Skilled plant employees	5.1	16.4
Machine operators	26.8	47.5

Women must be given the place that is their due in business enterprises. How is this to be achieved? I would like to examine this question now by taking IBM as my example.

In 1970 Mr T.V. Learson, then Chairman, announced a policy of promotion for women; it was no longer a matter of simply hoping that heads of departments and executives would do their duty, but rather of making the job advancement of our women employees compulsory. Voluntary programmes were continued by Frank Cary and John Opel: top management in the group certainly got the message. The following lines are taken from Chairman John Opel's editorial, which appeared in the June 1984 issue of *Think Magazine*, IBM's principal house journal:

> Our recruiting figures for 1983 have been very good. Of our 10,000 new employees, 19 per cent belong to minorities (Blacks and Hispanics) and 45 per cent are women.
>
> The number of 'minorities' and women in the very highest managerial posts has risen. Nevertheless much remains to be done. We intend to carry on with our total commitment to equal opportunities.

Not only did the percentage of women in the total work force increase from 15.1 per cent in 1973 to 26 per cent in 1983, but more importantly the number of women managers rose from 760 in 1973 (4.9 per cent) to 3,665 in 1983 (12.5 per cent). Finally, the number of women occupying positions at the start of their careers, which would give them the best chance of access to managerial posts (engineers, systems analysts, sales engineers) rose from 4,948 in 1973 to 18,410 in 1983, i.e. from 9 to 19 per cent of the total in ten years. Women also occupy more than 29 per cent of sales and systems engineers positions. Furthermore, in 1983 25 per cent of the participants in management courses organized by the company were women.

In Europe, however, we were lagging behind the United States. Of the overall number of managers of local IBM companies, women represented the following percentages in 1984: England, 3.5%; France, 3.4%; Germany, 3.2%; Italy, 3.2%.

Fortunately recruitment changes have affected Europe, too. The number of women now hired represents: 36.7% of total recruitment in Italy; 25.5% in France; 24% in England; 15.6% in Germany. It must be acknowledged that the large number of women now attending university has had a great influence on recruitment figures. For example, the percentages of women engineers who graduated in 1983 were as follows: England, 15.3%; France, 14%; Italy, 12%; Germany, 7%.

To obtain these results, we had taken the following steps in the USA:

1. Managers were appointed to run 'Equal Opportunity' programmes. Their role was to ensure that each department in the company had well-defined programmes and to oversee their functioning. In particular we fixed targets which were regularly reviewed.

2. We established 'awareness' programmes for top management. All our senior executives took such courses, the aim of which essentially was to uproot prejudices against women who rise to high managerial positions.

3. We mapped out career plans for all our women employees who appeared to have sufficient potential to reach a high position in the company.

4. We improved our social programmes, notably by giving special maternity leave, which allowed the employee to return to the same or an equivalent job.

5. Since each department set up its own scheme for the promotion of women, we now have multiple programmes. In Europe it was possible to improve the situation quickly, because as I have already pointed out, the hiring of women with degrees had increased considerably during the last ten years.

It is evident in spite of this that companies cannot resolve this problem on their own. Society as a whole must change its attitudes. It seems to me that one acute danger threatens women.

If women's entry into the world of business is an irreversible phenomenon, then too many women may find themselves assuming the double burden of work at their place of employment plus work at home. Many women are doing two days' work instead of one. Is this really progress? This situation is tolerable only if it represents a transitional stage. We must reform our work-patterns; in particular we must allow working mothers to devote sufficient time to the upbringing of their children (special leave, opportunities for part-time work, flexible working hours, etc.). But the company cannot alone bear the cost of such reforms. I am thinking specifically of part-time work which entails increased costs for the employer. What is needed is a thorough-going revision of government legislation. For example, the building of crèches is a burden that must fall on the government.

Far many more men must also be willing to share family responsibilities, and the household chores with their wives, especially if the latter are working. In addition they must recognize that the task of raising a family devolves on men as well as women, contrary to the widely-held view that bringing up the children is the prerogative of women. Many young people have already adopted such new attitudes, but they are far from being universal. Women must also be given real opportunities to choose their own future: a working life of complete equality with their male colleagues; home life; or a third course which allows for both.

How will such developments be possible? The women's liberation movements in the United States, France and many other countries, constitute only a first stage: they have awakened public opinion. However, the demands of feminists – often greeted with a smile – do not seem to me to be the best way to bring about a transformation in our thinking. It is also debatable whether the appointment in France, of a Secretary of State for Female Working Conditions constitutes a prelude to genuine transformations. To my way of thinking, it is at the heart of every ministry, every business enterprise and every department that new attitudes must be forged. No one can claim any longer to be ignorant of the profound change which has already taken place.

I have not spoken about female managing directors or vice-presidents of business. There are as yet very few of them and this proves what a long road we still have to travel. A social problem has not been solved when one can point to the example of a mere ten or fifteen people out of hundreds of thousands who have escaped the statistical curves.

With regard to very high-level jobs American women have fared no better than European women. In the list of the 500 largest companies published by *Fortune*, one finds only ten women in key positions in 1978. In an article published in *French-American Commerce*, Winter 1982, Marie Monique Steckel (a graduate of the Institute of Political Sciences, Harvard) quotes a survey by Burson Marsteller which indicates that, out of the 1,300 largest American companies only 332 have a woman on their board of directors. But it also shows that progress is on the march and women are organizing themselves. Mme Steckel makes particular mention of Catalyst, an organization which is privately financed by American businesses, which has launched a unique service, the Corporate Board Resource. Dating from 1977, this service has selected and kept on file the names and qualifications of 850 women who are likely candidates for boards of directors. In 1980 sixty-three companies consulted the service and forty-four of them added a woman to their boards. Progress is slow, but there *is* progress.

Mme Steckel concludes:

Women can and must transform the current pattern in the business world so as to occupy their true place in it. Their challenge to the hierarchy must stimulate a new dialogue at the heart of business firms.

Not all women will want to take an active part in the business world and it is not my aim that they should do so, but it is time to fight for a greater number of women to have access to real responsibilities.

Women of tomorrow must have the opportunity to become businesswomen in the fullest sense.

I agree with you, Marie Monique, and so do my four daughters, but you will need the help of some responsible men: you can count on me.

13

My Last Three Years at IBM

Transition periods are never long at IBM and indeed that is one of the company's strengths. After several days spent passing on the baton to Kap Cassani, who had long been ready to receive it, I left once more for Armonk. On arrival I took part in my first meeting of the management committee which, at that time consisted of John Opel, President of the company, and four Senior Vice-Presidents: Paul Rizzo, Dean McKay, Spike Beitzel and myself.

My office was temporarily furnished; we were waiting for the permanent furniture, and this took as long to arrive in the USA as it does in France. My assistant, Mike Forster, did everything possible to help me. I had asked the Director of Personnel at HQ, Marty Penn, to help me staff my office. Not only did he do this instantly, but you can imagine how surprised and delighted I was to discover that he had managed to recruit Barbara Baerman, who had worked in my Paris office some years before, and Diane Chiquette, whom I had also known in Paris. He had brought them in from other departments. Both were French-speaking, dynamic, cheerful and competent. I almost felt I had a little corner of Paris, there in Armonk, and when Marty Penn came in to ask me if I would like to have a Millet from the IBM collection in my office, I felt even more at home for the same Millet had been in my New York office from 1968 to 1974. These friendly gestures gave me a warm feeling of welcome.

Several years earlier, when there was talk of the 'management gap' between the United States and France, I had suggested that there were four reasons, among others, to explain it:

1. The higher percentage of American executives with diplomas from business schools. France has, however, made good progress in this sphere, thanks in particular to the action of the *Foundation de la gestion* [Management Foundation].

2. The precise job descriptions drawn up by the majority of American companies. Here, too, we have made some progress.

3. The attitude of Americans who, having definite tasks, carry them out efficiently, without wasting time pondering on what they would do if they were in someone else's shoes. In this respect we have some way to go.

4. Finally, the average level of training given to staff in the secretariat and the administration allows executives to delegate to the maximum. In France progress has been made, but we must do more to raise the standard of training for young people. In my office in Paris, from 1974 to 1981 I tried to reproduce these American characteristics, and it worked very well.

Each member of IBM's management committee is responsible for certain functions or operational departments. It would have been simple to give me responsibility for the operational units of the World Trade Corporation, all the more so since I was Chairman of the holding company. But, in fact, the organizational solution chosen was much better. It would not have been a good thing for Kap Cassani if I had remained his 'boss', undoubtedly Ralph Pfeiffer would not have liked me to become his boss either, and, besides, it was good for me to learn new things. Perhaps it was necessary for the greater good of the corporation, that other members of the management committee should take on international responsibilities and that there should be a change at the top. John Opel therefore decided that the following people should be accountable to me:

—Walt Burdick, the Vice-President of Personnel. We had worked together in the World Trade Corporation and I already considered him to be the best personnel executive in the whole of American industry.

—Vic Macdonald, the Vice-President of Communications. We

had worked together in a Task Force in 1972. He was a brilliant and likeable man who knew his job through and through.

—Wally Doud, the Vice-President of Industry Relations, and another old acquaintance. Wally had held this post for some years and I had met him often. Among his responsibilities were the department of patents, which in a high tech industry is of great importance, and the department in charge of relations with the data processing industry.

—Billy Christensen, the Vice-President and Managing Director of the World Trade Corporation. Billy and I started work together in 1955. He had succeeded me as President of IBM Europe (the old formula) in 1967, and we were on the very best of terms.

These four men welcomed me in a perfectly normal way. They were not in the least shocked at having a foreigner come to intervene between them and the American top management. Never at any time did any of them make me feel I had been 'grafted on' or 'parachuted in' and I remain grateful to them for this. Moreover, they were top class international managers; they knew their business inside out and did not need to be supervised.

My first months were spent attending numerous committee meetings, sometimes two or three a week, lasting all day long, which gave me my apprenticeship into the functions for which I was responsible. I spent the greater part of my time with personnel and communications, because I had little experience of how either worked in an American setting and because it was in these areas that my experience from 'abroad' could be most useful. Of course there were daily problems to be solved, but Walt and Vic did not need me to solve them: they simply kept me informed. But there were also the questions of how new policies could be applied, and how relations could be better developed between the two companies, IBM Europe and IBM the Americas/Far East.

The functioning of the management committee is an interesting example of management techniques. In 1982, for example, there were sixty-six meetings, of which twenty-five lasted almost all day, from 9 a.m. to 4 p.m., and the others half a day. This meant that the top executives of the company saw each other at least sixty-six times during one year. In addition, there were quite often meetings between pairs of them. This shows the importance IBM attached to internal communication and to 'collegiality of management'.

It was the committee's secretary, an experienced and 'promising' manager, who decided how we spent our time, and he would send us the agenda a few days in advance. Every meeting began with what were called 'Executive Items'. Each of us informed the others of some current question, good news or bad, or a problem that had arisen. Then reports were presented. The president of one division, the vice-president responsible for a certain area of operations, the company economist, the treasurer, the auditor and many others gave, with the assistance of their colleagues, reports on a great many subjects for which they required the committee's agreement and decision.

All the plans — two-year budgetary plans, five-year strategic plans — of all the operational units were thus covered. All major programmes for new products and all important investments were discussed, as were the replacement tables for high-level managers, and the list of young people with rapid promotion prospects in sight. In addition, improvement to personnel policies, new sales policies, proposals for the announcement of new products, etc., etc. were also looked at. Everything, which had an important bearing on the company's future, was gone through with a fine-toothed comb.

Having had occasion during the preceding years to give presentations on IBM Europe, I knew what a lot of work went into them, how many 'rehearsals' were needed, and how anxious the 'presenters' were before going into the boardroom. As a result, the quality of the presentations was exceptional. Several directors from other companies have told me how astonished they were at the professionalism exhibited by IBM managers when expounding problems and their solutions!

Marshal Foch* once said: 'To kill a project, all you need is to form a committee to study it!' This was absolutely not the case at

---

* Supreme Commander of the Allied Armies on the Western Front in World War I.

IBM. I must say without giving away any big secret that the voice of the Chairman was preponderant. In the discussions that followed each presentation his opinion carried a great deal of weight, but he never made a decision without listening to the opinions of the other committee members.

The inconvenience of this system was that the Chairman and the President had to spend a lot of time at these meetings and perhaps not enough on long-term planning. In March 1983 reorganization took place aimed at overcoming this problem. Two committees replaced the original one: a 'Policy Committee' composed of the Chairman, the Vice-Chairman and the President, assisted by the Director of Finance and the President of the 'Business Operations Committee' and a 'Business Operations Committee' composed of the Senior Vice-Presidents and chaired by the one I considered the best, Dean Phypers. The first committee was exclusively concerned with long-term planning, but the second with all planning. The advantage of this reorganization was that it brought a larger number of managers into the overall planning procedures of the company and gave the three top executives more time to concentrate on future planning.

I was a member of the 'Business Operations Committee' and continued to plague my colleagues about their lack of attention to international affairs. At the end of the first year, Dean Phypers sent us each a personal cartoon with an appropriate bubble. Mine read, 'Well now, what effect will this decision have on IBM World Trade?'

It was in 1983 that John Opel informed me that the Board of Directors of the IBM Corporation had decided to elect me. John could not have made me happier for I also knew he was the one who had proposed me. This allowed me during my last year with IBM to meet an absolutely outstanding group of men and women who had all accomplished something great for their country. I cannot hide the fact that I was proud of my election. It was the final proof I could give to all the non-American IBMers that it was possible for a foreigner, who had started at the bottom, to become a member of the top decision-making body of a very large corporation.

*

During the first months of my new appointment I was once again alone in New York. First, I had to find an apartment and, since the early part of 1982 was a period of very high interest rates, we decided to rent rather than buy. What a mistake! I went back to look at the house in Bronxville which we had liked so much; it was for sale at four times the price I had got for it in 1974. The years 1973 to 1982 had seen the greatest increase ever in real estate prices in the New York area. Every weekend I went to look at several apartments, finally found one that my wife liked, and in May 1982 we moved into 1192 Park Avenue between 93rd and 94th Streets. The *Lycée Français* was on 93rd between Park and Madison. We could see the school building from one of our windows; what a convenient spot for Anne-Sophie!

Life took up its normal course once more at the end of the summer when my wife and Anne-Sophie came to New York. Anne-Sophie entered the top form in the French *Lycée*, passed her *baccalauréat*, then spent a year at Barnard where two of her sisters had been a few years earlier. The President of the College was Helen Futter, who graduated at the same time as my daughter, Sylvie; she was the youngest president of any American college. Anne-Sophie spent one scholastic year at Barnard and worked sufficiently hard to be given credits for her *baccalauréat* and finished with the equivalent of two years spent at an American college. She decided, with a little help from us, to prepare for admission to a French business school and entered Sainte-Geneviève in the autumn of 1984. François, after finishing his service at the Embassy, had worked in the IBM Washington office for nine months and was then accepted by Harvard Business School where he enrolled in September 1983.

In October 1983 my father had to undergo an intestinal operation. We spent as much time as possible in Paris, and at Christmas he was well enough to join in the family festivities. The anxiety and distress we were feeling, however, prevented us from enjoying to the full the birth of our fourth American grandchild on 9 November. Kevin made his entry into the world at the very moment when his great-grandfather was about to leave it. On each visit I found my father thinner and visibly weakening. In

February 1984 I went to Paris and I found him so ill that, after discussing it with my son-in-law, a Professor of Medicine at Cochin Hospital, we very quickly decided to put him into hospital. On Saturday 25 February, I went back to New York intending to return to Paris in a week's time. On Sunday the 26th, my wife left to take my place at the side of my poor mother who was finding it hard to bear her ordeal.

During the night of the 27th to 28th, my father died, alone in his hospital room; I shall never forgive myself for not having stayed in Paris during the last moments of his life. Fortunately, my wife was with my mother and could assume responsibility for all the painful tasks. A few days earlier my father and I had had a long conversation. He spoke about the future, but also about the joys he had known, many of which he attributed to me. How proud he was of his son, how he loved my wife and his grandchildren!

I left immediately for Paris, and thought intensely about him during that long night flight! What a wonderful father and husband he had been! What an example! I was able to spend three weeks in Paris helping my mother to organize her business affairs. How sad it was to see her, listening attentively to everything we would explain to her. As her eyesight was failing, she could not read a single document, but in any case she had never had to bother about even such a simple thing as checking a bank statement for my father had always taken on all these responsibilities himself.

We had definitely decided to return to France at the end of 1984 after my retirement from IBM. And now, at the time of my father's death, I began to reflect on what I should do after leaving this company to which I was so deeply attached. This did not, however, prevent my carrying out to the full all my duties and taking advantage of the exceptional experience this post gave me.

If I say that I discovered America all over again, it will seem that I am a very slow learner. And yet ... what a long time it does take to know a country that is so vast and so full of variety! During these three years I made a real effort to understand IBM America well, and not simply the corporate HQ. I visited several branch offices, numerous factories, and laboratories; I met hundreds of employees. I took part in numerous sessions in our management schools. I gave a lot of lectures at conferences and at reunions of employees who belonged to the 'Quarter of a Century Club' (those who had more than twenty-five years' service with the company).

I observed the characters of the men and women who made this enormous machine work, their professionalism, their eagerness to learn, their open-mindedness and their confidence in the future of their country. How different the atmosphere was from the one I had encountered in 1973–4 during that period of *mea culpa* that swept across the United States! I no longer had to lecture on 'What's right with America'. The country had reawakened. Time had allowed people to forget; the Vietnam War was long past and so was Watergate, but I think President Reagan's first election campaign had something to do with it. One of the themes of his campaign was: 'We must no longer seek to be loved, we must strive to make ourselves respected.' His appeals to traditional values had a great impact; his new economic policy got growth started again. Of course he didn't lack critics: the budget deficit was very high, as was the deficit in the balance of payments, and the stabilization of domestic expenditure in the Federal budget had been achieved at the expense of various reductions in welfare programmes for the poor and in the allocation of federal funds to universities and local government. In any case the result has been considerable economic recovery, the creation of new jobs, and a relatively low rate of inflation.

Throughout the country the penetration of Japanese products on the American market came as a shock. There had been more and more talk about Japan, but now the talk became incessant. Although many Americans would have liked to see protectionist measures taken, the great majority still preferred to fight; fight in the sense of being economically competitive against Japan, and now with the new strength of the dollar against European countries, too.

Since 1981 studies of the Japanese miracle have multiplied and there have been numerous business missions to Japan. Firms

273

have introduced Japanese methods, which twenty years ago were American methods the Japanese subsequently improved upon. In 1980–1 Japan's production capacities were being used at between 50 to 80 per cent of their total capacity depending upon the industry. Investments were therefore oriented towards productivity and not towards creating new production capacities. Robotics, word processing, data processing and micro-data processing experienced an extraordinary development.

IBM, like all companies in the electronics industry, was hard-hit by Japanese competition; in Japan itself, most particularly in terms of data processing, and everywhere in micro-data processing and word processing. In 1982 manufacturers of electronic components did not use their own production capacity to the full, and during the same year Japanese companies sold 75 per cent of the 64,000-position chips which were delivered to American customers.

What was IBM's reaction? Nobody dreamed of going to Washington to ask for protection. At the start-of-the-year meeting of the three hundred most important managers, John Opel fixed precise objectives:

1. to grow at least as fast as the rest of the industry to which we belonged;
2. to be the leader in new technology;
3. to be the lowest cost producer;
4. to maintain our level of profits.

These objectives were added to our basic principles.

Some months later I was able to confirm how well communication was working. In every sales office, every factory, and every laboratory I visited, the manager who reported his activities to me always based his presentation on these objectives established by the Chairman. I was astonished to see that an awareness of them had spread very rapidly throughout the entire company. Results were rapidly achieved, helped by considerable investment in automation. Today, in the United States, IBM manufactures typewriters which are competitive with Japanese machines. Many American industrialists reacted in the same way and, while 1985 was not such a good year as the preceding two in terms of growth, I believe that the restructuring of industry has made a leap forward which will put it in a strong position as soon as the dollar falls.

I have explained that I became a partisan of the market economy after discovering the United States in 1948–9. My conviction that a market economy is superior to all other systems was reinforced over the years through my professional experience, and also through my frequent contacts with high-ranking officials, academics and students.

Having been a member of the boards of trustees of Barnard College, the International Institute of Education, the *Ecole Centrale* in Paris and the Lauder Institute of the Wharton Business School in Philadelphia; having also been a member of a Task Force for Cornell University's Business School, Director of the French Houses at both Columbia and New York Universities; having taught at the *Institut Auguste-Comte,* and in 1985 at the School of Political Sciences and at the International Institute of Management in Geneva, I believe I know what sort of society young men and women, and the younger executives, want to live, work and find fulfilment in.

I have also been involved in certain forms of associative life; the Franco-American Foundation; the Franco-American Chamber of Commerce; the Foundation for Biological Research; the Foundation of the American Hospital in Paris; the Rogosyn Research Center of the New York Hospital. As a result of these activities I have learned the value of private initiative.

The attitude of certain liberals (in the French sense of the word), who have just discovered liberalism and speak of Hayek or of Friedman as if they were very young men, seems to me, however, excessive. Undoubtedly we need less State intervention, less control, and more freedom of enterprise. But it seems to me that first of all we must alter the relations between different groups within European society, make it easier to move from one to the other in any direction, and do whatever is necessary to change certain mental attitudes.

The system of education in most European countries tends to

divide people into separate groups, and from a very early age there is little interchange between them. Apart from a very few childhood friends, our young people tend to mix mainly with those who have had identical types of higher education, and still worse with those who have chosen the same type of career.

In 1970 I suggested to President Pompidou that he should organize an exchange programme, comparable to the President's Exchange Program in the United States: choose forty to forty-five executives from the civil service every year and send them to work in the private sector for two or three years, while a similar number of executives from the private sector should be sent to spend an equivalent period in the public sector. It is no use sending them for a three-month stay which is too short to learn very much; they must be involved in a serious job. One must also choose younger executives, from thirty-five to forty, who are still capable of shedding their prejudices.

Another approach is to offer posts within ministerial departments to specialists from the private sector. In the case of research and development, we should have teams which include engineers and scientists from industry and those from State laboratories. People in the higher echelons of the civil service should not be allowed to go over to the private sector unless this is matched by a movement in the opposite direction – senior executives coming from the private sector into the civil service. Within the civil service, as in the private sector, a system of evaluations and planned careers should be practised to prevent people snoring away happily in 'established positions'.

The Americans in all the dealings I have had with them during these last three years have shown me what enthusiasm can achieve. At the same time I have been surprised to find that many of them are almost entirely ignorant about Europe. I cannot help wondering whether in some cases this is not a phenomenon based on the rejection of their country of origin. In the majority of cases, immigrants left Europe not – as is believed and too often said – in search of adventure, but because poverty and oppression drove them to seek refuge elsewhere. Americans of French origin are few because, apart from those who left because of the revocation of the Edict of Nantes, or explorers, or men who volunteered to fight in the War of Independence, the French have always been content in France.

During my last three years at IBM I continued my efforts to establish good public relations. I received a great many European clients and escorted them on their visits. In New York, as in Paris, I met French ministers and their entourages. The Consuls-General in New York, first M.B. de Lataillade and then M.A. Gadot, invited me every time some French personality was passing through. For me it was always a great pleasure to meet my compatriots. We did not always agree, admittedly, but I think I was able to explain the United States to them as I had spent so much time explaining France to Americans.

The Franco-American Chamber of Commerce decided to create a trophy for the 'Man of the Year', to be presented each year to an American or a Frenchman who had accomplished something outstanding to aid co-operation between the two countries. At the meeting of the Chamber at which this was discussed, I voiced my opposition because I thought it would be difficult to make a choice – every year there would be at least ten people worthy of receiving it and thus nine of them would be disappointed. The other members of the Chamber rejected my objections. A few months later I was astonished to find that I was to be the first to receive the trophy, in the form of a magnificent crystal pyramid! So I was the Chamber's 'Man of the Year' for 1984. Pierre Salinger had made a special trip to be the evening's principal speaker. It was 29 October 1984; I had already retired.

During my speech of thanks I could not resist letting off a few volleys against a Professor of Economics, John K. Galbraith who, a few days earlier during a seminar in Boston, had said: 'François Mitterand is on the wrong track. Instead of spending enormous sums to make France into a modern technological nation, he would do better to concentrate his efforts on the things the French do well: fashion, wine, good cooking and a little art.' He had added that France would never produce a good electronics engineer.

I launched into a demonstration of his ignorance and this experience reinforced my conviction that we have a lot to do to change our country's image abroad. In 1984 I spent a great deal of time trying to do so, and I still do. Whatever his political opinions may be, I believe that a Frenchman who resides and works abroad must do everything in his power to explain what modern France is. At the end of my speech, since I was already uneasy at that time about the fascination the Pacific area exerts over Americans, I introduced a word on behalf of Europe: 'We must fight Euro-pessimism as we have fought for liberty because, without a strong alliance between Europe and the United States, we will lose that liberty.'

I have just said that I was uneasy. For my part I believe that every man of action, every leader, must always be motivated by a certain anxiety and transmit this feeling to those who work with him. Nothing annoys me more than people who are so sure of themselves that outside events always take them by surprise, or those industrialists who year after year watch their company's profits dwindling, and continue to display a rare complacency right up to the moment when the company goes bankrupt or they have to appeal to the government for support.

The French poets of the nineteenth century often stressed the influence of suffering on creativity; I have often recited the 'Pin des Landes' to my children. It is one of the rare poems I remember in its entirety, and it contains these lines:

> In the wilderness the poet roams, a man apart,
> Compelled to bear a deep wound in his heart
> Whence flow his verses, those sacred tears of gold.

I believe that 'good bosses' are those who have a healthy anxiety in their guts or who, as Dick Watson used to say, are never satisfied with the status quo. But this anxiety is healthy only when it is accompanied by the will to act, to struggle against all the crises that a fertile and well-controlled imagination enables one to foresee.

In 1983 and 1984 discussions continued concerning the Statement of Objections which had been sent by the EEC Commission. Nick Katzenbach and Tom Bar, freed from the Anti-trust proceedings of the US Department of Justice, were actively engaged in them.

Kap Cassani proved himself to be a remarkable leader by co-ordinating the actions of all the subsidiaries implicated. He had to do a great deal of explaining to ensure that the same message would be given by all those dealing with experts from their own governments and from the Commission who specialized in the question of competition. I realized just how well Kap had succeeded when the Vice-President and Commissioner of Industry for the European Commission, M. E. Davignon, said in a meeting: 'It's incredible to hear all the people from IBM giving the same message. I wish it was the same in the Commission.'

It was necessary to hold many meetings in Brussels and a lot in Armonk before IBM undertook to change certain commercial policies. I will not go into all the details of the litigation, which was extremely complex, and ended with an agreement that was satisfactory to both parties (especially to the Commission's Directorate of Competition). Ironically, everything the Commission wanted to make us do, however, was essentially favourable to our Japanese competitors! I hope that in future cases where companies receive Statements of Objections, economic and social considerations will be given at least as much attention as the application, *stricto sensu*, of Articles 85 and 86 of the Treaty of Rome, especially when these articles lead to conclusions which are different from those reached by controllers of competition in certain European countries.

But in August 1984 I was very happy that this long drawn-out litigation had been settled. I had been unhappy at not being able to find the solution before I left Europe in 1981. Even today, I consider this as the greatest failure of my career. Neither Frank Cary nor John Opel have reproached me in any way, and I must say that however hard I have searched I have not been able to find anything I could have done to resolve the problem before 1981. And yet perhaps I could have got its importance understood more quickly, and I could have asked for Armonk's help earlier. Once again I fell victim to the sin of pride. I thought that we Europeans would be able to find a solution without the aid of the 'mother company'. This is a normal situation in a decentralized multinational: those in charge of the subsidiary always think they know better than the people at HQ what is going on in their own territory. And they are usually right, except when it is a question of problems that directly affect the parent company.

Since 1982 there had been in IBM, as I said, two top level management committees, the Policy Committee and the Business Operations Committee. A little while after their creation, a Corporate Management Board was set up whose members were the same as the other two committees, plus four Operational Directors and the Vice-President and Chief Scientist. This board met approximately every two months and formed in some ways an internal board of directors.

In February 1983 John Akers, who had been President of the Sales Division, then Senior Vice-President responsible for several development and manufacturing divisions, was elected President of IBM. Paul Rizzo was elected Vice-Chairman. However, I was still with IBM when there was yet another change in structure at the top. After the Business Operations Committee was set up it was recognized that it had too many members to operate at maximum efficiency, and that above all some of its members held operational positions of responsibility which made it impossible for them to be totally objective. As a result the Business Operations Committee was restructured in August 1984. It now consisted of: John Opel – Chairman; Paul Rizzo – Vice-Chairman; John Akers – President; and four Senior Vice-Presidents: G.B. Beitzel, Alan Krowe (Financial Director), Dean Phypers and myself.

I mention the composition of the committee to show how careful IBM is to have a collegiate management and to prepare for future successions. In October 1984 John Opel was to announce that John Akers would become President and Chief Executive Officer, in other words IBM's Managing Director. It was this committee I left on my retirement.

In a previous chapter, I quoted some figures showing the increase in the power of computers from 1955 to 1975. As I was about to bring my career to a close, I often thought of the extraordinary adventure I had lived through. Participating in the birth of an industry, being present during its growth, acting to promote its progress, and leaving it at a time when it has almost become 'mature', had been absolutely enthralling.

Where were we in 1984? IBM had fulfilled all the objectives John Opel had set:

1. IBM's growth rate in 1983 and 1984 had been at least equal to that of the data processing industry as a whole.

2. Manufacturing costs had come down, and IBM by manufacturing in the USA, Europe and Japan was able to be competitive against Japanese companies.

3. Our technological leadership was acclaimed.

4. Profits had increased more rapidly than turnover.

Nearly 400,000 people throughout the world had contributed to achieving these results.

To illustrate IBM's progress I will compare figures for 1955 and for 1984. I would have liked to compare 1948 with 1984, but computers did not exist in 1948.

	1955	1984
Time of execution	375 seconds	1 second
Cost	14.54 dollars	7 cents
Technology	Electronic tubes	Very dense chips
	Magnetic cores	New packaging of the components
	Magnetic tapes	New and more powerful architecture
	Magnetic drums	Thin film reading heads Cartridge mass memories
MIPS (millions of instructions per second)	0.011	14

I should add that the period 1980–4 was one of profound change regarding the distribution of data processing and micro-data processing. The PC (personal computer) had made a successful entry into the market; it had reached the end user and thus the general public was in touch with data processing services. I do not think there is a single industry in the world that has made comparable progress in thirty-six years and IBM has been its driving force. I am proud to have been among those who participated.

During my last months at IBM, I was often invited to speak at international meetings and at conventions. I gave twenty-nine lectures at meetings of company employees, of which twenty-two were in the United States and only six abroad. Unconsciously, I wanted to say *au revoir* and pass on a few messages. Anxious not to lose contact, I always managed to slip in a word: 'If you need an outside speaker, don't hesitate to call on me in future. I won't charge you very much!' They took me at my word, and in 1985 I was invited several times to speak to groups of my former colleagues. It remains a great joy for me to meet them and I avoid speaking about my memories, confining myself instead to the lessons I have learnt.

14

Some Contemporary Debates on Data Processing

The development of computers between 1948 and 1984 has been absolutely extraordinary as some of the figures I have given have already shown. To put it simply, computers are probably the only products which have regularly offered their users steady improvements of 20 to 25 per cent per annum in the performance/price ratio over the last twenty-five years. Right now, as I am bringing my part of the story to an end, what does the future hold in store?

First, as regards technology, the miniaturization of circuits continues, the density of recording on magnetic supports is increasing, the speed at which data can be processed is going up all the time, and the CRAY super-computers are on the market. The press has announced IBM's launch of a huge project to produce a parallel-functioning super-computer. The Japanese have launched what they call 'the fifth generation of computers', which they define as machines which do not have a Von Neuman architecture. The technology which will make the manufacture of computers of this type possible has been announced in the United States as well as in Japan. For example, disc memories with thin film heads are in production. Micro-chips with a million positions have been presented by several manufacturers at scientific meetings, and production is starting. It is estimated that within a few years we shall reach the limit of miniaturization permissible with silicon, and there will therefore be more and more work done on gallium arsenide.

But technology is not an end in itself; its essential function is to permit the manufacture of better products that allow us to find a quicker and more satisfactory solution to the problems encountered by men and women in every profession. The great transformation in human work that we have witnessed will continue. During the fifties the use of computers for scientific calculations began. During the sixties, we saw the development of large data-bases with long-distance link ups connected by terminals, and the beginning of telematics. During the seventies, computers made their entry into laboratories and factories. Conception and design were assisted by computers, specifically those with new high performance software. Robotics began before the name was invented. The eighties have already seen rapid progress made in robotics. I should quickly mention the IBM robot 7565, which is controlled by computer, and can be adapted to its work environment to the extent that it can see, touch and even handle fresh eggs without breaking them.

The most important change in the last few years has been the introduction of personal computers in homes, offices and schools. This has been the 'take-off' of text processing, which has brought in its wake a major reorganization in the sales departments of the manufacturers of equipment and software. Personal computers have become a widely-sold product. Now the end user has access to data processing. In 1974 IBM in the USA provided one terminal for every twenty employees; in 1984 there was more than one terminal for every two employees.

Not all this progress has resulted solely from technological breakthroughs; the exponential growth of the treatment of information is the principal cause. How could the post offices, banks, and airline companies resolve their problems without installing a substantial number of central computers and thousands of terminals? How could the manufacturing industries produce whole lines of high quality articles without systems for recording orders, and then beginning and controlling the process of production without computers and without robots? But perhaps it has not yet been sufficiently understood that traditional or mature industries need computers in order to be competitive. Such change, here described in a few words, moves quickly and entails much, hence the fear it inspires.

Every time a computer has been used in a new profession, frightened voices have been raised. Then later the members of that profession have come to understand how much such an innovation can benefit them. Like me you will have heard people say that the utilization of personal computers has had an adverse effect upon the young and that their studies of French, History and Geography have suffered as a consequence. This is absolutely incredible for none of these young people, whether graduating from secondary school, the universities or whatever, has ever — except in rare cases — used a personal computer throughout the entire period of his education.

Young doctors, who have difficulty in finding a job because too many doctors have been trained, will also claim that new technologies applied to medicine, and medical data processing, are to blame. One can only be astonished at their reaction, when one knows that medical data processing is just taking its first halting steps.

I could cite many other examples, but I will confine myself to just two subjects of debate: data processing and liberty, and the impact of data processing, word processing and robotics on employment. I want to speak about these topics because people's fearful reactions to them have been a constant preoccupation of mine, as they have of IBM.

I believe, in fact, that a man who conceives a product, or a system of organization, must assume a certain degree of responsibility for the social consequences of his invention, but I also believe very strongly that he cannot take on the whole responsibility — the legislator and the consumer carry the major share of this burden. I will try to argue my point by using two examples.

We must never forget that it is *man* who makes all the important decisions. As I write these words I have just learned of a train disaster at Argenton-sur-Creuse, the third railway accident in France in 1985. In all three cases there was human error and in all three cases sophisticated electronic equipment could have averted the tragedy. The headline of *France Dimanche* of

1 December reads: 'Trains That Kill'. Trains do not kill, cars do not kill, knives do not kill, lancets do not kill, computers do not kill, *except as a result of human error or – human decision*. On the contrary, modern technologies can help save men's lives if they are correctly used. Electronic systems can help the driver of the train or the car, the computer user or the surgeon. As far as the knife is concerned, that is a matter for the law.

Man tries to blame the machine so as to shed his own responsibility. It is so easy to attack something that cannot defend itself. Several times in recent years I have been faced with the same problem on arrival at a hotel in the United States:

'My name is Maisonrouge, there should be a reservation for me.'

A few touches on the terminal.

'No, sir, we have no reservation in that name!'

'Look under Rouge, Christian name Maison.'

'Ah, yes, you're in Room 245. The computer made a spelling mistake!'

DATA PROCESSING AND LIBERTY

Does the computer threaten the liberty of the individual? On 8 May 1973 I had the honour to deliver an address on this theme to the Academy of Moral and Political Sciences – I mention the date to show that this is no new concern of mine. The history of man is in large part the story of his constant struggle for freedom. From the 'suicide' of Socrates to the Magna Carta, from the French Revolution to the Declaration of the Rights of Man, the great heritage of the Western world is its belief in individual liberty.

Liberty is seen to entail certain fundamental rights: the right to inherit property; the right to express oneself; the right to live in safety; the right to do what one likes as long as this does not interfere with the rights of others. And there is also the right to protect one's private life – which is, however, difficult to define. Article 9 of the Civil Code states that 'everyone has the right to demand that his private life shall be respected'. The German courts recognize the *Personlichkeitsrechte*, the right of the 'personality', but are not more specific. This right is also recognized in the USA, but the definition varies from state to state. In the case of England, Common Law does not recognize any particular right in this sphere. The protection that does exist is linked with the laws on personal property.

The concept of private life is difficult to define; nevertheless many have tried. Judge Brandeis of the US Supreme Court called it: 'The right to be left in peace'. Professor Alan Westin has defined it as 'The right of individuals, groups or institutions to determine for themselves how, and in what form, information concerning them may be supplied to others.'

Whatever our definition may be, we are all agreed on the fact that protection of one's private life is more than a right, it is a psychological necessity. This right is also a safeguard of democracy. And the great fear is that, if this right is not respected, the next step may be surveillance of our personal activities.

Traditionally, our private lives have been protected by the centralization of the information contained on index cards recording censuses, taxes and social security, and in medical files and police dossiers. Our protection was in part a result of inefficiency and the difficulty of communication. Today, it is technically and economically possible to gather all this information together in the memory of a computer and, thanks to teleprocessing, make it available over great distances.

Let us take as an example the United States, which has the largest number of computers of any country in the world:

— The tax authorities store all the fiscal data known about 75 million Americans.

— Social Security has detailed information about the salaries of 90 million people.

— The FBI has the fingerprints of 86 million people stored in electronic data banks.

— The Secret Services have detailed information on 50,000 people who, it is believed, might pose a threat to the lives of government or political personalities.

— And so on and so forth . . ..

Another simple example is that in most countries we have to fill in a form every time we go into a hotel. If these forms are assembled in a central data bank, it becomes easy to reconstruct the movements of every individual very rapidly. It is the computer's ability to reorganize information, to evaluate it, and to utilize correlating techniques that is mainly responsible for provoking our fear. For some people the danger lies in the fact that the evaluation of a vast amount of information gives it, in effect, a different aspect. Another anxiety springs from the belief that any alteration made to a conventional file is obvious, whereas one cannot detect alterations made to electronically-recorded data. It is feared that:

— A disgruntled programmer could tamper with the contents of a memory.

— An unauthorized person could gain access to confidential information.

— Above all there is the fear that it will be too easy for everything about us to be known.

Without the slightest doubt, grave problems do exist, and data processing specialists are aware of them, not only because they are at the centre of the debates concerning their industry but because they, too, are anxious to protect their own private lives. But let us not forget that every major technological advance brings with it a potential danger and, if there are dangers in the use of data banks, we must also take into account their positive aspects:

— At the medical centre of the University of California, a data bank is used to keep an inventory of the kidneys available for transplants. The computer also makes it possible for all the transplant centres in the United States to find compatible organs.

— In Sweden a network of computers enables all the large hospitals to obtain the medical case-histories of casualties the moment they arrive in the emergency ward.

— NASA has ten centres for the distribution of scientific information which allow industry and the universities to benefit from its research.

— In France data processing centres assist in the speeding-up and systematization of preventive medicine.

— And in most countries computers enable the police to capture criminals more swiftly.

The computer is only a machine. It gathers, records and classifies information. It can reproduce it if asked to do so. It is neither moral nor immoral, but amoral. The computer is neutral.

As Mme Gallouedec-Genuys wrote in a work entitled *Data Processing and Secrecy in the Administration*: 'Power does not belong to the technician any more than to the user of the machine; it belongs to the man who gives them orders. Power, therefore, remains with the powerful, and the computer does nothing to change this; all it does is to modify, by reinforcing, the means of power.' Since it is men who decide what the computer will do, it lies within the power of men to establish safeguards which will protect them from possible abuses in the use of this marvellous tool. Responsibility must be shared among five groups: the public; the government; professional associations; the users; and computer manufacturers.

The public and the government

Citizens get the laws they deserve. I interpret this to mean that well-informed people, conscious of their responsibilities and able to express themselves articulately, are the best insurance against bad executive power. And since all citizens could be affected by the wrongful use of computers they must demand new laws, ethical codes and standards of government practice aimed at defining and protecting what belongs exclusively to the individual, and the information that can be obtained concerning him. They must decide what information can be gathered and to what extent particulars gathered with one specific aim can eventually be used for another. They must also decide who can have access to this information and what the limits are to its use.

We must applaud the efforts of Ralph Nader in the United States who has made himself the advocate of a law to protect private life. This proposed law insists that the individual's consent must be obtained before any enquiry or any distribution of information concerning him can be made. In the same vein Professor Westin has proposed the creation of a *'Habeas* data', the right for everyone to know what is recorded about him in data banks.

The role of the legislator in the establishing of records, in the protection of individuals, and in the protection of access to information has been recognized in almost every country in Europe. Over the last fifteen years numerous commissions have studied the subject and laws have been passed: 1973 – Sweden; 1974 – the Federal Republic of Germany; 1978 – Austria, Denmark, France and Norway; 1979 – Luxemburg; 1981 – Iceland and Israel; 1984 – the United Kingdom. Other laws are in the course of preparation and will be promulgated in 1985–6.

The various States of America have chosen different methods of control, but overall they have created a specialized government agency responsible for the application of the law that, in general, includes clauses concerning the creation of files, the gathering of information, the right of the individual concerned to alter information collected about him and control access to it. In France the National Commission on data processing and civil liberties, presided over by M. Jacques Fauvet, exercises the same function.

International organizations have also not remained indifferent: the Organization for Economic Co-operation and Development published some directives in September 1980. In the same month the Council of Europe proposed a convention 'For the protection of individuals against the risks involved in data processing files'. This convention was ratified by Sweden in 1982, France in 1983, Spain and Norway in 1984, and West Germany in 1985. It has been in force since October 1985.

Professional associations

Security and secrecy depend very much on the integrity of those in charge of computer operations. The extreme mobility of operators, programmers and systems analysts renders the problem all the more complex and urgent. Some amongst them could succumb to the temptations their work offers, and this gives rise to the following questions:

— Should they be licensed?

— Should professional standards be established?

— Should we ask them to make a commitment similar to the Hippocratic Oath?

— More simply, should we establish a deontological code of data processing?

These questions must be answered by professional associations. One example comes to mind. Employees of the Bank of America, the world's largest bank and one of the best-equipped with computers, have to sign a contract of employment which states: 'All information regarding clients' accounts and the bank's transactions must be kept secret and must not be imparted to anyone whatsoever, within the bank or outside it, without the written consent of a superior authority.'

The users

There is nothing new about the protection of data being a cause for anxiety, nor has it been provoked solely by computers. For a very long time now, industrialists have been trying to protect their manufacturing secrets, their formulae and their cost prices. But now that all this information is recorded in computers, they must ensure the safety of the machine.

The Bank of America, which I have already mentioned, spends 1 million dollars per annum to ensure the safety of its installations. Access to its computer room is strictly controlled; television cameras keep it under constant surveillance. The magnetic tapes are all recopied every day and taken to a separate place. In the case of the FBI all requests for information are automatically recorded and the magnetic tapes duplicated; no operator is ever left alone in the machine room; he is under perpetual supervision.

However, the problem became more complex when the teleprocessing of information began. In effect, thanks to terminals linked to a computer by telephone lines, access to the data recorded in the memory can be obtained, but it must not be imagined that this is easy.

Personal computers create another danger since young people for the sake of amusement try to penetrate the most secret files, just as older people do the same thing with different ulterior motives. One way of protecting access to information is to give a password to those who have the right to communicate with the files. But by spending some time trying out possible passwords with the aid of a personal computer, it is possible to find the correct one. The original user must, therefore, set up an efficient system of protection by using special software. Such programmes exist, but they cost more and sometimes companies and civil service departments with installations will not make the necessary expenditure until an incident actually occurs.

Listening in to telephone calls is no new phenomenon. When information is being transmitted from the terminal to the computer, or between computers, whether by telephone or by radio, it is obviously possible to overhear it. Here again defensive measures can be taken in the form of cryptography, and the electronic and software means for carrying this out exist.

The manufacturers

It is necessary to find methods for the protection of recorded data and the makers of computers have suggested some important measures. One of them consists in verifying the identity of those who are using the system. Let us take the case of a social security department. Only two or three people will have the right to research certain information. To ensure this, it is sufficient for the operator to be the only person who knows the password or the number that opens the line of communication.

In other cases a special key can be used or a 'magnetic identity card'. The two can easily be combined. To obtain an item of information, it is necessary to enter a number with the aid of a keyboard, and at the same time insert the identity card. The two are then compared so as to avoid the use by a third party of a stolen or lost card.

Programmes can be written in such a way that one obtains a hierarchy of information. In certain systems a security profile exists for each person using it. The profile permits access to certain information and not to anything else, and can also prevent the insertion of new data or any change to existing data. Another frequently-used system consists in printing a checklist of all interrogations, so that the computer can automatically detect any unauthorized questions.

Indeed these methods of protection, whether identification of the enquirer, restriction on the issue of data, or control over interrogations are much more efficient than the security measures adopted for protecting information contained in manual files. The difficulty in using the techniques involved, and the training required for operators, are themselves a very considerable protection.

In addition to these methods IBM invested $20 million in 1972 in order to set up four centres to study security, three in clients' installations and one in its own departments. The goal of these centres has been to develop new access-to-information techniques. IBM's investment in this project was stimulated by our conviction that the legislator's responsibility is to decide who should have access to what, while it is the manufacturer's job to limit access to those who have the right to it. In other words the protection of private life is everybody's responsibility, but security for the data is also security for the manufacturer.

We are convinced that the problem of security of information is relatively simple to solve. The techniques needed to do so are available. However, no technique can address itself to some fundamental questions:

— What information should be recorded?
— For what purpose?
— Who should have access to it?

These questions require human decisions.

The manufacturer is duty-bound to encourage the solution to

such questions of national policy, and, as a citizen, to help in the understanding of what the real problems are. But there can be no doubt that, although there are already a great many of them, data banks will proliferate in the years ahead. That is an irreversible trend because the services they provide will alway outweigh the risks they might entail.

There are two principal problems to be resolved here:

1. Control of data recorded in files.
2. Control of access to the files and of the dissemination of the information.

I do not believe that the merging of several files into one, in itself, constitutes a danger. Let us suppose that criminal records and social security indices were combined into a single computer complex. The risk is no greater than if the two sets of records were in different buildings, for whoever wanted to obtain information would in any case have to find a great many accomplices. Yes, you may say to me, but what if it is the government who is asking for information, wouldn't that make it much easier? But, there again, are two telephone calls any more of a threat than one? It does not make that much difference!

The control of recorded information must be based on laws or government regulations, but there is no reason why electronic files, even if centralized, should contain more information about each of us than the existing manual files. It is simply that we must insist on knowing what these memories contain concerning us. Moreover for technical reasons the storing of data is a complex operation, and the more there is to store, the higher the costs of recording and storing it in the computer's memory will be. Files are not built up for the fun of having a lot of information — they are created to answer certain questions.

What worries us most is not that our medical history, our tax returns and our genealogical tree are in the memory, but that more intimate information may be put there, too. In a democratic regime, at least, there is no reason why these facts should be gathered systematically. Only where a government has reason to take a special interest in an individual will it seek out this kind of information. And in such a case, electronic memory or no electronic memory, nothing has changed. In a totalitarian regime the situation is the same. The powers-that-be can always obtain the desired information; the fact that they can get it in one hour instead of in two days will not alter the outcome for the individual.

In relation to industrial security, which I know rather well, I can state positively that anyone who wants to steal a company's secrets can do so much more easily by chatting to the engineers, and by photographing documents than he can by hunting for the data in computer memories.

Is it possible to conclude that the computer is a threat to individual liberty? On the surface, perhaps, but only in as much as modern chemistry, biology or psychology pose such a threat. Unscrupulous men can use certain drugs and certain psychological techniques to manipulate people; on the other hand, a proper use of the same products and techniques can relieve or cure mankind.

Mme Gallouedec-Genuys has also written: '. . . the responsibility of data processing has no common yardstick with that of government. More than ever it is the quality of the latter which will guarantee secrecy; all the more so in that the computer itself suggests safeguards and it is sufficient to have the will to use them.' It is not the lancet which is to blame for a bungled operation, it is the surgeon. It is not the typewriter which is to blame for a defamatory pamphlet, it is the writer. It is not the computer which is a threat to our individual liberty, it is man.

I would also like to quote Georges Duhamel: 'I do not mistrust the machine that I examine inquisitively as it stands on its base or under its casing. I mistrust the machine that is within me; I mistrust my way of using the machine.'

Data processing and employment

The argument I am about to advance is relevant to the impact of all new technologies. This argument began several centuries ago, each time a new tool was invented permitting a single man or woman to do the work formerly done by several. The weaving trade is one of the most celebrated examples. In the more recent past all the industrialized countries experienced a considerable reduction in the number of people employed in agriculture, owing to the use of tractors and new machinery. This happened in France, particularly during the years that followed World War I. In the little village in the Normandy Vexin where I spent my holidays every year from 1931 to 1945, the farmers still used carthorses, and their most modern pieces of equipment were reaping-machines.

From 1950 to 1973 population movement from the country to the town involved 100,000 people per annum. But it was a period of growth, and jobs in industry and in the tertiary sector were sufficiently numerous to avoid a rise in the rate of unemployment. France, like many of the industrialized countries of Europe, even had to bring in foreign workers. Obviously, one may regret the depopulation of the countryside; however, the disappearance of thousands of jobs in agriculture did not provoke a great outcry because plenty of other jobs were created elsewhere.

It is a very different situation today when it comes to automation in all its forms – data processing, text processing and robotics – because growth is greatly diminished and there are certain jobs Europeans do not wish to do. On the other hand, it is much easier to understand the micro-economy than the macro-economy, and the media have really made an issue of automation. I remember reading some absolutely crazy articles written after the publication of Messieurs Simon Nora and Alain Minc's book of telematics. One journalist raved: 'In a few years, a car will consist of nothing but a chip surrounded by a bit of sheet-metal.' Soon afterwards I met him at a dinner given by mutual friends and he had to concede that a car would still have to have wheels with tyres, an engine, a steering-wheel, etc., and that the addition of a micro-chip would simply provide new functions. What has changed, and will change still more in car production, are manufacturing methods, thanks to the use of robots, numerical control of machine-tools and the design and release of components to production by computers.

M. Nora and M. Minc also stated in their book that the

installation of data processing in banks would entail a 30 per cent reduction of staff between now and 1988 . . . for the same workload. Many commentators simply omitted the words 'for the same workload'. Actually an examination of the changes in staffing in the most automated banks shows that today the number of employees has increased not fallen, because the number of transactions has increased faster than productivity.

It has always been thus. In the United States it has been estimated that, if new technology had not been applied, the total American telephone network would have required 400 million employees to deal with the number of calls made in 1981 (i.e. nearly twice the entire population of the USA). In spite of regularly introduced technological advances, the number of employees has risen from 121,000 in 1910 to 874,000 in 1981.

For several years now I have made a study of almost everything that has been published about the effects of automation on employment, and I must say that nowhere have I found clear and definite conclusions. In the March 1980 issue of *The Economist* − a very serious paper − two articles appeared on two different pages about micro-electronics. One was headed 'Micro-electronics will increase the number of unemployed by 500,000 in five years'; the other forecast 'Micro-electronics will create 200,000 jobs in England by 1985'.

In order to get a better grasp on this problem I set up two study groups within IBM at the beginning of 1984, one on 'Technology and Employment', the other on 'Robotics and Employment'. The conclusions drawn from these studies were that the principal causes of unemployment are poor economic growth and a failure to restructure in time.

Almost at the same moment Kap Cassani, President of IBM Europe, asked several universities to carry out a study on 'Information Technology and Employment'. Their conclusions, presented at a seminar in la Hulpe in June 1985, were more or less the same.

Since 1982 the number of jobs in the United States has grown by several millions, and unemployment has gone down to 7.2 per cent of the working population. And yet the penetration of data processing in the running of businesses in the US is the highest in the world, and the use of robots in factories has risen at a faster pace since the Americans realized the need to be competitive. The growth rate of the American economy in 1985 was much lower than it was in 1984: the gross national product grew by 1.9 per cent during the second quarter as against 7.5 per cent during the second quarter of 1984. The unemployment rate remained stable, but, while jobs in the manufacturing industries dropped by 210,000 between January and July, the total number of jobs in the private sector (excluding agriculture) increased by 1.1 million during the same period. On 6 September unemployment figures had again dropped, reaching their lowest figure for five years.

For years Japan has been the country with the highest number of robots per thousand workers. Sweden is second in this field, but their levels of unemployment are amongst the lowest in the industrialized countries.

I have already said that there is no question of a nation's industry choosing between exports and foreign investments, but that it is imperative to produce goods abroad to sell them there; I am equally sure there is no question of choosing between automation and the old methods. Without the use of data processing, text processing and robotics, a modern country cannot be competitive. Once you accept this fact, the real debate centres on what qualifications will be required in the future. I have already spoken of this, but the problem is so important for men and women of every nation that I will not hesitate to repeat myself.

The US Department of Labor has published an estimate of the growth in employment, in all professions, from 1982 to 1995. This type of analysis seems to me very useful, provided the citizens of a country — and more particularly its educators — take note of it. It must become basic knowledge for those whose task it is to guide young people. The survey shows that, while the working population will increase from 20 to 29 per cent, some professions will suffer a drop in employment. A self-evident truth! Yes, but if we know where employment will grow, and where it will decline, we can learn some lessons from it.

The following figures are extracted from a report of the Statistics

Office of the US Department of Labor; they include only the professions in which there will be the creation of more than 30,000 jobs during the period under consideration. Classification is given in decreasing order in terms of the number of new jobs.

	Period 1982 – 1995	
	New Jobs	Percentage increase in 1995 employment as against 1982
Employees in retail businesses (shops, supermarkets, etc.)	898,000	27
Security guards, caretakers of buildings	779,000	28
Cashiers	774,000	47
Secretaries	719,000	29
Nursing assistants and qualified nurses	642,000	49
Qualified engineers	584,000	49
Lorry drivers	578,000	24
Hotel and restaurant employees	562,000	34
Schoolteachers	511,000	37
Medical assistants	423,000	35
Cooks and chefs	402,000	33
Accountants and auditors	344,000	40
Factory workers on assembly lines	332,000	25
Employees in wholesale businesses	327,000	30
Garage mechanics	324,000	38
Factory foremen	320,000	27
Watchmen, porters, etc.	300,000	47

The following table concerns jobs, classified in the decreasing order of their rate of increase (only those with over 50 per cent growth).

	New jobs 1982–1995	
	Percentage increase 1995 as against 1982	No. of jobs created
Data processing operators	97	53,000
Clerks in lawyers' offices	94	43,000
Data processing systems analysts	85	217,000
Programmers	77	205,000
Office machine mechanics	72	40,000
Electrical engineers	65	209,000
Technicians in electronics	61	222,000
Physiotherapists	60	15,000
Administrators in health services	58	175,000
Mechanical engineers	52	109,000

I have of course seen long-term predictions proved false. But whatever the errors may be in absolute terms, the tendencies are probably exact, and a whole book could be written on the basis of these three tables.

Finally, listed opposite are the jobs where there will be a decrease in employment.

I will make only one comment. There is no reason to suppose that Europe, Japan and the other industrialized countries will not experience the same evolution in the distribution of qualified jobs in the future, and yet I am convinced that the table showing new jobs to be created does not correspond to the results we would get if we carried out an opinion poll. I do not want to make a value judgement, but I am convinced that on the whole European

	Jobs lost	
	Number	*Percentage rate of decrease*
Postal workers	55,000	18
College teachers (secondary education)	111,000	15
Stenographers	20,000	7
Typographers	7,600	7
Butchers	12,000	6
Postmen	11,000	5

society will not change in a way that will be very different from that of American society. The actual creation of jobs in Europe will not be the same as it will be in the USA for a great many reasons to do with culture, social traditions and social safeguards, but the distribution of jobs in the years to come is not likely to be very different. If we practise a little humility, we can predict what is already happening in the United States. And if we do this well we can even avoid the pitfalls that have already caused a good many human problems in the USA.

These two debates, on data processing and liberty, and on automation and employment, are not the only ones that have been provoked by the very rapid development of the information industries. There has been the debate on decentralized data processing as against centralized data processing — which was a false one — and there are all the arguments about standards, telecommunications and the transfer of data across borders. It is a good thing that these debates are taking place; they certainly help the inventors and the constructors of new technologies to be aware of their responsibilities. We must, however, be aware of the seriousness of these discussions and avoid sensationalism. Front page 'shock headlines' will only delay the general public's understanding of the benefits to be derived from the new technologies.

What is perhaps more serious still is that by dint of making the young believe that only the high tech industries have any future, false discussion can steer too many in that direction, and neglect the training required by more traditional industries. I have noticed, for example, that mechanics was not an option favoured by the engineering students at the *Ecole Centrale*. Now if we want to have a good robotics industry in France, for example, we shall need very good mechanical engineers.

15

The Conditions for Success

The best days are those in which one learns something. I am thinking not only of the study of new subjects or delving deeper into old ones, but of very intimate communication with one's loved ones, of the interest one takes in their careers and their problems, of the discovery of one's grandchildren's progress, of long walks in the country, and of meeting people who are very different from those with whom one works every day.

My review of the past, which I have just undertaken on a professional level and also a little on the family level, has revived a great many memories which lead me to a simple conclusion: I am a happy man. I have experienced difficulties, painful times, sorrows and failures, but the happy moments, the professional successes, and the joys of family love and friendship have far outweighed them. I have been given a great deal, and I believe I can say that I have given a great deal in return. Therein lies the secrets of success and happiness. Happiness, however, does not preclude anxiety, an anxiety that compels us to ask ourselves some questions, above all the most important one, have I done all that I could have done?

The answer is no! On many occasions in life, every man and every woman could have foreseen the imminent problems earlier, dealt with them more successfully, understood sooner the difficulties of the people surrounding him or her, been more generous and given him — or herself more completely to others. I have often reproached myself; sometimes I have shared these reproaches with my bosses, often with my subordinates, and always with my wife.

In every case I have tried to draw a lesson from my mistakes: I have acknowledged my responsibility for them and made every effort to prevent the people around me suffering from them. As far as possible I have applied the lessons I learned in business to all my activities. Tolerance, for example, has led me to the belief that the distinction made in France between the Right and the Left is totally outdated. Starting from a so-called 'left' consciousness, I have discovered liberalism, true liberalism, the kind Sorman speaks about in his latest book *L'Etat Minimum* [The Minimum State], and long ago I suggested to Messieurs Jacques Duhamel and Fontanet that they should adopt the slogan 'Neither Right nor Left, but Forward!' I still believe in this, as I believe – not through ideology but as a result of my international experience – in a certain number of ideas and principles of action:

1. The importance of education, including one's family upbringing.

2. Equality of opportunity.

3. Non-discrimination whatever the criteria may be.

4. The chance for everyone to improve his position through continuous training.

5. The search for a consensus of opinion when making decisions.

6. Social promotion.

7. Respect for others.

8. Rejection of chauvinism and xenophobia.

9. The need for a business company to have principles, ethical standards, and objectives which are clearly explained and known to everyone.

10. Training in human relationships.

11. Freedom of individual decision.

12. The need for every man and woman to justify his or her position all through their working lives.

13. Rejection of the status quo.

14. The immense potential for creativity in all the employees in a company, and consequently the management's duty to set

up structures, methods, and the necessary team spirit that will make it possible for this creativity to express itself.

There are some small things that mark an individual. I have often mentioned them in this book: my discovery at Endicott and Poughkeepsie that all the factory employees, from the unskilled workers to the managing director, took their meals in the same company cafeteria, and on my return from the United States finding the same situation in IBM France, showed me how certain barriers can be broken down. This remark may seem very naïve, but there are many simple things that make life within a company more pleasant!

My American bosses, who were always available, taught me very early on that one of the conditions for good labour relations is a systematic development of internal communications. Again in America, I realized how much better the climate was when there were not too many classifications between the employees, and when the foremen and all the first line managers were part of the management.

Later in my career I realized how difficult it was for women to rise up through the hierarchy, either because they lacked the initial training necessary to make progress or because they came up against the absurd prejudices of their petty male bosses.

I have experienced what it means to have a company ethic and learned that one has to be prepared to lose a deal rather than betray one's principles. The need to adapt to changes in the external environment; the need for flexibility which can be interpreted as physical and intellectual mobility of staff and workers; and the need to prepare all restructuring well in advance so as to reduce the shock changes caused by it, also became apparent to me very early in my career.

A constant battle against bureaucratization has to be waged with a will. I quickly realized this is the only way to allow a growing enterprise to respond quickly to all unexpected events. I have seen, too, how increased interference by the State can be damaging to the successful running of businesses, to the prosperity of a country, and, what is too often forgotten, to the happiness of its citizens.

I know now that the people who achieve the best performance are those who accept their responsibilities to the full, and do not see 'the others' as the cause of everything unpleasant that happens to them.

It is said repeatedly that each country defends its own interests, and this is true, but people forget quickly so that one sees heads of State, politicians and citizens outraged because some foreign government has taken a decision which seems to be against the interests of their own country. A proper understanding between nations must be founded on the search for a solution which throughout the world will have the least negative impact on each of them. We must find common grounds of interest. It is practically impossible for a decision which affects several countries, like those within the Common Market for example, to have the same beneficial results for them all.

I have described the extent to which common principles and policies, plus precise objectives, created an *esprit de corps* amongst the 400,000 employees of IBM throughout the world. Could we not dream a little and apply the same methods, first to the nation, then to the Western world, then to the United Nations? (Now that really is a dream!)

Some years ago the authors of *Global Reach* criticized me for stating publicly that the organization of multinational companies was more advanced than that of nation States. They saw in this affirmation the alleged greed for power of the great capitalist companies, who want to see the world organized in such a way as to make their task easier. I do not believe companies have the 'power' that some attribute to them. Undoubtedly they can try to bring their influence to bear on governments, but they are not at this moment a pressure group like any other. As several successive presidents of IBM have said, 'a business enterprise, no matter how large it is, must not dictate its country's foreign policy; that is the task of government'.

Running a State is very different from running a company, the qualities, the experience required of the men and women in charge are not at all the same. One may well ask oneself, however, whether certain conditions for the success of the great companies are not also the conditions for the success of a nation. The more important a role the economy plays in political decision-making, the more the factors for success in a micro-economy can be applied to the running of a State.

The reasons for Japan's success from the point of view of the economy have been examined many, many times. For myself, I have not the slightest doubt that the good understanding and the exchange of men between government and industry are important factors. The extraordinary success of some Japanese firms has been due to a certain humility on the part of their leaders, who have never hesitated to learn from others. They strove to understand the things that the other industrialized countries did better than they did, then adopted the same methods while adapting them to Japanese culture.

In France, as well as in several other European countries, we are too inclined to believe that our own ideas are sufficient, and other people's ideas superfluous. That is a dangerous mental attitude for eventually it leads one to spending time and considerable sums of money on catching up with the others. To be really creative, one must have a profound knowledge of the latest advances in technology, the methods of work and the social systems of the industrialized countries, and adopt and adapt what is well-done elsewhere.

Can the principles and objectives of a company like IBM be examined (I do not say copied) by other companies, and even by the State, to see whether their application could bring about improvements? As far as other companies are concerned, my answer is yes. Naturally people will reply that a small or medium-sized company cannot do what a company the size of IBM can do. It is true that if one examines IBM's actions and programmes in absolute terms some things would be impossible. But I recall that some of IBM's principles and objectives were announced and applied before World War II, when IBM was a medium-sized company. I remember that in 1949 IBM had only 7,000 employees working outside the United States, but was already operating in sixty countries.

Let us return to my years in data processing. In reviewing the various stages of my career, one question has occurred to me. For a long time now I have been one of the 'number two's' or 'number three's' in one of the largest corporations in the world. Certainly I derive immense personal pride from this, but above all I enjoy the satisfaction of having demonstrated, along with other people, that a Frenchman and a European can do as well as an American or a Japanese, and that he can also feel perfectly at ease in a management team which is foreign to his culture, and is multinational.

My friends and associates think that I must have taken a vast number of decisions during my twenty-eight years in management positions. I took some all alone, especially when it was a matter of staffing problems. I have experienced the famous 'loneliness at the top' when I promoted various men and women, and more especially when I had to convince someone that he had not fulfilled the objectives set him. I have also made many suggestions and proposals, which led to decisions being taken by my boss of the moment and later by the Board of Directors when I was President of the IBM World Trade Corporation, but chiefly I have participated in decisions made collectively by a number of people. In some cases it was my voice which predominated – when I was president of IBM Europe, for example – in others, it was the voice of my immediate boss, the Chairman of the company who in his turn often had to refer a decision to the Board of Directors in compliance with clearly laid-down regulations. Obviously I am speaking here of major decisions, such as the launching of a new product, steering a research programme, building a new factory, installing a subsidiary in a country where IBM had never operated before, stopping or restructuring a programme and many others. But the taking of collective decisions in no way relieves a boss of his individual responsibilities. Even in a very decentralized system of management, there are some decisions which can only be taken by the man at the top and which he cannot delegate. As President Truman said, 'The buck stops here.'

All limited companies have a board of directors and in the United States the directors carry heavy responsibilities. They must therefore be well-informed, and they must take their share of important decisions, particularly in view of the fact that they are accountable for their actions to the General Assembly of Shareholders, who elect them.

IBM has pushed to the limit its system of 'Checks and Balances', which sometimes causes a slight delay in arriving at a decision, but is an excellent insurance against gross blunders. The custom of consulting specialists and asking those who are responsible for the development of a project to present well worked-out reports, listing all the pros and cons, makes decision-making easier, and more especially ensures that a large number of executives will be involved.

This is not far removed from the Japanese management by consensus model. This method avoids decisions taken on the spur of the moment, and those which a boss might be tempted to make when a collaborator 'sells' him a brilliant idea that has not been studied sufficiently in depth. It provokes frustrating moments when one is convinced of being in the right, when one can see a swift solution to a problem yet cannot apply it until two or three people – sometimes as many as ten – have examined it from every angle. I experienced some of these frustrations at the start of my career. It was not the wisdom of age, nor custom, that diminished or eliminated these feelings; it was the conviction, acquired with time, that an important decision cannot be successfully applied unless it has to some degree been shared by all those who have to execute it.

What is important to the company is that the total time which elapses between the birth of an idea, the decision to launch a programme, and the delivery of the finished product to the client, must be as short as possible. It is not a good thing to make rapid decisions if those who have to execute them have not properly grasped them, or if, as often happens, they are not entirely in agreement with them and so set to work with a kind of passive resistance that delays the time of execution.

The system of shared decision making creates a strong *esprit de corps*. The proverb – 'Success has many fathers but failure is an orphan' – does not apply if one has a collegiate system of management.

In the United States when someone who is retiring or leaving the company for any other reason is called upon to make a farewell speech, the opening words (provided he or she is still on good terms with the company) are almost always the same. 'I have spent x number of years with you in this model company and I have enjoyed every minute of it.' I did not say that in my farewell speech, but I did say that I had enjoyed tremendous satisfaction *almost* every minute of the time.

Inside and outside IBM I have met remarkable men and women. My confidence in the possibility of building a united Europe has been strengthened. Over the years I have grasped which conditions are necessary to the success of a large company, and which are necessary to the success of the men and women who work for it. These conditions are implicit in everything I have written. Nevertheless I would like to end by summarizing what I believe to be essential to individual success, at least in a multinational. For me fundamentally this is the most important element, since I believe (and have even heard it from the lips of Mr T.J. Watson himself) that 'the major assets of a company are the men and women who work for it.'

Conditions for individual success

1. An adequate level of training and personal competence. Such a level may already have been reached at the time of joining the company, or it may be acquired through continuous in-job training. Everyone must understand that the knowledge he has gained to pass his degree becomes obsolete very quickly and he will need to go on learning.

2. Hard work.
There are, of course, highly intelligent people who do not need to make as strenuous efforts as other people to achieve the same results. But they will find out along the way that others, who are

310

equally intelligent but who work hard too, will go much further. The complexity of managing a huge enterprise demands a constant up-dating of knowledge and skills: one must read, listen, discover, meet people, go out towards them, and one must explain. All this takes time.

3. Whatever you have to do, do it well.

I have met people who are intelligent, gifted, and well-trained yet they did not progress through the hierarchy as fast as other people because they only did well those things they enjoyed. Some of them had chosen a personal way of life that suited them, and that was fine as long as their subordinates did not suffer as a result; but there were others who did not understand why they were not promoted more quickly and became embittered. To rise up through the hierarchy implies that you will have to take on more and more tasks that have nothing to do with your original vocation. For example, an engineer may find that organizing human resources does not interest him in the least, but when you have subordinates, it is their psychological needs and not your own that must be satisfied. Besides, if you do whatever you have to do well, you will not waste time wishing you were in somebody else's shoes.

4. Give to human relations all the attention they deserve.

You cannot rise to the highest positions in a company which has a well-organized system of promotion unless you have shown your capacity for motivating the men and women with whom you work. To motivate people, you must constantly set a good example. You must have proved that you respect those who work under you and are ready to give them total support.

If morale is better in companies that practise a system of internal promotion, instead of 'parachuting in' outsiders, it is not only because the executives know their career progress will not be blocked by the engagement of someone from outside, but also because those who are responsible for making promotions know what kind of reputation the man they are moving up has amongst his peers and his future subordinates.

5. Have character and be capable of taking decisions.

I have known executives who had all the intellectual qualities to fit them for brilliant careers, but who spent an eternity examining the pros and cons before they could come to a decision. They caused a great deal of frustration amongst their associates as well as for their bosses. If serious and capable people hesitate for a long time between two possible decisions, it means that neither is really superior to the other. It is then preferable to choose one of them and get on with it quickly.

A man or a woman of character does not need to demonstrate it by too often taking a negative stand, but rather by being coherent in his or her attitudes and decision-making. 'Bawling people out' is not, to my way of thinking, a proof of character.

6. Rid yourself of prejudices acquired during your youth.

We are all profoundly influenced by our family environment, by our education, and by the characteristics of the nation to which we belong. Respect for others is, as I have already said, one of the conditions for success, and it often shows itself in the form of humility which consists in refraining from bragging about your family, your degree, and especially, if you work with foreigners, your nationality.

7. Know how to seize an opportunity when it presents itself.

Napoleon always tried to choose generals who were lucky. If this type of man exists, so much the better for the company. I do not believe in luck, except the kind that allows certain people to explain away the success of others. On the other hand, I believe that there are opportunities which present themselves to companies and to individuals. One must be ready to seize them and basically this requires hard work, ambition, and a little intuition.

8. Be well-balanced.

Balance can only be achieved if marital and family life are happy. The husband or wife of an executive who is progressing rapidly must not only understand and accept the fact that the road to the top is hard, and imposes absence, separations, household removals, and when an urgent decision has to be made sudden changes to family plans, but he or she must also move ahead with the marriage partner and take an interest in his or her professional life. This is of vital help. My wife has played a considerable role throughout my career, and if my colleagues have sometimes remarked on my even temper, it is thanks to her.

9. One last word of advice: Choose your boss carefully!

I have known all too many young people who have chosen their careers well but did not know how to choose the right company to work for. The best of them changed to another company, but the less enterprising submitted to their fate and waited impatiently for the weekends. In today's conditions it is often difficult to choose, but what I would suggest is that you take your destiny into your own hands and build a future. Never submit!

We had just come back from our holidays. Two very enjoyable weeks on board the boat belonging to our friends, Jacques and Colette Dauphin, in the waters off Sardinia and then Corsica. It was not the first time they had invited us and it was a pleasure and a delight to be with them. Scarcely had we arrived home than the telephone rang: 'Hello! Is that Happiness House?' It was our friend, Louis Bertagna, the father of our son-in-law Xavier, giving us news of our mutual granddaughters.

Summer in this house was a little different from previous summers. Up until then we had succeeded in gathering all our children together, with their spouses and their children for two to three weeks in July. That year only Christine and Xavier with their three children, Florence with her four little Americans, and Anne-Sophie were able to be with us. François paid us a flying visit, while Ketty and their son had to remain in the United States to wait for her green card. I spent two weeks in New York and so was able to see them, but my wife did not have her full share of the children's company. All the same there were several weekends during which four generations were present, and my mother and my mother-in-law were able to enjoy their seven great-grand-children. Bob and Sylvie had just spent a fortnight in Paris and we were lucky enough to see them often.

For me it is always a real relaxation to find myself amidst a large family party in our country house which we had always intended to be a family gathering-place, to see our neighbours who have become friends, and after long trips away 'to live among my dear ones a part of the life that remains to me' (thank you, Du Bellay!).

My retirement from IBM was not at all what I thought it would be, and I worked just as many hours as before. I spent a lot of time in the Air Liquide group mostly in the United States, but also in Paris because I had to learn a new 'trade'. I discovered that the concept of 'professional manager' is not as easily applied as I had believed. Fortunately I found within this great French company a 'culture' that was not so very different from IBM's: the same will to hold to principles and the company ethic, and also to hold to precise objectives. I was happy to discover that in a classification of French companies according to overall profits Air Liquide came second . . . after IBM France!

I also spent a lot of time giving lectures and courses, and attending meetings of employers, executives and instructors who were conscious of where they were going.

And I thought a great deal about all the men and all the women with whom I had travelled part of the road. I would have liked to say more about them in this book, and particularly those who worked very closely with me. Some time ago IBM set up a system of administrative assistants. These were promising young executives, thirty-five to forty years old, who came to work with a top executive for eighteen months to two years, to deal with certain multi-functional problems for him and ensure the best possible organization of his time. This job is full of frustrations, but one learns a great deal. Every one of them saved me from a great many mistakes and became a friend. Over the years, I tried to pick people of various nationalities. There was one Belgian, two Germans, two Italians, two Englishmen, several Frenchmen and several Americans (one of them a woman). Each of them taught me a little more about his or her country and I am very grateful for that. Two of them died, and I was deeply grieved.

The summer of 1985 was marked by a good many tragic accidents in the world and in France. Seven employees of IBM died

THE CONDITIONS FOR SUCCESS

in the accident in Dallas; two in the Air India disaster; three in the air crash in Tokyo. As I write I have not yet received any information, but it is probable that several Mexicans from IBM were victims of the earthquake in Mexico. Conversely, a few months ago I was overjoyed to learn that one of our ex-managers in an African country, condemned to death for political reasons, had been pardoned by the president of his country. Here is an aspect about participating in the life of multinational companies that would never occur to most people. A responsible manager who has made friends throughout the whole world, and acquired a certain loyalty to his company, will be distressed by anything that causes suffering to those who have been a part of the group in any region of the world whatsoever. What better means could there be to make one more sensitive to the rights and the sufferings of man? I remember how the directors of IBM took immediate action whenever there was a catastrophe anywhere in the world. I saw what efforts were made to find satisfactory jobs for any of our ex-employees who were forced to leave their countries. I saw Michel Faucon, for example, devoting his time tirelessly and without stint to helping those of our colleagues from IBM Vietnam who managed to make their way to France.

This attitude on the part of management exists in many multi-national companies, no matter which country the parent company is in. Mr T.J. Watson chose as his slogan, 'World Peace through World Trade'. It was a little ambitious, but I am absolutely convinced that companies can contribute to a better understanding between nations and that in particular, international managers can come to understand after a few years' experience the cultural differences between countries. They cannot run a business with French, or German, or American, or Japanese methods. They must adapt to managers and subordinates of every nationality, without sacrificing their own integrity.

My conclusion is obvious: *to manage is to motivate*. If one accepts this principle, it follows that one has only to understand what forces motivate employees in different countries. This is not an easy task and requires careful study. Fortunately, no matter what their nationality, men and women in a company react enthusiastically to people who like and respect them. 'Hard' bosses and cynics, the technocrats of management, those who do not know how to arbitrate fairly between the different responsibilities of the company, will find me naïve, or if they speak English will consider me a 'do-gooder'. Ah, well! I would rather have a reputation for being naïve than one for being hard.

Love of one's neighbour must remain the basis of our Judaeo-Christian civilization. It is love of others that leads to success in one's profession and in one's family life. The companies that have the best image are those which have the best human relations, and – this is interesting to note – they are very often the ones that are most profitable.

20 September 1985